ALTERNATIVES IN JUDICIAL RESEARCH

DECISION MAKING
IN
THE SUPREME COURT OF INDIA
(A JURIMETRIC STUDY)

Vijay K. Gupta

Kaveri Books
New Delhi - 110 002

Edition 2019

ISBN-13: 978-81-7479-006-4

Published by
Kaveri Books
4832/24, Ansari Road
New Delhi-110002 (India)
Tel: 011- 4707 2321
E-mail : info@kaveribooks.com
kaveribooks@gmail.com
Website: www.kaveribooks.com

PRINTED IN INDIA

To
Tipi and our children
Natasha and Vivek

Preface

The present work is a revised version of my doctoral dissertation submitted to University of Delhi. The study is unique and unorthodox as it is for the first time an attempt has been made to analyse the Supreme Court as an institution to provide a close insight into the internal dynamics of its decision making process.

It is unique in the sense that it makes a complete departure from the traditional common law technique of judicial research. It shifts its focus from what the judges say in their opinions to what do they do by casting their votes in favour of one or the other party to the litigation before them. Essentially, therefore, analysis of the judge's performance is vote based rather than opinion based. By analysing the votes of the judges during a particular time span, an attempt has been made to determine their value orientations.

Besides, it seeks to analyse quantitatively a whole range of factors that go as essential input into the Supreme Court's decision making process. For instance, several assumptions relating to interplay of factors operating in the appointment of judges, the Chief Justice's role in the appointment process and his leadership of the court, the business environment, the structural arrangement of its decision making panels, the opinion assignments, the nature of voting response of the judges in decision making process and the character of dissent, concurrence and unanimity in the court are some of the areas which have remained unexplored thus far, and for the first time subjected to a close rigorous quantitative analysis in an overall institutional setup.

The term institution here is used in a general sense referring to the Court as a formal organisation which is characterised by a code of norms and regulations and a role structure within which specific patterns of relationships are evolved among its members. The Court as an institution, therefore, implies a concrete apparatus with clearly defined rules and an exclusive personnel carefully hand picked for carrying out its functions. But like all social institutions the Court cannot sever its links with the wider society. In fact, the Court as an institution has its significance only in its role within the society.

It is assumed that the decision making process in the apex court is not a stereotype activity where the decisions are arrived at mechanically within the strict confines of 'legal logic' but involves a complex interaction of factors which lay the institutional fabric of the system. The Court is not only a part of the political system with which it continuously interacts but also an ongoing concept of political life. It is at the same time a functional organism whose functional autonomy although secured to a large extent from external influences, inevitably undergoes changes due to its internal dynamics. Both the external and the internal factors create a set of interactions which seek to cope with the stresses generated by the environment in which it functions as one of the conditions of its own survival. The study focuses on those processes, activities, or conditions which it undergoes and which in turn influence its decision making functions over a period of time.

The method of analysis employed is an extension of jurimetrics as developed and refined in the United States and applied to judicial behaviour research in that country. The method has for reasons explained in chapter 1 escaped the Indian Scholars but holds a key to unravelling the mysteries of judicial process even at the level of elementary descriptive analysis.

The information was collected from cases reported in the All India Reporter covering almost one decade and was reduced into a number of variables. These were statistically analysed to elicit emerging response patterns which in turn were used to test several hypothesis. This method was supplemented by historical and political behavioural analysis to a limited extent. The analysis is essentially descriptive and not predictive except a brief attempt made in chapter seven which deals with value orientations of judges. The reasons will be obvious as explained in the text and as one goes along and examines the primary nature of the data on the Indian Supreme Court which, it will be noticed that by virtue of its very character, does not lend itself to any attempt on a sustained predictive analysis.

The work is divided into four parts. The first part consists of chapters two and three which deals with the appointment of the

Chief Justice, and the selection and appointment of judges. The second part comprises chapters four and five which concerns itself with work environment and the structural arrangements in the decision making process of the Court. The third part comprises chapters six and seven mainly devoted to voting response patterns and the value orientations of judges. The last part is the concluding part with a postscript and an Appendix introducing the background characteristics of 39 judges who served on the court during the period covered here.

Chapter one which is an introductory part explains the conceptual and methodological orientation of the study and seeks to establish credentials for jurimetrics in judicial behaviour research in India which hitherto has remained almost unexplored.

Chapter two discusses the appointment of the Chief Justice of India which has been the subject of controversy several times in the past. The seniority convention in the appointment of the Chief Justice has played an important role, and has survived the onslaught of the two supersessions. The chapter examines the controversies from the overall institutional perspective and their possible consequences on the leadership in the Court.

Chapter three deals with the appointment and selection of Supreme Court judges and their background characteristics. According to the Constitution the appointment of judges can be made by the President in consultation with the Chief Justice of India. The chapter examines the role and influence of the Chief Justice in the appointment of his colleagues in the Court. An analysis of the background characteristics of seventy one judges appointed to the Court upto the end of the year 1981 reveals factors upper most in the minds of those entrusted with the task of appointing judges to the apex Court.

Chapter four quantitatively projects the court's docket jurisdiction wise, in terms of regional inflow of appellate work, and analyses the character of court's response in terms of overrulings and affirmations of appeals from the various High Courts. Who uses the court and for what purpose ? It has been alleged that the Supreme Court of India has been a battle ground for the rich and the powerful, and its response has been largely pro big business. The analysis presented in this chapter and chapter seven do provide some justification for this assumption.

Chapter five addresses itself to one of the most important

institutional variables i.e., the fragmented structure of the decision making panels and the role of the Chief Justice in determining the extent to which his colleagues in the court participate in the decision making process. The formal and informal rules and practices regulating the discretion of the Chief Justice in assigning benches and allocating work to his brother judges has been discussed. The quantitative data on bench assignments made by four successive Chief Justices, Sikri, Ray, Beg and Chandrachud has been analysed with a view to ascertain differences and similarities in their approach, method and styles. Similarly, the data has been further analysed in terms of assignment patterns under the four successive chiefs to find out the possible influences circumscribing their discretion.

Chapter six is the subject matter of judges' response patterns in terms of their oral and written behaviour; the extent to which they have simply agreed with the opinion written by one of their colleagues on the panel - a silent acquiescence, or they have actively participated in the sense of writing opinions of the court, concurring or dissenting opinions. In determining the character of a judge's response several institutional factors come into play like, the role of the Chief Justice, opinion assignment principle followed by the decision making panels and the frequency of participation of judges on different bench formations. The chapter examines these factors along with the character of dissent, concurrence and unanimity in the court.

Chapter seven attempts to provide a plausible explanation of the judges' value orientations in terms of their aggregate voting response. In determining variations in the aggregate response of judges, the two important variables used are: who the litigants are, and what is the nature of dispute before them providing stimulus for their response.

The study concludes with inferences drawn from the overall analysis with a postscript incorporating post study period changes in the membership of the court, its leadership and the validity of the inferences drawn from the study in the context of such changes.

The author wishes to place on record his particular gratitude and indebtedness to Professor Upendra Baxi for his advice and encouragement in the preparation of the original work which forms the basis of this book. I deeply cherish the time I spent with him and it has been a continuous source of inspiration.

I owe special thanks to my friends and colleagues Padam Vir Singh for hooking me on to the computer which immensely facilitated the completion of this work; Ranjan Dwivedi for showing his interest in my work; P.S.Dutta for sharing my pains over the loss of a part of my revised manuscript particularly when I was hard pressed for time and my old friend Dharam Paul Sharma who was kind enough to arrange material which helped me updating my information on the subsequent appointments to the court . In fact, there are always people without whose help, encouragement and good wishes it would not be possible to accomplish a work of this nature and I gratefully acknowledge their debt. I am also thankful to the Academy for providing me with time and opportunity to complete the book.

My sincere thanks are due to Ajay, the Senior Steno in the Academy and my personal assistant, who ungrudgingly typed the first draft of the manuscript with all the complicated tables in it, and Poonam and Aslam of the Reprographic unit for helping me out with formating and print-out.

Before I close, I should like to express my sincere appreciation and gratitude to my publisher who not only patiently waited for the manuscript which I had originally promised them by August, but also ensured the timely publication of the book.

Vijay K. Gupta

Contents

List of Tables

List of Cases

1. *A.D.M. Jabalpur* V. *Shivkant Shukla*, AIR 1976, S.C.1207.
2. *A.K. Gopalan* V. *State of Madras*, AIR 1950, S.C. 27.
3. *Azad Rickshaw Pullers* V. *State of Punjab* (1981) 1 SCC, 366.
4. *Bachan Singh* V. *State of Punjab*, AIR 1980, S.C. 898.
5. *Bandhua Mukti Morcha* V. *Union of India* (1984) 3 SCC. 191
6. *Bela Banerjee* V. *State of West Bengal*, AIR 1954, S.C. 170.
7. *Brij Bhushan* V. *State*, AIR 1950, S.C. 129.
8. *Dr. Upendra Baxi*, V. *State of U.P.* 1981 (3) SCALE 1136.
9. *Fateh Chand* V. *State of Maharashtra*, AIR 1979, S.C. 1825.
10. *Francis Carolee Mullin* V. *Delhi Administration*, (1981) 1 S.C.C. 608.
11. *Golaknath* V. *State of Punjab*, AIR 1967, S.C. 1643.
12. *Hussainara Khatoon* V. *State of Bihar*, AIR 1979, S.C. 1360; AIR 1979, S.C. 1369; AIR 1979, S.C. 1377; AIR 1979, S.C. 1819.
13. *Indira Nehru Gandhi* V. *Raj Narain*, AIR 1975, S.C. 2299.
14. *In re Special Court's Bill*, AIR 1978, S.C.478.
15. *Kesavananda Bharati* V. *State of Kerala*, AIR 1973, S.C. 1461.
16. *Kharak Singh* V. *State of U.P.* AIR 1963, S.C. 1295.
17. *Labourers Working on Salal Hydro Project* V. *State of Jammu & Kashmir*, AIR 1984, S.C. 177.
18. *Madhav Rao Scindia* V. *Union of India*, AIR 1971, S.C. 530.
19. *Maneka Gandhi* V. *Union of India*, AIR 1978, S.C. 597.
20. *Manohar* V. *Marotrao* AIR 1979, S.C. 1084.
21. *Minerva Mills Ltd.* V. *Union of India*, AIR 1980, S.C. 1789.
22. *Mohd. Ahmed Khan* V. *Shah Bano Begum*, AIR 1985, S.C. 945.
23. *Neeraja Chaudhary* V. *State of Madhya Pradesh* (1984) 3 S.C.C. 243.
24. *Olga Tellis* V. *State of Maharashtra* 1985 (2) SCALE 5.
25. *Organo Chemical Industries* V. *Union of India*, AIR 1979, S.C. 1803.
26. *People's Union for Democratic Rights and others* V. *Union of India*, AIR 1982, S.C. 1473.

27. *R.C. Cooper* V. *Union of India*, AIR 1970, S.C. 564.
28. *Ramesh Thapar* V. *State of Madras*, AIR 1950, S.C. 124.
29. *Sajjan Singh* V. *State of Rajasthan*, AIR 1964, S.C. 854.
30. *Sakal Papers Ltd.* V. *Union of India*, AIR 1962, S.C. 305.
31. *Satwant Singh* V. *A.P.O. New Delhi*, AIR 1967, S.C. 1836.
32. *Shankari Prasad* V. *Union of India*, AIR 1951, S.C. 458.
33. *Sheela Barse* V. *State of Maharashtra*, AIR 1983, S.C. 378.
34. *S.P. Gupta* V. *Union of India* (1984), Supp. S.C.C. 87.
35. *State of Bombay* V. *Vaidya* AIR 1951, S.C. 127.
36. *State of Madhya Pradesh* V. *Baldev Prasad*, AIR 1967, S.C. 1170.
37. *State of Madras* V. *V.G. Row*, AIR 1952, S.C. 196.
38. *State of M.D.* V. *Bharat Singh*, AIR 1967, S.C. 1170.
39. *State of Maharashtra* V. *Prabhakar*, AIR 1966, S.C. 424.
40. *State of Rajasthan* V. *Union of India*, AIR 1977, S.C. 136.
41. *St. Xavier's College* V. *State of Gujarat*, AIR 1974. S.C. 1389.
42. *Sunil Batra* V. *Delhi Administration*, AIR 1978, S.C. 1675; AIR 1980, S.C. 1579.
43. *Tara Prasad Singh* V. *Union of India*, AIR 1980, S.C. 1682.
44. *Tulsi Ram Patel* (1985) 3 S.C.C. 369.
45. *V. Dhanpal Chettiar* V. *Yasodai Ammal*, AIR 1979, S.C. 1745.
46. *V.C. Shukla* V. *State*, AIR 1980, S.C. 962.
47. *Virendra* V. *State of Punjab*, AIR 1957, S.C. 896.
48. *Wamanrao* V. *Union of India*, AIR 1980, S.C 178.

1

Jurimetrics : A Note on Methodology

The term 'jurimetrics' was introduced into the legal vocabulary by Lee Loevinger in the late forties and, signifies the scientific investigation of legal problems.[1] Loevinger employs the term 'jurimetrics' to denote a different set of activities from those that are normally performed under the umbrella of 'jurisprudence'. According to him, "jurisprudence is engaged in asking questions such as; what is the nature of law? What is the end or aim of law? ... these are questions that seek ultimate answer, like the 'why' of a 'curious child'.[2] They are "the unanswerable questions of life which belong to the domain of philosophy, and jurisprudence is the philosophy of law".[3] On the other hand, in science question is meaningless unless it is possible to find some operation by which answers may be given to it. Loevinger believes that the questions of science, in contrast to those of philosophy, are likely to be of the 'How' variety; How do you know that? How do you do this? These questions seek 'immediate; rather than 'ultimate' answers, "subject to further correction and modification as additional questions are formulated".[4]

Loevinger's above characterisation not withstanding, both the scientific and the philosophic methods seem to have considerably contributed to the growth of what we today know as "Jurisprudence". It was the great French scientist and philosopher, Descartes who, in rejecting any doctrine of final causes and insisting on strict methods of precise observation and on Logical and mathematical calculation, had given to rationalism a new intensity and direction enabling a traditional body of ideas to be readapted repeatedly to changing situations.[5]

Leibniz seems to transcend all such distinctions when he says,... "the plan I have had for a long time to reduce all human thinking to a calculation, such as we know it in algebra ... so that many arguments could be solved, the certain could be distinguished from the uncertain and even grades of probability could be measured... then, if two were arguing, they could say to each other Let us calculate".[6]

The birth of empiricism and its later culmination into positivism by gradual steps not only accomplished a shift from teleological to a causal and empirical view of the nature of man, but also brought about a strong temptation to apply the methods used in the natural sciences to the realm of social sciences. Thus, positivism was described as a scientific attitude which rejected all *a priori* speculations and confined itself to the data of experience. It sought to exclude value considerations from the science of jurisprudence and to confine the task of this science to an analysis and dissection of a positive legal order.[7] This emphasis on the 'given' as opposed to the 'speculative', was to guide and shape the methods in jurisprudence and the various approaches which flourished under the banner of 'legal positivism' in the nineteenth and the twentieth centuries. The emergence of analytical positivism, historical, anthropological, sociological and the realist approaches in law gradually widened the scope of legal inquiry. This would not have been possible if jurisprudence was not receptive to advances made in other disciplines, and had not readily adopted their techniques in its continuous search for alternatives. Jurimetrics in this sense is but a step towards seeking new alternatives in the field of legal inquiry and may not be treated as a 'new science'. As early as 1895 Justice Holmes had asserted that "An ideal system of law should draw its postulates and its legislative justification from sciences".[8] Undoubtedly, what he meant was that, at least potentially, the techniques of physical sciences could solve the most basic problems of law. For the rational study of law, he declared, "the man of the future is the man of the statistics,"[9] and he projected the ideal of "an ultimate dependence upon science" because, "it is finally for science to determine, so far as it can, the relative worth of our different social ends..."[10]

Unless, therefore, one wishes to be too dogmatic about drawing distinctions between a scientific method and philosophic method the ultimate test of any approach or method should lie in its ability to advance knowledge which can be utilised in solving manifold human problems as, methods are only means to an end.

In this respect no matter how jurimetrics is placed whether within or beyond the boundaries of jurisprudence, the primary concern ought to be with its ability to help in the understanding and investigation of legal problems.

Assumptions of Jurimetrics

Quantitative analysis of judicial behaviour (Jurimetrics) can be regarded as the work of second or third generation of American legal realists.[11] The legal realists juxtaposed the essential characteristics of positive and sociological approaches, and treated the law both as fact and as a social phenomenon. This new approach was highly empirical. To the realists, only the "reality" of law mattered in fact, and reality was what actually happened in the courts and no more. Law, therefore, was to be found in the decisions of judges which, according to them were the product of ascertainable factors. Included among these factors were the judges' personalities, their social environment, the economic conditions in which they are brought up, business interests, trends and movements of thought, emotions, psychology and so forth.

Since legal realism was not just one approach, but a compendium of several view points, it may be instructive to refer briefly to some of its major emphases. For Holmes, realism was a temper, the mood of pragmatism,[12] while for Llewellyn, realism was only a method, and the 'method' was to get at the real facts and issues that underlie legal controversies and the procedures employed to resolve them.[13] For Cardozo, realism meant to understand the values of the judge, since the judge's personality was the only funnel through which policy norms could enter into judicial decisions.[14] Frank, who was more influenced by Freudian psychology, shifted the focus to the sets of unique life experiences of judges which shaped their individual value-patterns;[15] Felix Cohen offered the contemporary view that the decisions of individual judges whatever might be the forces that shaped their individual value-patterns, acquired social significance only when evaluated in the context of complex antecedent and consequent processes involving the interaction of many human besides the judge.[16]

All these major exponents of legal realism, however, had a common theme in that they "directed attention away from the manifest content of judicial opinions,[17] and away from a concern for "logical consistency among sets of legal norms".[18] This was "an attempt to break away from an older kind of sterility - a sterility of abstractions and mechanical deductions unrelated to reality".[19] A knowledge of what judges do and say is important, but it is by no means enough; a realistic understanding of judicial decision-making demands that "the acts of judges be examined like any other form of social behaviour".[20]

Western Experience in Jurimetrics

A systematic quantitative analysis of judicial behaviour was inspired by Pritchett's pioneering work *The Roosvelt-Court*[21] published in 1948. This study initiated dramatic shift in the character and focus of judicial research. Pritchett addressed himself to the problem, "what moves Supreme Court Justices to decide cases as they do ?" and dealt with it with the aid of elementary statistical devices, undertaking quantitative analysis of judicial voting patterns in non-unanimous decisions of the United States Supreme Court 1937-1947. He demonstrated that justices could be aligned on policy dimensions such as attitudes towards organised labour, freedom of speech and religion, criminal justice, and economic regulation. He also devised a method for measuring the extent of agreement and disagreement between pairs of judges which enabled him to identify the existence of group patterns , which he termed "blocs", and to chart their stability over a span of time.

Pritchett thus foreshadowed and stimulated two new research emphases, namely, methodological - the utilization of quantitative techniques and, a shift in target from what do judges say to what makes judges believe as they do? His hypothesized explanations in this regard fall into four broad categories : a) policy oriented values, b) perceptions of role, c) background characteristics, and d) small group interaction.[22] Much of the systematic research on these hypothesized determinants can be traced back to the simple action stimulus response (S-R) model of the *Roosvelt Court*. The S-R model conceptualizes the votes of judges as responses to stimuli provided by cases presented to them for decisions.

The late fifties and sixties brought on the frontiers of judicial research men like Schubert,[23] Danelski,[24] Ulmer,[25] Nagel,[26] Kort,[27]

Tanenhaus,[28] Grossman,[29] and others[30] who contributed greatly to the growth of quantitative analysis of judicial behaviour. Among these, Schubert[31] occupies a prominent place. In fact, judicial behaviour research reached its high mark in the United States with the publication of his work *The Judicial Mind* in 1965.

By utilizing the votes of judges, these researchers were able to establish that judges exhibit consistent patterns of behaviour in relation to each other, in respect to the particular class of litigant before the court, and in responding to subject matter. Thus, judges on collegial courts often coalesce in highly stable blocs or cliques.[32] It was also established that certain litigants are more successful than others before the United States Supreme Court. For instance, in the 1959 term of the Court, the federal government won seventy five per cent of the opinion cases in which it participated. This compared with a success rate of sixty two per cent for labour organisations, fifty three per cent for state and local government, and twenty two per cent for corporations and other business enterprises. Moreover, the responses of the court to certain classes of litigants were found to be consistent over time.[33]

Voting records of some judges in the United States Supreme Court have shown that they are highly tilted in one direction or another in cases involving certain kind of litigants, particularly, the aliens, communists and the negroes.[34] Similarly, regularized response to subject matter has been observed at both state and federal levels and, there is evidence for the view that democratic judges are more likely to vote for the workmen in workmen's compensation cases,[35] for the unemployed in unemployment compensation cases[36] and for defendants in criminal cases.[37]

These and other similar studies have not only revealed that there are stable patterns of behaviour but, also that these are precisely those factors which make prediction possible. Research to date suggests that even though judicial behaviour may be in part a function of attitude rather than law in the narrow sense, it may still be fairly predictable since "mature judges do not change attitudes, habits, perspectives, or values with each setting sun".[38] Having discovered how a particular judge or court responds in certain kinds of situations and that such responses are regularised, the researcher could anticipate a continuation of the same behaviour patterns, and relate them to decisional outcome in such a way as to make prediction of such outcome possible.

Other studies in this area are focused upon a host of factors such as, the background characteristics of judges; interplay of influences and interests in the selection of judges; interaction among several background variables like political party affiliation, previous judicial experience, parent family socio economic status, family tradition of judicial service, religion, and geographical origin. Attempts have been made to correlate some of these background characteristics to the decision making process.[39]

There is another important aspect of judicial behaviour research which is essentially non metric in character and utilizes political process approach. It seeks to analyse judicial decisions in the broader context of social, economic and political conflicts treating judiciary as the party to the conflict of interests. The position that what courts and judges do is part of and effected by the entire political context in which the judicial task is performed was most coherently stated by Jack Peltason in his study *Federal Courts in the Political Process* in 1955.[40]

According to Pritchett, this study stands as the 'manifesto' of what he called the "judicial process movement".[41] Pritchett himself had advocated for a "political jurisprudence" which to him, was an amalgam of judicial process and judicial behaviour.[42] Whereas, the former is important to understand the "external world" of political context the later concerns the "internal world" of judicial personality, and in as much as it influences the judges' exercise of discretion, it provides a key to the understanding of the law. To the extent to which the external and the internal worlds interact and influence one another, they form part of an integrated process.

Extension of Jurimetrics to Asian Countries

Quantitative analysis of judicial behaviour made its appearance in the literature on the judicial process not only in the United states, the country of its origin, but also in several other countries like Canada, Australia, the Philippines, Japan, Korea, and to some extent in India.[43] The extension of jurimetrics beyond its American home, however, appear to have raised certain problems. These problems are essentially of two kinds. One cluster of problems concern the structure and composition of the courts and their institutional norms and practices. It is generally felt that the United States Supreme Court, and even the state Supreme

Courts lent themselves to jurimetric analysis perhaps more readily than any other court elsewhere in the world. The factors which facilitated the application of statistical methods to the United States Supreme Court are wide ranging. They concern its composite character - the strength of judges being neither too large nor too small to be insignificant, fairly long uninterrupted tenure of the judges on the bench, known political party affiliations of the judges, select controversies eventually finding access to the apex court, full court hearings and most of all, the institutionalization of dissent on the court. These factors would readily allow for statistical observation of judicial behaviour in substantial number of cases displaying similar patterns and over a long period of time. This is possible because adequate data can be extracted not only on the court as a whole or for one group of cases, but for each individual judge whose behaviour is to be characterized. Since the American jurimetricians have exclusively relied upon judicial disagreement in studying judicial behaviour, the presence of a large quantity of dissent on the American Supreme Court which is not only regular but well institutionalized, has been considered as one of the most significant factors in their studies.

The other variety of reasons seem to concern the accepted content, style, and sophistication of ordinary, nonmetric comment on the judicial process in the United States.[44] Plenty of literature is available dealing with almost every aspect of the court, its decision-making process, and the judges. There is a well settled tradition of writing judicial biographies which provide rich source of information about the individual judges and their interpersonal relations. Availability of information enables the jurimetricians to cross-check their findings, and once checked, can naturally fall into place into the mainstream of academic comment.[45] Comments concerning the division of judges between conservative bloc and liberal bloc on the court, or, that an individual judge is a conservative or a liberal are taken for granted in both scholarly as well as popular circles, and no shadow of embarrassment attaches to the making or hearing of such propositions. Accordingly, no shadow of scepticism or surprise clouds their universal acceptance.[46]

It is true that none of the apex Courts in Asian countries where jurimetrics has been extended to varying degrees of ambitiousness and sophistication in the study of judicial behaviour, matches the description of the United States Supreme Court. Perhaps, one may also argue that the courts in these countries, including the apex Courts, are so fashioned in terms of their institutional norms and practices that they "stubbornly defy" the application of statistical methods in the analysis of judicial behaviour.[47] But these differences surely do not transcend the basic assumptions of jurimetrics. Despite these differences, the fact remains that the Collegial Courts decide cases by votes. Votes are indispensable to the process of adjudication by these courts and, therefore, provide sufficient justification and premises for the extension of jurimetrics in Asian countries.

In the absence of institutionalized dissent on the courts in Asian countries, the focus of analysis can very well be shifted to the unanimous decisions. Vast amount of data on unanimous decisions was left unexplored by the American jurimetricians on the assumption that it is of no consequence to the analysis of individualistic behaviour. One may not completely agree with such an assumption and instead, put to test an alternative proposition that, "individual judges are likely to reveal stable patterns in their attitudes in their aggregate voting response, by utilizing data on both the unanimous and non-unanimous decisions. For this purpose, one may have to develop additional statistical models particularly suitable to the requirements of such data where overt dissent on the apex courts has been usually too insignificant to be relied upon exclusively.

Jurimetric research can be undertaken at two different levels i.e. the descriptive and the predictive. Whereas, the descriptive analysis may be undertaken with the aid of elementary tools of mathematics, the predictive analysis has often involved the use of highly sophisticated statistical models. Even at the level of descriptive analysis, jurimetrics can contribute significantly to the research on judicial process in Asian countries. Large amount of data on voting behaviour of judges can be quantitatively analysed and classified so as to reveal certain patterns and uniformities suggesting several new hypotheses. It would also provide a better understanding of judicial process in Asian countries because of its ability to encapsule vast amount of information and present it in a systematic manner which is not possible under the conventional common law tools of research in this area.

The other difficulties arising out of the cultural differences in terms of the accepted content, style and sophistication of ordinary nonmetric comment on judicial process appear to be transitional in nature. Even in the United States, none of this was salient just about forty years back. It is because of the introduction of a pragmatic approach in legal education, better coordination among scholars from different disciplines and persistent efforts by the jurimetricians, that a new culture and orientation could be acquired. The differences are not inherent in the two systems, and the difficulties which are being felt by the jurimetricians at present as a result of the absence of such a culture in Asian countries may not necessarily continue as jurimetric research establishes its credentials among the prevailing orientations of the contemporary Asian intellectualism.

Since, jurimetrics has often been associated with classifications, tables, graphs and diagrams, ordinarily considered alien to legal culture, lawyers trained in the glorious traditions of the Common Law rhetorics, would normally consider it as sheer waste of time and energy meddling with cumbersome calculus. They may, on the other hand, find these statistical representations as too technical to comprehend. In the alternative, some may entertain the feeling that jurimetrics is an unwaranted "American neo-imperialism"[48] of the intellect and, this "outlandish"[49] intrusion into our lands must be resisted with all the might. Whatever may have been the reason besides some of the difficulties actually felt by the jurimetricians, there has not been sufficient interest in these countries in the possibility of application of the quantitative methods in judicial research.

Scope of Jurimetrics in Judicial Research

Jurimetrics involves substantially the use of quantitative methods in judicial research. Quantitative methods are essentially aids to description. They help to bring out in details the regularities in the data researcher has collected. Means, ratios and per centages are ways of summarizing the features and relationships in data. Statistical measures based on the theory of probability go beyond the mere quantitative data and use devices to bring out the association between variables emerging out of data.[50] Such associations at times can be used to test the existing hypotheses, or else, they may suggest modifications, refinements or reformulation of the old one. Quantitative methods are generally suited to the handling of large quantities of data, and wide range of variables.

The bulk of the data and the complexity of the variables involved may make it extremely difficult to handle the data manually. For this reason, it is desirable to make use of the computer which has opened up, in all scholarly fields, unprecedented opportunities to look beyond our fragmentary items of unconnected knowledge.

Any social scientist making a study of the judicial process would no doubt be struck by the great quantity of relevant data systematically recorded and accessible to one who wishes to use it. This is not always true in social science research. In the common law countries, particularly, because of the binding nature of precedence, the decisions of the higher appellate courts assume special significance for the subordinate courts. For this reason at least it becomes almost inevitable that such decisions are systematically recorded and published as far as possible. The researcher can extract variety of information from these reports, information which is otherwise considered to be as of no consequence under the traditional approaches to the study of judicial process. Information such as the parties to the litigation before the court the kind of subject matter litigated, the nature of the Court's response, the voting response of the individual judges and so forth. This information when classified and presented in tabular form is likely to reveal certain patterns and regularities. A simple exercise like this itself can reveal much that ordinarily remain embedded under the plethora of reports, and can be utilized in testing several propositions which are often made but never really tested. The associations between these regularities can then be projected into a predictive fashion. Moreover, when observed consistently over a period of time in a category of cases, these regularities are likely to bring to the surface those elements in judicial decision-making which are highly subjective, non-rational and stubbornly value charged. Thus, if jurimetrics reduces our judges to ciphers, it does so far a paradoxical reason: "to reduce them to ciphers may be the best way to discover and explore their humanity".[51]

While all this may seem impractical to many, perhaps some will agree that the ideas and concepts that such an approach attempts to express are not substantively competitive with established approaches to the law. Jurimetrics is not a substitute for the basic elements of judicial reasoning. Essentially, it involves putting a series of questions that are capable of investigation.

It seeks not sudden revelations or universal laws, but, the slow accretion of tested information. Perhaps the greatest and most obvious advantage of jurimetrics lies in that it helps us determine how fully they rest on historical accident or on practical limitations inherent in the traditional approaches to the law.[52] Certainly, jurimetrics does not offer any social panaceas. Since it seeks primarily to understand judicial behaviour through mathematical analysis of judges' voting records often regardless of judicial talk, it suffers from certain obvious limitations. One such limitation flows from its inability to discriminate between decisions according to their meritorious worth. It has to assume, on the other hand, that all cases are of equal worth in determining judges' attitudes. While, this may appear absurd to many, yet differential treatment of cases is not possible within the ambit of mathematical analysis.[53] Likewise, vote base response often ignores multiple issues that are raised and answered in several decisions. Jurimetric has also been criticized for completely disregarding motives as it is argued that in discounting motives it discounts a crucial perhaps, the most crucial element in human conduct.[54]

But then limitations are as integral to jurimetrics as to any other approach, method, or thought process seeking to unravel the mystery of human nature. This is what seems to have prompted Francis Bacon to remark, "it cannot be that axioms established by argumentation alone can suffice for the discovery of new works, since the subtlety of nature is greater many a times over than the subtlety of argumentation".[55]

Notes

1. See Lee Loevinger, "Jurimetrics - The Next Step Foward", 33 *Minn.L.Rev.* 455 (1949).
2. Loevinger, "Jurimetrics: The Methodology of Legal Inquiry", 28 Law and Contemporary Problems 7 (1963) see also *id.*, "Jurimetrics : Science and Prediction in the Field of Law", 46 *Minn.L.Rev.* 255 (1961).
3. Loevinger, "Jurimetrics : The Methodology of Legal Inquiry," *ibid.*
4. *Id. at 7.*
5. Cited in Julius Stone, *Human Law And Human Justice* 68-69 (1965).
6. *Ibid.*
7. Bodenheimer, Jurisprudence, *The Philosophy and Method of the Law* 92 (Harvard Univ. Press Cambridge, 1970).
8. Cited in Loevinger, "Jurimetrics : The Methodology of Legal Inquiry,".
9. *Ibid.*
10. *Ibid.*

11. See, A.R. Blackshield, "Quantitative Analysis : The High Court of Australia, 1964-1969" 3 *LAWASIA* 2(1972).
12. Holmes, *The Path of the Law*, 10.
13. Karl N. Llewellyn, "Some Realism About Realism", 44 *Harv.L.Rev.* 1222 (1931).
14. Benjamin N.Cardozo, *The Nature of the Judicial Process* (1927).
15. Jerome Frank, *Law And The Modern Mind* (1930).
16. Cohen, "Transcendental Nonsense and the Functional Approach", 35 *Colum.L.Rev.* 847 (1935).
17. Glendon Schubert, "Judicial Attitudes and Voting Behaviour : The 1961 Term of the United States Supreme Court". 28 *Law and Contemporary Problems*, 10 (1963).
18. *Ibid*.
19. Blackshield, *supra*, note 11 at 2.
20. Glendon Schubert, supra, note 17 at 101.
21. C.Herman *Pritchett, The Roosvelt Court: A study in Judicial Politics And Value, 1937-1947* (New York, Macmillan, 1948).
22. J.B. Grossman and J. Tanenhaus, "Towards A Renascence of Public Law" in *Frontiers of Judicial Research* (John Wileg & Sons, 1969).
23. Schubert, *Quantitative Analysis of Judicial Behaviour* (Free Press of Glencoe, Illinois, 1960); *Id., Judicial Behaviour: A Reader in Theory and Research* (1964); Id., The Judicial Mind (1965); Id., *Judicial Policy Making* (1974 edn.); Id., *The Judicial Mind Revisited* (1974); G.Schubert and D.Danelski (ed.) *Comparative Judicial Behaviour* (1969).
24. David J.Danelski, "The Influence of the Chief Justice in the Decisional process" in Walter F.Murphy and C.H. Pritchett (eds.), *Court Judges and Politics* 497-508 (New York : Random House, 1961); *id.*, also see *supra*, note 23 and *id., A Supreme Court Justice is Appointed* (1964).
25. Sidney Ulmer, "The Analysis of Behaviour Patterns on the United States Supreme Court", 22 *J.Politics* 629 (1960); *id*, "Supreme Court Behaviour in Racial Exclusion Cases, 1935-1960", 56 *Am.Pol.Society Rev.* 325 (1962); id., *Courts as small and not so small Groups* (New York; General Learning Press, 1971); id., "Quantitative Analysis of Judicial Process; Some Practical and Theoretical Applications: 28 *Law and Contemporary Problems* 164 (1963).
26. Stuart S.Nagel, "Off the Bench Judicial Attitudes", in Schubert ed., *Judicial Decision-Making* 43 (1963); id., "Political Party Affiliation and Judges' decisions" 55 *Am.Pol.Sci.Rev.* 843 (1961); *id.*, "Ethnic Affiliations and Judicial Propensities", 24 J.*Politics* 92 (1962).
27. Fred Kort "Predicting Supreme Court Decision Mathematically; A quantitative Analysis of the Right to counsel cases". 51 *Am.Pol.Sci.Rev.* 1(1957); see also id., "A Reply to Fisher's Mathematical Analysis of Supreme Court Decisions," 28 *Law and Contemporary Problems* 143 (1963); id., "Quantitative Content Analysis of Judicial Opinions" in Schubert, Judicial decision Making (1963).
28. Joseph Tanenhaus, "The cumulative Scaling of Judicial Decisions" 79 *Harvard Law Rev.* 1583 (1966), J. Tanenhaus and Walter Murphy, *The Study of Public Law* (New York; Random House 1972); Id., "Supreme Court Attitudes Toward Federal Administrative Agencies", 22 *J. Politics* 502 (1960); Grossman and Tanenhaus (eds.), *supra* note 22.
29. Joel B. Grossman, "Social Backgrounds and Judicial Decision Making", 79 *Harvard Law Rev.* 1557 (1966) *id.*, "Social Backgrounds and Judicial Decisions: Notes for a Theory,: 29, *J.Politics* 334 (1967); *id.*, "Further Thoughts on consensus and conversions: A Reply to Professor Goldman" 31 *J.Politics* 223 (1969).

30. For Instance, see Sheldon Goldman, "Background, Attitudes and the Voting Behaviour of Judges: A comment on Grossman's Social Backgrounds and Judicial Decisions", 31 *J.Politics* 214 (1969); John D. Sprague, *Voting Patterns of the United States Supreme Court* (Indian apolis; Bobs Merrill, 1969); Harold Spaeth, The Supreme Court Policy Making (W.H. Freeman, San Francisco, 1979).
31. See, *supra*, note 23.
32. Pritchett, *supra* note 21; Schubert, *Quantitative Analysis of Judicial Behaviour* (1960), Snyder, "The Supreme Court as small Group," 38 Social Forces 232 (1958); Ulmer, "The Analysis of Behaviour Patterns on the United States Supreme Court", *supra* note 25.
33. Schubert, *Constitutional Politics, The Political Behaviour of Supreme Court Justices And the Constitutional Policies That They Make*, see Ch. 3 (1960); See also, Tanenhaus, *supra* note 28.
34. See, Ulmer, "Quantitative Analysis of Judicial Process", *supra* note 25 at 167.
35. Ulmer, "The Political Party variable in the Michigan Supreme Court", *J.Public Law* 352 (1962); Schubert, *Quantitative Analysis of Judicial Behaviour* (1960).
36. Ulmer, *supra* note 35.
37. Nagel, "Political party Affiliation and Judges' Decisions", 55 *Am.Pol.Sci.Rev.* 843 (1961).
38. Ulmer, "Quantitative Analysis of Judicial Process," *supra* note 26 at 170.
39. By far the best account of the background characteristics of the United States Supreme Court Judges is to be found in John R. Schmidhauser, "The Justices of the Supreme Court; A Collective Portrait", 3 *Midwest Journal of Political Science* 1-49 (1959); *id.*, "Stare Decises, Dissent and the background of the Justices of the Supreme Court of United States" *XIV U.Toonto L. Journal* 194 (1961-62); *id.*, *The Supreme court: Its Policies, Personalities & Procedures* (New York, 1960), Henry J. Abraham, *Justices and Presidents: A Political History of Appointments to the Supreme Court* (Oxford University Press, 1974); Joel B. Grossman, *Lawyers and Judges; the ABA and the Politics of Judicial selection* (Wiley, 1965); See also, Ulmer, *supra* note 35, Nagel, *Supra* note 37; Grossman, *Supra*, note 29; Harold W. Chase, *Federal Judges; The Appointing Process* 3-47 (1972).
40. Jack W. Peltason, *Federal Courts in the Political Process* (New York, 1955); *id.*, "A political science of Public Law", 34 South Western Social Science Quarterly 51 (1953); Rosenblum, *Law as a Political Instrument* (Random House, 1964) Martin Shapiro, *Law and Politics in the Supreme Court*. (Free press, New York, 1964), The Political Process approach seems to have impressed legal scholars and political scientists in other parts of the world as well. For instance, see, J.A.G. Griffiths, *The Politics of the Judiciary*, (1977); Upendra Baxi, *The Indian Supreme Court and Politics* (1980) see also id., *Courage Craft and Contention: The Indian Supreme Court in the Eighties* (1985); George H. Gadbois, Jr., "The Supreme Court of India as a Political Institution", in R. Dhavan, R. Sudarshan and S. Khurshid (Eds.) *Judges and the Judicial Power* 250 (1985).
41. Pritchett, "The Development of Judicial Research", in Grossman and Tanenhaus, *supra* note 22 at 7.
42. *Id.* at 7.
43. A.R. Blackshield, *supra* note 11, also see the literature on other countries cited therein in foot note 7; In addition to these, see articles on Japan, West Germany, Swiss Federal Court and Australian High Court in Grossman and Tanenhaus, *supra* note 22. Quantitative studies on Indian Supreme Court are largely the

work of an American Political scientist, George H. Gadbois, "Indian Supreme Court Judges-a Portrait", 2 *Law and Society Review* 317 (1986); *id.*, "Selection Background characteristics and voting Behaviour of Indian Supreme Court Judges, 1950-59" in G. Schubert and D. Danelski (ed.) *Comparative Judicial Behaviour: Cross-Cultural Studies of Political Decision Making in the East And West* 221 (1969); *id.*, "Indian Judicial Behaviour", 5 *Economic and Political Weekly* 149 (1970) *id.*, " The Supreme Court of India: a Preliminary Report of an Empirical Study", 4 *Journal of Constitutional and Parliamentary Studies* 33, (1970); *id.*, "Supreme Court Decision-making" 10 *Banaras Law Journal* 1 (1974); *id.*, "Participation in Supreme Court Decision-Making" 24 *Journal of the Indian Law Institute* 1 (1982); id., "The Decline of Dissent on the Supreme Court, 1950-81", in Ram Avtar Sharma (ed.) *Justice and Social order in India* 261 (1984); and *id.*, "The Supreme Court of India as a Political Institution: in Dhavan, Sudharshan and Khurshid (ed.) *supra* note 35 at 250. Besides, the use of quantitative methods can also be seen in V.S.K. Haranath "Supreme Court of India, 1950-70: An Empirical Enquiry into Judicial Behaviour:, 7 *Journal of Constitutional and Parliamentary Studies* 94 (1973) and Rajeev Dhavan, *The Supreme Court of India: A Socio-legal critique of its juristic techniques* (1977); *id.*, *The Supreme Court Under strain: The Challenge of Arrears* (1978); Dhavan & Jacob, *Selection and Appointment of Supreme Court Judges;A case study* (1978).

44. See, Blackshield, *supra* note 11 at 5.
45. *Ibid.*
46. *Ibid.*
47. *Id.* at 6. Also see Gadbois, "Supreme Court Decision Making", *supra*, note 43 at 38-39.
48. Blackshield, *supra* note 11 at 4.
49. *Ibid.*
50. A.L. Epstein (ed.), *The Craft of Social Anthropology*, 20 (1979).
51. Blackshield, *supra* note 11 at 3.
52. Reed Dickerson, "Some Jurisprudential Implications of Electronics Data Processing". 28 *Law and contemporary Problems* 69 (1963).
53. For a critique on this and other accounts, see, Wallace Mendelson, "The Neo-Behavioural Approach to the Judicial Process : A critique", 57 *Am.Pol.Sci.Rev.* 593 (1963); see also, Dahl, "The Behavioural Approach in Political Science: Epitaph for a monument to a successful protest", 55 *Am.Pol.Sci.Rev.* 763 (1961).
54. Mendelson, *supra*, note 54 at 596.
55. Cited in Selltir, Jahoda, Deutsch, Cook, *Research Methods in Social Relation* 32 (1959).

Part I
The Decision Makers

2

Appointment of the Chief Justice of India

The Chief Justice of India occupies an important position in the institutional framework of the Court. This importance may be accorded to him for various reasons. He plays an important role in the appointments of his colleagues in the Court. He is responsible for constituting division benches and determine their composition which perform the decision making function of the Court. He is also the administrator, the manager and the leader of the Court. In addition, he is normally consulted by the government in all matters relating to the judiciary and in particular to the Supreme Court. All appointments of the officers and servants of the Court are to be made by the Chief Justice.[1] The Chief Justice is also to be consulted in all appointments and transfers in the High Courts. He is thus an important structural link between the judiciary as such and the executive.

The Chief Justice is to be appointed by the President after consultation with such of the judges of the Supreme Court and of the High Courts in the States as the President may deem necessary for the purpose.[2] However, in this case, unlike in those of appointment of judges other than the Chief Justice, the Constitution is silent on whether the outgoing Chief Justice need to be consulted at all. There being no Constitutional obligation for the President to consult the outgoing Chief Justice, it would appear that the appointment of the Chief Justice is purely at the discretion of the executive. Nevertheless, it is a moot point whether the consultation with the judges of the Supreme Court and the High Courts can be regarded as a precondition to the appointment of the Chief Justice and, the failure on the part of the executive to fulfill this requirement could be invoked to challenge the appointment?[3] It would be useful, however, to examine some of the available evidence on the appointments of successive Chief Justices since the court's inception in 1950, and try and examine the role of the executive in such appointments and its implications for the court as an institution.

Seniority Convention

In November, 1951 when the Chief Justiceship fell vacant for the first time due to Chief Justice Kania's untimely death, Home Minister Katju is believed to have made an offer to Setalvad the then Attorney General of India to succeed Kania. It appears that the Home Minister's mind was working on the English pattern of the Attorney General becoming the Lord Chief Justice, but Setalvad had already passed the age of retirement for Supreme Court judges (65 years) which the Home Minister had not realised.[4] Patanjali Shastri, then the senior most judge[5] in the Court, who was appointed as the acting Chief Justice, was later appointed as the Chief Justice.

Evidence, however, suggests that something more had transpired before Patanjali Shastri was finally confirmed as the Chief Justice of India. M.C. Chagla, in his autobiography recalls that, "when Kania died, I understand Setalvad, unknown to me, strongly pressed my claim with Nehru".[6] Earlier, Chagla was offered puisne judgeship in the Federal Court before the Constitution came into force. Chief Justice Kania, according to the author, had assured him that in the ordinary course he (Chagla) should succeed him as the Chief Justice when he retires, but Chagla had declined the offer as he thought he was doing more useful work as Chief Justice of Bombay High Court than he would be doing as a puisne judge in the Supreme Court.[7] He further claims that he had consulted Setalvad, "who agreed with him that he should not accept a puisne judgeship, but should accept the Chief Justiceship (if) it was offered after Kania's retirement.[8] "Nehru", therefore says the author, "seemed agreeable but ... the judges of the Supreme Court threatened to resign if the seniority rule was not followed, and the Government yielded to the threat".[9]

This is perhaps the first account of its kind which suggests that the Supreme Court judges had started thinking of promotion to the Chief Justiceship in terms of seniority way back in 1951 itself. The collective threat of the judges to resign if the seniority rule was not followed was an indicator to a possible crises which may erupt in future in the event the government decided not to follow the criteria insisted upon by them.

Not long after Shastri was confirmed as the Chief Justice of India, there occurred another incident which created unnecessary feeling and heart burning among some of the judges of the Court. Setalvad was reported to have remarked that a frequent succession in the office of the Chief Justice of India was undesirable and that care should be taken while appointing the Chief Justice to see that the person appointed to the office would have a fairly long tenure so that he could have the time to leave an impress on the judicial performance of the Court.[10] A story thus went round that Setalvad had recommended to the government that in appointing a successor to Chief Justice Shastri they should give effect to this policy and appoint as a successor to him not Justice Mahajan or Justice Mukherjea who would have each a short term but Justice Das who was next in seniority so that the Court could have a Chief Justice with a long tenure. The two senior judges whose succession he was supposed to have urged 'naturally took umbrage at the idea and threatened to resign their office as judges'.[11] This account further provides a measure of the intense feelings of the senior judges against any attempt at being bypassed in the appointment of the Chief Justice.

Since Chief Justice Kania and Home Minister Sardar Patel were responsible for Mahajan's appointment to the Federal Court much against the wishes of Prime Minister Nehru in 1947,[12] it is quite likely that Nehru was not very happy at the prospects of Mahajan succeeding Patanjali Shastri as Chief Justice in 1954. It is in this context that the above incident assumes importance as at least Mahajan did seem to have real apprehensions about being bypassed. Otherwise, the threat to resign could not have emanated from mere rumours. Both Mahajan as well as Mukherjea were, however, elevated to the Chief Justiceship respectively on the basis of seniority rule, and the practice thereafter continued until 1964.

The appointment of the Chief Justice once again created an unprecedented situation when Chief Justice B.P. Sinha was due to retire. Justice Imam, who was then the seniormost judge, should have been the obvious choice, but was not considered for appointment to the office of Chief Justice because he was believed to be medically unfit to discharge the function of a judge. P.B.

Gajendragadkar, the next seniormost judge in the Court was designated Chief Justice to succeed B.P. Sinha. Gajendragadkar, however, found himself in a rather embarrassing situation to take over as Chief Justice as long as Justice Imam continued to be a member of the Supreme Court Bench, as that would clearly amount to supersession of the seniormost judge in the Court. In order to avoid this kind of a situation, Justice Imam was persuaded to resign before Gajendragadkar was actually sworn in as the Chief Justice of India.[13] In other words, one may argue that this was done, not so much in order to avoid embarrassment to the new Chief Justice, as to avoid creating a precedent in favour of bypassing the claim of the seniormost judge, a situation that had become almost inevitable under the circumstances. In view of the fact that Justice Imam was prevailed upon, though much against his wishes, to resign before the new Chief Justice took over technically there was no supersession as Gajendragadkar automatically stepped in the shoes of the seniormost judge.

But what is significant about this incident is the executive's role in bringing about the much needed resignation of Justice Imam which was viewed both at the Bar and the Bench as of crucial importance. Prime Minister Nehru told the delegation consisting of Setalvad and Daphtary, the then Attorney General, of various steps the government had already taken in the direction they had desired, and that in fact a report by a competent medical man from the All India Medical Institute had indicated that Justice Imam was not fit to discharge his judicial duties. "The Prime Minister assured us", says Setalvad, "that, in his view, it would be possible to bring about Justice Imam's retirement without moving the Parliament".[14] Nehru ultimately succeeded in persuading Imam to resign in February, 1964. The executive, thus, by its own actions gave credibility to promotion strictly by seniority - a principle to which it was neither legally nor morally obligated, particularly, under the circumstances.

It may be relevant to mention here that prior to this, in 1958, the Law Commission had considered the prevailing practice of promoting the seniormost judge to Chief Justiceship, and had observed in this regard:

> "It would appear that such a promotion has become almost a matter of course. We have referred to the high and important duties which the Chief Justice of India is

called upon to perform. It is obvious that succession to an office of this character cannot be regulated by mere seniority."[15]

Therefore, at least for the executive which is entrusted with the responsibility of appointing the Chief Justice, there was no urgency in seeking the resignation of Justice Imam. In doing so, the executive had linked the appointment of the new Chief Justice with resignation or removal of the incumbent judge to clear the way for the implementation of the seniority rule.

Does this mean that the executive was committed to promotion to Chief Justiceship strictly in terms of seniority, and that was why it did not heed to the Law Commission's suggestion? The later developments do not in any way vindicate this suggestion. For instance, an editorial comment on changes in the Chief Justiceship of India in January 1971 clearly suggested the possibility of supersession of the then seniormost judge, Justice J.C. Shah. It had observed that, "speculation was quite rife and disquieting rumours were circulating that political considerations may influence the choice of a successor to Hidayatullah C.J., when he retired".[16] Significantly, the editorial also portrayed the prevailing mood towards any kind of executive interference and the kind of fear and apprehensions which will be aroused if any such motivation operated in regard to the Chief Justiceship. The editorial went on to remark that, "it would have been calamitous and the one institution in India which has commanded universal respect because of its reputation for integrity and independence would have suffered a loss of prestige both at home and abroad".[17] Contrary to the speculations, Justice Shah, the seniormost judge was, however, appointed Chief Justice, and he served the Court in that capacity for the briefest period of 36 days before he retired from the Supreme Court.[18]

Again, in January 1971 there were speculations that Sikri, the next seniormost judge may not be appointed as the Chief Justice. It was believed that the government was considering some one (possibly Kumaramanglam, the then Minister of Steel and Mines in the Union Cabinet) from outside the Court for the appointment. This impression was not a mere exercise in vague speculations as later developments partly confirmed. Defending the appointment of A.N. Ray as Chief Justice of India in April 1973, Kumaramanglam is believed to have said in Parliament that, "the social philosophy of the superseded judges (Shelat, Grover and Hegde) did not coincide with the thinking of the Government which had won a massive mandate from the people. *We did not want to appoint even Sikri but, at that time our plate was too full because of the dispute over the crisis within the Congress Party (emphasis supplied).*[19] This frank admission reveals a perceptible change in the government's attitude towards the judicial appointments as such, and the Supreme Court appointments in particular.

Implicit in this admission is the clear denial of the myth that judges are neutral and the process by which they arrive at decisions is a stereotype mechanical function which operates within the confines of legal logic. It also assumes that judges cannot be treated as interchangeable parts of a machine, neither can they be looked upon as 'powerful robots who strike institutional thunderbolts' without ever realising the impact of their momentum.[20] Kumaramanglam's statement was a clear recognition of the reality of the judges' role in the political system. One would, therefore, think that the executive's attitude towards Supreme Court appointments must have changed radically during this period which made it possible for the executive to reassert its privilege and bring about the supersessions on the eve of Sikri's retirement in April, 1973.

The Supersessions

The appointment of the fourteenth Chief Justice had suddenly made a departure from the past practice of following scrupulously the seniority convention and appointing the seniormost judge next in line as the Chief Justice. The executive chose A.N. Ray as the next Chief Justice who was then occupying the fourth position amongst the senior judges overlooking the claims of three seniormost judges, Shelat, Grover and Hegde. The decision superseding the three judges was announced on the day following the delivery of the judgment in the *Fundamental Rights* case[21] which by majority overruled the *Golaknath*[22] decision and conceded to Parliament the right to amend Part III of the Constitution. This may have its relevance in view of the timings of the two significant events occurring one after the other leading to a general belief that the position taken by the three judges, not being too favourable from the government's point of view, had possibly led to their supersession. For instance, Nayar writing on supersessions later recalled how when Grover, one of the superseded judges, learnt about it, "he could not believe his ears. He had never expected it. He knew his judgment in *Fundamental Rights* case went against the governments' thinking but he never thought he could be "punished" if he said that Fundamental Rights were beyond the pale of Parliament".[23]

This statement characterises the kind of response which supersessions generally evoked. But, the move certainly could not have been so direct a repercussion as suggested, neither did it emanate so suddenly as it appeared to be. In this context it would be important to note that though there were protests from the politicians (mostly among members of the opposition), the press, some prominent sections of the Bar and the retired judges of the High Courts and the Supreme Court, yet no protests of any description came from anyone of the sitting judges of the Supreme Court against the supersessions this time. Not even the seniormost amongst the sitting judges who might have been affected in future[24] by this decision joined their three superseded brethrens in raising the protest. All this suggests at least, that the 'seniority rule' did not draw any support from within the institution and perhaps no longer enjoyed the strong commitment of the members of the Court as it did at one time. It is understandable that the sitting judges would feel constrained to air their views against the supersessions while on the bench, none of them even after retiring from the court is known to have expressed their stand on the issue.

It is also, important to take into account the overall political environment within which the supersessions could be possible. Kumaramanglam's statement referred to earlier indicates that what happened in 1973 could have been brought about even earlier but for the internal political crisis within the Congress party. By 1973 Mrs. Gandhi had not only established her supremacy over the party, but had led the country successfully through a war, had obtained a massive mandate from the electorate, had nationalised the major Indian Banks, extinguished the privy purses of the former Indian rulers, and had amended the Constitution in a significant manner. Although, the Supreme Court decisions in *Bank Nationalisation*[25] and *Privy purses*[26] cases had the effect of postponing the implementation of her policies for a while, she had overcome most of the hurdles by then. All these factors did help

Mrs. Gandhi in a significant way to take the plunge, even if it meant possibly a loss of popularity which perhaps she knew would be short lived.

The storm of protests and the debates which followed the supersessions have been sufficiently documented by now and it is not necessary to recall them here, except to say that the storm disappeared and the debates which essentially had political and emotional overtones subsided without achieving any purpose. The resolution adopted by the eminent leaders of the Bar at the Ashoka Hotel in New Delhi on the Eleventh and Twelveth of August, 1973 and duly presented to the President, Prime Minister and the Minister of Law and Justice is an indication to this effect. The resolution had proposed that the appointment to higher judiciary at all levels be recommended by Committees of Chief Justices, prescribed number of seniormost justices, and prescribed number of senior advocates. Once this was institutionalised, the norm of seniority should ipso facto apply in elevation of a justice to Chief Justiceship of India or of the High Courts.[27] The method suggested by the resolution was in fact a retrograde step in the sense that it sought to shift the venue of power to appoint judges from an accountable body to a body which was neither representative nor would be accountable to anyone whatsoever.[28] This was perhaps the reason why the Constituent Assembly did not favour to vest a veto on judicial appointments even in the Chief Justice of India by providing for consultation in place of concurrence in article 124(2) of the Constitution. The resolution failed to evoke substantial support.[29]

Consequently, in view of the virtual lack of a principled opposition the executive did get away with supersessions not only in 1973 but in 1977 too when Beg instead of H.R. Khanna, the then seniormost judge, succeeded Chief Justice A.N. Ray on his retirement.

Recollecting the events preceding to his supersession, Justice Khanna writes in his autobiography, "as the date for the appointment of new Chief Justice came closer, I started feeling somewhat uneasy and would be seized occasionally by some inner tension. I, however, decided not to see anyone or talk to anyone in connection with my appointment".[30] Once again when the supersession took place, no one from among the sitting judges of the Supreme Court raised any protest. Justice Khanna was to suffer it alone and perhaps he did undergo mental anguish on this account since the very day he decided to write a dissent in *Habeas Corpus*[31] case during the emergency.[32]

Although protests were raised from various quarters, the intensity of criticism against the government did not appear to be so strong as it was in 1973. After Justice Khanna's dissent in *Habeas Corpus* decision, like him, others too had almost anticipated this action. Moreover, this time the situation was a little different from the earlier controversy. Justice Khanna had a relatively short term left on the Court, and the government conveniently resorted to the argument that because of his short tenure there was no point in elevating him to the office of Chief Justice. It was clearly an argument without much substance because atleast three Chief Justices (Sarkar, Subbarao and Shah) had served shorter terms in the past than the term which would have been served by Justice Khanna if he were elevated in accordance with the seniority principle. One possible reason why supersession of Justice Khanna did not evoke prolonged reaction could be because the general elections had been called in India after the nineteen months emergency and while the nation prepared to elect their representatives, the controversy died down.

The Janata Government which came to power in the post-emergency period rededicated itself to the 'seniority rule', and despite opposition this time from certain quarters to the government's resolve to follow scrupulously the seniority convention,[33] elevated Chandrachud, the then seniormost judge to Chief Justiceship at the retirement of Chief Justice Beg in February, 1978. The opposition to Chandrachud being appointed to the highest post was obviously prompted by the position he took in *Habeas Corpus* decision during the emergency. A few months before the decision to appoint Chandrachud as Chief Justice was announced, laying at rest various speculations about whether the Janata Government would reinstate the status quo disturbed by supersessions in 1973 and 1977, Prime Minister Morarji Desai made it known that it is the government and not the lawers who make judicial appointments.[34] In 1985 the elevation of Justice P.N. Bhagwati, the seniormost judge, to Chief Justiceship and thereafter all the appointments to this apex office till date seem to have finally resolved the controversial issue by a silent acquiescence to seniority convention.

Chief Justices and the Court

The Supreme Court had seventeen Chief Justices including Chief Justice Bhagwati who was appointed w.e.f. July 13, 1985 at the retirement of Chief Justice Chandrachud. The table below shows the Chief Justices of the Court from 1950 upto 1981 spread over a period of thirty one years.

Table I: Chief Justices of India, 1950-1981

Sl. No.	Name	Term		Tenure			Remarks
		From	To	Yrs.	Mts.	Dys.	
1.	Kania	26.01.50	06.11.51	1	9	12	Died in Office
2.	Shastri	07.11.51	03.01.54	2	1	27	
3.	Mahajan	4 .1.54	22.12.54	0	11	20	
4.	B.K. Mukherjea	23.12.54	01.02.56	1	1	10	Resigned due to ill health
5.	S.R.Das	02.02.56	30.09.59	3	7	28	
6.	B.P.Sinha	01.10.59	31.01.64	4	4	1	
7.	Gajendra-gadkar	01.02.64	15.03.66	2	1	15	
8.	Sarkar	16.03.66	30.6.66	0	3	15	
9.	Subbarao	01.07.66	11.04.67	0	8	11	Resigned to contest Presidential election
10.	Wanchoo	12.04.67	25 .02.68	0	10	15	
11.	Hidayatullah	26.02.68	17.12.70	2	10	0	
12.	J.C.Shah	18.12.70	22.01.71	0	1	5	Held Office for shortest period
13.	S.M.Sikri	23.1.71	26.4.73	2	3	5	
14	A.N.Ray	27.04.73	29.01.77	3	8	2	First Superession
15.	M.H.Beg	30.01.77	22.07.78	1	1	22	Second Supersession
16.	Y.V. Chandrachud	23.02.78	12.07.85	7	4	14	Longest period served as C.J.

During this period, seventy one judges were appointed to the Court, and sixteen i.e. 22.5 per cent of these were elevated to the highest office of the Chief Justice of India. On an average, therefore, a Chief Justice had less than two years term on the Court, which means that a Chief Justice had to be appointed almost every two years. There are noticeable exceptions where Chief Justices served the Court for longer period. Prominent among them was Y.V. Chandrachud who had the singular distinction of heading the Court for the longest period of over seven years followed by B.P. Sinha, S.R. Das and A.N. Ray.

The death of Chief Justice Kania in November, 1951 brought an early end to what would have been a fairly long lasting[35] Chief Justiceship as in the normal course Kania would have retired in November, 1955. This would have deprived both Patanjali Shastri as well as Mahajan of leading the Court and would have substantially cut down on Mukherjea's tenure as Chief Justice too. Chief Justice Mukherjea, however, resigned because of ill-health almost seven months before he was due to retire.

Thus, during the first six years, the Court had as many as five Chief Justices. The next eight years were relatively stable as during this period the Court was led only by two Chief Justices, S.R. Das and B.P. Sinha respectively. This stability, however, did not last long and as the table clearly shows, the next seven years (1964-1971) had as many as seven Chief Justices four of whom served the Court for very short terms ranging approximately between one month (Shah) and ten months (Wanchoo).

The Period 1973-81

This period recorded some of the most eventful happenings in the history of appointments made to the office of the Chief Justice of India as discussed earlier. Three Chief Justices were appointed during a period of nine years. But for the two supersessions in 1973 and 1977 respectively, this period would have seen on the basis of seniority rule a quicker turnover of Chief Justices in the Supreme Court.

Accordingly, A.N. Ray would not have become Chief Justice if the government had not decided to jump him over the heads of three seniormost judges. Promotion by seniority, on the other hand, would not have affected Beg's chances of becoming Chief Justice as Khanna would have retired in the normal course in July 1977, except in so far as a little cut in the term which Beg would have had in his tenure. Instead of three there would have been six appointments to this office, reducing the average term from three to one and a half year for each Chief Justice during this period. Relatively speaking, in terms of continuity, the Court was under more stable leadership than it would have been if Chief Justices were appointed strictly by seniority.

The 1973 supersessions, it may be argued, had brought about a relative stability in the office of the Chief Justice, and the government did not fail to make use of this argument while justifying supersessions. The government had argued that pursuant to the Law Commissions recommendations in its *Fourteenth Report*, its action was fully in compliance with the institutional interests. But the past record was a clear indication that it could not have been the desire to implement those recommendations which prompted it to supersede the three seniormost judges. Such a step could have been taken in 1966, the year which witnessed the turnover of three Chief Justices.

Distinctive Role of the Chief Justice

The Law Commission, in 1958 had drawn the attention of the Government towards the rapid succession in the office of Chief Justice of India, and had observed: "A continuity in the office of the Chief Justice of India appears to us to be essential in the interests of judicial administration throughout the country. On him rests the tone and tradition of the highest court of the land, the law laid down by which, is the law of the country. Apart he carries in a measure responsibility for the satisfactory administration of justice in the whole of India".[36] The Law Commission, therefore, felt that only a Chief Justice who has a tenure of five to seven years can render that necessary and useful service which is expected of the Chief Justice of India.[37]

There were two ways in which this could have been achieved: by appointing younger persons to the Court and elevating only those to the office of Chief Justice who have at least five to six years to go before they retire; and secondly, by appointing a Chief Justice from outside the sitting members of the Court. Both these methods impinge upon the seniority rule which made the quick turnover of Chief Justices possible, in addition, of course, for the reason that judges invariably have made their entry to the Court at a very late stage of their careers. But if the seniority rule were to be followed strictly appointments of younger judges ipso facto could not always ensure long term and stability to the office of the Chief Justice of India. On the other hand, a selective use of 'seniority rule' without fixing a minimum term for the Chief Justice, would invite all those objections which would be raised if seniority rule is violated as it was done in 1973 and 1977.

It is clear that seniority rule may not always ensure the stability in the office of Chief Justice which seems to be so essential for an effective management and functioning of the Court.

Assuming that the Chief Justice is to be appointed for a longer term disregarding the seniority rule either from outside the Court or from amongst the younger judges in the Court, what kind of considerations other than a long tenure ought to influence the choice?

The Constitution nowhere provides for separate qualifications for the selection of the Chief Justice of India. Neither did the Constituent Assembly debate upon this issue. For the first time the Law Commission had emphasized that, "the qualifications needed for a successful Chief Justice are very different from the qualifications which go to make an erudite and able judge".[38] The Commission, therefore, suggested that, "for the performance of the duties of Chief Justice of India, there is needed, not only a judge of ability and experience, but also a competent administrator capable of handling complex matters that may arise from time to time, a shrewed judge of men and personalities and above all, a person of sturdy independence and towering personality who would, on the occasion arising, be a watch dog of the independence of judiciary".[39]

Since, in the appointment of the first thirteen Chief Justices, the seniormost judge almost automatically stepped in the highest judicial post as soon as the incumbent retired, the question of suitability of the candidate for the post of Chief Justice of India never assumed any significance. It was almost taken for granted that anyone who is good enough to be a judge is equally good to be promoted to Chief Justiceship. Neither did the two supersessions make any significant difference in this behalf. Consequently, men who served as Chief Justices of the Court were not selected on the basis of any special qualifications which endowed them particularly with leadership qualities, but because they happened to be judges of the Supreme Court and were invariably next in line by virtue of their seniority in the Court.

Despite the Law Commission's attempts to articulate the distinctive role of the Chief Justice and emphasise the considerations which should govern his appointment, the executive does not seem to have given any thought to this aspect. It must be recognised that the Chief Justice requires something more than the skill of judging particularly in view of his added responsibilities. Apart from a certain amount of stability in his tenure which would enable him to understand the problems, he must possess a mixture of administrative, management and leadership qualities. Perhaps in today's context, managing the docket is one of the foremost priorities which would require more than ordinary skill to effectively deal with the problem of mounting arrears in the Supreme Court, an aspect discussed later in chapter four.

In the ultimate analysis, it would not be inappropriate to say that the appointments to the highest judicial office were completely relegated to a mere promotion by seniority perhaps on the assumption that one who is competent to be a judge of the appex court is equally good to be elevated to the office of the Chief Justice of India. The role of the executive in this regard simply amounted to formalising the arrangement rather thrust on it and not in conceptualising a distinctive criterion for the selection of the Chief Justice keeping in view the institutional imperatives, not withstanding the two supersessions.

Notes

1. The Constitution of India, Art. 146(1).
2. *Id.* Art.124(2).
3. Such an argument in fact was raised by some-ex-judges and lawyers in the context of the 1973 supersession controversy. See, A.R. Antulay, *Appointment of a Chief Justice* 1 (Popular Prakashan, Bombay, 1973).
4. M.C. Setalvad, *My Life: Law and Other Things*, 185 (Tripathi, Bombay, 1971).
5. M. Fazal Ali, who was senior to Patanjali Shastri had retired in September 1951, but was reappointed-ad hoc judge w.e.f. October 15, 1951.
6. M.C. Chagla, *Roses In December* 171 (Bhartiya Vidya Bhavan, Bombay, 1974).
7. *Ibid.*
8. *Ibid.*
9. *Ibid.*
10. Setalvat made a similar recommendation in his capacity as the Chairman of Law Commission of India. See, *Law Commission: Fourteenth Report* 38 (1958).
11. *Supra*, note 4 at 189-190.
12. M.C. Mahajan, *Looking Back* 191 (Asia Publishing Houses, New Delhi, 1963).
13. *Supra* note 4 at 507-508.
14. *Id.* at 508.
15. *Supra* note 10 at 39.
16. Supreme Court Journal 1 (1971).
17. *Ibid.*
18. An attempt was made to impeach Justice Shah about the time Chief Justice Hidayatullah was due to retire. See, M. Hidayatullah, *My Own Boswell Memoirs*, 263 (Arnold-Heinemann, New Delhi, 1984).
19. Kuldip Nayar (ed.), *Supersession of Judges* 36 (Indian Book Company, New Delhi, 1973).
20. The Phrase was used by Anthony Lewis, *Gideon's Trumpet* 11 (Random House, New York, 1964). See also H.R. Gokhle's (the then Minister of Law and Justice) speech in Lok Sabha defending the appointment of Mr. Justice Ray, wherein he said: "The impression which was given was that judges, as it were, were like

supermen or demigods; that they have no opinion, have no predilection have no prejudices, have no biases, etc, Every judge, whether of the Supreme Court or of the High Court or for that matter of any other court, like any other man, is subject to all these prejudices, all these opinions, the biases and the predilections". Cited in Kuldip Nayar, Supra note 19 at 99.

21. *Kesevananda Bharti* V. *State of Kerala* A.I.R. 1973 S.C. 1461.
22. *Golaknath* V. *State of Punjab*, A.I.R. 1967 S.C. 1643.
23. *Supra* note 19 at 10.
24. At the retirement of A.N. Ray in January 1977, H.R. Khanna the then seniormost judge was superseded by his junior colleague M.H. Beg.
25. *R.C. Cooper* V. *Union of India*, A.I.R. 1970 S.C. 564.
26. *Madhav Rao Scindia* V. *Union of India*, A.I.R. 1971 S.C. 530.
27. The text of the resolution is cited in a key-note paper at p.5, read by Upendra Baxi on "Appointment of the Chief Justice and Justices of the Supreme Court" at the Bar Council Seminar on Judicial Appointments held on October, 17-19 (1980).
28. Rajeev Dhavan & Alice Jacob, *Selection and Appointment of Supreme Court Judges : A Case Study* 46 (Tripathi, Bombay, 1978).
29. *Id.* at 4.
30. H.R. Khanna, *Neither Roses Nor Thorns* 83 (Eastern Book Company, Lucknow, n.d.).
31. *A.D.M. Jabalpur* V. *Shivkant Shukla*, A.I.R. 1976, S.C. 1207.
32. *Supra* note 30 at 89.
33. Bombay Memorandum which, according to The Times of India (7 January, 1978) consisted of fifty two public men and advocates, stated, "to restore the convention of seniority blindly now would be to perpetuate a hierarchy built on commitment; a hierarchy so arranged that the two seniormost sitting judges outlive sitting judges of the Supreme Court, many of whom have unexceptional records. It is a hierarchy sedulously built up by Mr. H.R. Gokhale, the then Law Minister, with an eye to guaranteeing the succession of committed judges to fill up the office of the Chief Justice". The criticism was obviously directed against the two seniormost judges, Chandrachud and Bhagwati, as both of them had a long term to serve on the Court. An alternative procedure was also suggested in this Memorandum as follows: "a judicial appointments commission should be at once constituted of five or seven persons, say three former distinguished and eminent members of the Bar (whether actively practicing or not) and the President of Bar Council of India (if elected and not otherwise). This Commission may have the power to co-opt two other non-official members who are not officers of the Government". See Dhavan & Jacob, *supra* note 28 appendix IX at 120 and 125 respectively.
34. Northern India Patrika, 13 January, 1977, cited in Id. at 124.
35. In the Indian context a period of five to six years can be considered a fairly long period in view of the fact that average term of the Chief Justice has not exceeded two years. Whereas, in America, during the last 180 years there have been as few as 15 Chief Justices in the American Supreme Court, giving an average of twelve years term to every Chief Justice. See, Henry J. Abraham, *The Judicial Process* 56-58, (Oxford University Press, 1980).
36. *Supra* note 10 at 38-39.
37. *Id.* at 39.
38. *Ibid.*
39. *Ibid.*

3

Selection and Appointment of Judges: Who Gets Appointed to the Court

The laws and the Constitution in India mean precisely what the Supreme Court judges say. The character and composition of the Court at any given point of time determines the judicial policies espoused by the Court as an institution. Any change in the composition of the Court is, therefore, likely to affect its policies as well. Consequently, any attempt to gain a proper understanding of the Court as a working institution must also take into account its decision makers.

Two questions may be asked at the outset, viz., how and why are particular men chosen to serve on the Supreme Court, and what manner of men are so chosen? The first question concerns the method of appointment and selection, and the second relates to their background characteristics. The characteristics of the men chosen for the Supreme Court are determined by a variety of factors, the more important of which include the method of their selection and appointment and the social and political conditions within which such a method operates.[1] In this chapter, we shall, first briefly examine the origin of the method in the Constituent Assembly; second, how this method has evolved over the years in the selection and appointment of puisne judges and the role of the Chief Justice in the appointment of his colleagues in the Court, and third, analyse the background characteristics of the seventy one appointees to the Court with a view to ascertain factors possibly considered important in such appointments.

The Origin of the Method

The report of the Union Constitution Committee which had considered the recommendations of the Ad hoc Committee on the

Supreme Court[2] had suggested in clause 18 that "a judge of the Supreme Court shall be appointed by the President after consulting the Chief Justice and such other judges of the Supreme Court as also such judges of the High Courts as may be necessary for the purpose".[3]

Sir N. Gopalaswami Ayyangar, who had moved this clause for discussion for the first time in the Constituent Assembly on July, 29, 1947, was rather disappointed at the abrupt manner in which the clause was disposed off. He began his concluding address by saying, "I really thought that so important an issue as the constitution and functioning of the Supreme Court of the would be Federation would occupy more time than it has this morning..."[4] The members of the Assembly at this preliminary round of discussions seemed to be generally convinced that the President will have the power to appoint judges in consultation with the Chief Justice and such other judges of the Supreme Court and the High Courts as may be necessary for the purpose. Mr. K. Santhanam had put forward an alternative proposal according to which the Chief Justice and other judges of the Supreme Court were to be appointed by the President "after consulting a joint standing committee of both Houses of the Federal Parliament consisting of six members from the House of the People and five members from the Council of States".[5] But the proposal was not pressed any further. The only other criticism that was offered against the method proposed in clause 18 came from Ananthasayanam Ayyangar who pointed out that it did not provide for the appointment of the Chief Justice himself.[6] The objection, however, was met by Sir Gopalaswami Ayyangar by saying that "even as the clause stands, a judge of the Supreme Court might be held to include the Chief Justice of the Supreme Court also".[7] This argument was clearly based on section 200(2) of the Government of India Act, 1935 which made no reference to the appointment of the Chief Justice of the Federal Court as distinct from its judges. By implication, therefore, the term judge of the Federal Court included the Chief Justice as well.

Various suggestions were considered at the time of framing the draft Constitution Article 103(2). Some members suggested that the consultation of the judges of the Supreme Court be obligatory while consulting the judges of the High Court be considered discretionary.[8] There was also a suggestion that the whole consultative process should be left informal.[9] Another suggestion was that the President should consult the Chief Justice, the Chief Justices of the High Courts and judges of the Supreme Court as regards the appointment of puisne judges to the Supreme Court. The list should then be placed before an Advisory Board of fifteen members of Parliament. A similar procedure should also be followed for the appointment of the Chief Justice of India.[10]

The method of appointing judges of the Supreme Court came up for discussion in the Constituent Assembly once again when the Draft Constitution Article 103 was moved on May 24, 1949. The drafting Committee had proposed in clause 2 of Article 103 that: "every judge of the Supreme Court shall be appointed by the President by warrant under his hand and seal after consultation with such of the judges of the Supreme Court and of the High Courts in the States as may be necessary for the purpose and shall hold office until he attains the age of sixty-five years.

Provided that in the case of appointment of a judge, other than the Chief Justice, the Chief Justice of India shall always be consulted..."[11]

Three different proposals emerged from the various amendments moved to the method suggested in the draft article. The first proposal was that the judges of the Supreme Court should be appointed with the concurrence of the Chief Justice; the other view was that the appointments made by the President should be subjected to the confirmation of two thirds vote by Parliament; and the third suggestion was that they should be appointed in consultation with the council of states. All the amendments incorporating these proposals were rejected by the Assembly. B.R. Ambedkar who had piloted the motion on draft Article 103, explained why such methods could not be adopted:

> "It seems to me in the circumstances in which we live today, where the sense of responsibility has not grown to the same extent to which we find in the United States, it would be dangerous to leave the appointments to be made by the President, without any kind of reservation or limitation, that is to say, merely on the advice of the executive of the day. Similarly, it seems to me that to make every appointment which the executive wishes to make subject to the concurrence of the legislature is also

> not a very suitable provision. Apart from its being cumbrous, it also involves the possibility of the appointment being influenced by political pressure and political considerations.
>
> With regard to the question of the concurrence of the Chief Justice it seems to me that those who advocate that proposition seem to rely implicity both on the impartiality of the Chief Justice and the soundness of his judgment. I personally feel no doubt that the Chief Justice is a very eminent person. But, after all, the Chief Justice is a man with all the failings, all the sentiments and all the prejudices which we as common people have; and I think, to allow the Chief Justice practically a veto upon the appointment of judges is really to transfer the authority to the Chief Justice which we are not prepared to vest in the President or the Government of the day. I therefore, think that that is also a dangerous proposition. A 'middle course', therefore, was adopted by the drafting Committee which provided for consultation by the President with persons who are '*ex hypothesi*' well qualified to give proper advice in matters of appointment of Supreme Court judges."[12]

Thus the method for the selection and appointment of judges of the Supreme Court as conceived by the Constituent Assembly was not a radical departure from the past, or a substantial innovation in any strict sense. The veto in matters of appointment of judges, like in the past, was vested with the executive but with a rider now attached to it in the form of consultation with the Chief Justice. The consultation with the Chief Justice of India in the appointment of puisne judges to the Supreme Court was evolved as a compromise check on the Executive's discretion in this matter. But, at the same time, it may be noticed that no such formula was evolved in the case of appointment of the Chief Justice himself. The Constitutional provisions thus remained largely favourable to the executive playing a predominant role in the judicial appointments and selections as was the case under the Government of India Act, 1935.

From the institutional point of view it would , however, be important to examine how the process of selection and appointment envisaged in the Constitution was worked out in practice and in particular the role played by the successive Chief Justices in the appointment of their colleagues in the Court through the consultative mechanism.

Appointment of Puisne Judges and the Role of the Chief Justice

Although the Constitution provides that appointments of the Supreme Court judges be made by the President after consultation with the Chief Justice of India and such judges of the Supreme Court and the High Courts the President deems necessary, appointments are actually made by the Prime Minister and the cabinet, and the President simply makes the formal announcement. In the appointment of judges other than that of Chief Justice, the Chief Justice of India must be consulted, but his concurrence is not a constitutional requirement.[13]

It seems that even before the Supreme Court came into being, a well developed practice as regards the appointment of the Federal Court judges did exist. The Government of India Act, 1935 had provided that the judges of the Federal Court shall be appointed by his Majesty by warrant under the Royal Sign Manual and shall hold office until the age of sixty five years.[14] There was no provision for consultation with either the Chief Justice or with any other judges of the Federal Court or High Courts. A similar provision governed the appointment of High Court judges before the Constitution came into force.[15]

It is, however, in evidence that both in the appointment of Federal Court judges as well as the High Court Judges, the respective Chief Justices enjoyed initiative as well as influence in the selection of their colleagues. The former Chief Justice of India, Mehar Chand Mahajan provides a glimpse of the existence of such a practice in the appointment of Federal Court judges in his autobiography. Recalling the events preceding his own appointment to the Federal Court, Mahajan records : "Chief Justice Kania had sounded me long before I was actually extended the offer of puisne judgeship on the Federal Court".[16] To which he replied that he would be quite willing to accept the offer. According to the author, Pandit Nehru, then heading the Congress Ministry, wanted Dewan Ram Lal, the then Chief Justice of East Punjab High Court, in preference to him. But, the Chief Justice of India and Home Minister Patel were of different opinion and eventually Mahajan was appointed. Referring to the correspondence between the Chief Justice and himself, the author recalls:

> "Chief Justice Kania wrote to me that he had recommended my name and there was nothing further to write till he knew that names submitted had gone through ... 'Everything has passed through as intended', he wrote to me later on and invited me to join the court ..."[17]

This shows that in the selection of nominees for the Federal Court the Chief Justice had the initiative and his recommendations carried weight with the executive. The practice of the Chief Justice initiating the process of selection seems to continue even after the Supreme Court replaced the Federal Court. In addition to this the executive was now under a Constitutional obligation to consult the Chief Justice in the appointment of judges which added a new dimension to the Chief Justice's role in this regard. Although Chief Justice's concurrence was not mendatory, the available evidence suggests that the executive has by and large respected the wishes of the Chief Justice.

All the first six judges (including the Chief Justice)[18] were appointed from the Federal Court. The seventh vacancy was filled up in September, 1950 with the appointment of N.C. Aiyar, a retired judge of the Madras High Court. Seventeen more judges were appointed to the Supreme Court by the end of the first decade. Some of these appointments were adversely commented upon by Setalvad, the first Attorney General of India, in his autobiography. According to him, Chief Justice Mahajan's choice of B.P. Sinha in 1954 was treated unenthusiastically and was felt rather awkwardly particularly when it was realised that in accordance with the Seniority Principle[19] Sinha would hold Chief Justiceship for much too long after Chief Justice S.R. Das retires. Sinha's tendency to avoid writing judgments was well known among the Nagpur Bar,[20] and for this reason he was regarded as a shirker. He had not shown any particular talent even during the years that he had been a puisne judge in the Supreme Court.[21] Similarly, commenting upon certain appointments made during the tenure of Chief Justice S.R. Das,[22] the author further remarked:

> "... though S.R. Das was a most distinguished Chief Justice, certain appointments made during his regime were unfortunate. It was believed that he (Chief Justice S.R. Das) had recommended Justice Govinda Menon in 1956 against his own inclinations and under pressure from high quarters. The appointment in early 1957 of Justices Kapur and Sarkar from East Punjab and Calcutta High Courts could not have been based on merit; Justice Kapur had shown no particular distinction as a judge ... Justice Sarkar's appointment in 1957 over the heads of some senior judges was said at Calcutta Bar to be due to his having read in early years in the Chambers of the Chief Justice."[23]

The Law Commission of India had also criticised some of these appointments and had remarked that "it is widely felt that communal and regional considerations have prevailed in making the selection of judges ... what perhaps is still more to be regretted is the general impression, that now and again executive influence exerted from the highest quarters has been responsible for some appointments to the Bench. It is undoubtedly true, that the best talent among the judges of the High Courts has not always found its way to the Supreme Court.[24] The matter was raised in Lok Sabha in 1959 and the government's attention was drawn to the remarks made by the Law Commission. Home Minister Pant emphatically denied any such suggestion when he said that "to say that the judges that have been recruited there have just been thrust on the court by somebody else is against the facts and is absolutely incorrect".[25] Citing figures, the Home Minister said that, "since 1950, seventeen judges have been appointed to the Supreme Court and every one of those judges was nominated and recommended by the Chief Justice of India".[26]

It is interesting to note that the comments, assertions and the counter assertions invoked by the appointments during the first decade had the mixed flavour of critically scrutinising not only the role of the Chief Justice but also questioning the legitimacy of the executive in influencing his choice of the candidate. So much so that the Home Minister had to defend the government's decision on the floor of the House emphatically denying that any appointee was thrust on the court against the wishes of the Chief Justice. But, given the Constitutional position, was it really necessary for the government to justify the appointments in the manner in which it sought to do.

At least two Chief Justices who served during the first decade partly substantiated the government's stand. Mehar Chand Mahajan who served as the Chief Justice in 1954, wrote in his autobiography that as the Chief Justice he had a say in the appointment of judges of the High Courts and his colleagues in the Supreme Court whenever vacancies occurred.[27] And B.P. Sinha who was the Chief Justice during the period 1959-64, admitted that the Chief Justice has the initiative in the selection process.[28]

The Chief Justice's role in the selection of nominees for the Supreme Court is also clearly brought out in the following description:

> "Though over a decade has passed since its inauguration, the Supreme Court had yet to recruit to the Court a member of the Bar. The new Chief Justice P.B. Gajendragadkar, who had taken over from Chief Justice B.P. Sinha in February, 1964 was very keen to appoint a judge from the Bar. When the Chief Justice talked to me about this, I suggested the name of Gupte, who was then the Additional Solicitor General. The Chief Justice was hesitant whether it would be right for him, a Maharashtrian, to recommend the appointment of another Maharashtrian. Gupte, however, did not accept the offer for personal reasons. Gajendragadkar then mentioned Sikri (then the Advocate General of Punjab) but wanted to be assured that Sikri had not been in any way concerned with the doings of Pratap Singh Kairon, the somewhat notorious Chief Minister of Punjab."[29]

Sikri was appointed a judge of the Supreme Court eventually after the Chief Justice had recommended his name after having cleared his doubts about the former's involvements.

The above account is corroborated by the former Chief Justice Gajendragadkar in his autobiography where he recollects that since he was eager that a member of the Bar should be appointed to the Supreme Court he had tried to persuade ... Palkhivala and Lal Narain Sinha to accept the offer but all of them declined.

Gajendragadkar then mentioned the name of Sikri to the outgoing Chief Justice Sinha and ... at his instance Sikri was asked to meet the Chief Justice at his residence. Narrating the incident, Gajendragadkar writes:

> "... the Chief Justice told him, "Sikri, I want you to join us on the Bench". He was absolutely taken by surprise. He said, "No, Chief Justice, I won't be able to do the work of a judge in the Supreme Court satisfactorily. ... Sinha said: "Leave that to me and my colleague Gajendragadkar. We have decided to recommend your name. We won't take a 'no' from you."[30]

Incidentally, it was during Sikri's tenure as Chief Justice that S.C. Roy, the only other member of the Bar to be elevated to the Supreme Court until 1981. Chief Justice Sikri has also gone on record suggesting that in all cases the opinion of the Chief Justice has been decisive.[31]

Another interesting version is to be found in the former Chief Justice Hidayatullah's memoirs wherein he writes:

> "...I was sorry that I was not called upon to appoint my colleagues A.N. Ray, P. Jagmohan Reddy and I.D. Dua as judges of the Supreme Court. It would have been interesting to see if I could consult myself ! I had recommended their appointments and it would have been a Gilbertian situation, if I rejected my own recommendations ! It would have been equal to Lord Chelmsford hearing an appeal from his own judgment and revising himself. I do not know if I could have changed opinion."[32]

While all this leaves no doubt in one's mind that, by and large, the successive Chief Justices have had a role in the selection of their colleagues in the Court, on the other hand, there are also indications of possible impositions or external pressures on their choice of nominees. The possibility of such impositions or conflict may not be ruled out particularly where the executive is not very well disposed towards the Chief Justice, or the Court as such. The early seventies appear to have witnessed some such situation which possibly might have led to the supersessions in the appointment of Chief Justice Sikri's successor in 1973. This move may as well be interpreted as the executive's attempt to make its pressure felt and assert its authority in the selection and appointment of Supreme Court judges. Never before had any one on behalf of the government categorically stated the need for inducting "committed judges" into the Court, neither did any one emphasise the executive's 'prerogative' to appoint judges.[33]

The Period 1973-81

The 1973 supersessions, therefore, marked a beginning of a new phase in the history of appointments to the Supreme Court. During the period 1973-81, twenty two appointments, were made. Ten judges were appointed during Chief Justice Ray's tenure; three during Chief Justice Beg's tenure; and, nine judges were appointed during Chief Justice Chandrachud's tenure upto 1981. It may also be recalled that during the first five months of Ray's tenure as Chief Justice four vacancies were filled up. Each one of these four appointments were distinctive in character. For instance, Justice Bhagwati was the youngest ever to be appointed to the Court; Justice Krishna Iyer was a known political activist, who had been a Minister between 1957-59 in Kerala, and had only about two years of working experience as a judge of the High Court; Justice Goswami was the first to be ever appointed from Gauhati High Court representing the North Eastern Region, and Justice Sarkaria was the first Sikh and well below in High Court seniority when elevated from the Punjab High Court.

Similarly, the appointments of Justices Fazal Ali[34] and Jaswant Singh from Jammu and Kashmir High Court within a period of one year also appear to be distinctive in character, particularly in view of the fact that the successive Chief Justices since 1950 did not find any one meritorious enough to be considered for appointment from that High Court. Three appointments[35] were made during Beg's tenure as Chief Justice, one of which had evoked considerable debate particularly in the Gujarat High Court Bar. While the Law Minister Mr. Shanti Bhushan tried to defend the government's decision by saying that, "the decision to appoint the judge was made on the advice of the Chief Justice of India",[36] the Prime Minister, Mr. Morarji Desai, on the other hand made it known that "it is the government and not the lawyers who make judicial appointments".[37]

The controversy over the appointment of Justice Desai was, however, different from the earlier controversies surrounding the appointments of the Chief Justice of India. Whereas, the supersessions of the three seniormost judges Shelat, Grover and Hedge in 1973 and that of Justice Khanna in 1977 in the appointment of the Chief Justice had clearly gone against the well established seniority convention, no violation had occurred in the appointment of Justice Desai from Gujarat High Court to the Supreme Court as seniority convention had never governed the appointment of High Court judges to the Supreme Court. Several junior judges from the High Courts were appointed to the Supreme Court in the past (see Table I *infra*).

Incidentally, in September 1977, two judges V.D. Tulzapurkar from Bombay High Court and D.A. Desai from Gujarat High Court were appointed judges of the Supreme Court. Both of them were elevated from among the puisne judges of their respective High Courts. But there was a storm of protest only about one of the two appointments then made. No less a person than M.C. Chagla went on record saying that:

> "... In the present case every principle had been violated and the appointment was either political or a glaring instance of jobbery and therefore deplorable and completely contrary to Janata Party's professed solicitude for the independence of the Judiciary."[38]

Mr. Chagla, however, did not elaborate upon how the appointment of Justice Desai was a 'glaring instance of jobbery'. The Gujarat High Court Bar passed a resolution castigating the Chief Justice of India along with his two senior colleagues for having stated that 'Justice Desai was the ablest judge of the Gujarat High Court, while recommending his appointment'.[39] The resolution further noted that "this was not a question of merely considering the judges of the Gujarat High Court only. Mr. Justice Desai held 66th rank in all India seniority of puisne judges and if all puisne judges had been considered other outstanding judges would also have been available".[40] These and other similar allegations made during the course of the controversy are well documented by Dhavan and Jacob,[41] and need not be reproduced here any further. It is unfortunate, however, that this controversy not only doubted the integrity of the government, but had also imputed motives to the Chief Justice and the sitting judges of the Supreme Court which was rather unprecedented. This was the second controversy within a year that overshadowed the appointments to the Supreme Court. The first being the supersession of Justice Khanna in the beginning of 1977. Towards the end of the same year, yet another controversy was in the offing which cast its shadow on the appointment of a successor to Chief Justice Beg who was due to retire in February 1978. The uncertainty surrounding the appointment of Justice Chandrachud as the Chief Justice has been dealt within the previous chapter.

Desai controversy is important at least in the sense that it reveals a significant change in the outlook towards the appointments to the apex court among the members of the Bar who ever since the first supersession in 1973 were clamouring for a decisive role in deciding who should sit on the High Bench. The unpalatable part of this controversy however, was the bad taste in which the matter was conceived and the manner in which it was allowed to drift.

Similarly the first three appointments made after Chandrachud took over as the Chief Justice in 1978 were distinctive with a common denominator in the sense that all the three judges[42] had been victims of the emergency transfers during the period 1975-76. This could not have been a mere co-incidence, and there is little one can say by way of an explanation in the absence of a policy decision to make a choice among those High Court judges who were subjected to this kind of victimisation.

The two appointments made in 1980 those of Justice Baharul Islam and Vardharajan were equally distinctive. For instance, Baharul Islam had an active political background with two successive terms in Rajya Sabha representing the Congress Party almost immediately before he was elevated to Gauhati High Court. He had retired from the Gauhati High Court as its Chief Justice long before he was offered puisne judgeship in the Supreme Court for a term which would have been in any case, the shortest term ever offered to a judge, even if he had not resigned but had retired in the normal course. Likewise, Vardharajan was the first from among the scheduled castes to be appointed to the apex tribunal since the country achieved its independence. Politically, it was a significant decision as so far none from among the socially disadvantaged sections of the Indian society had made it to the highest court in the land.

Thus, the post 1973 period recorded some of the most distinctive features in the appointments made to the Supreme Court. It was a decade of controversies, of building up of new attitudes and recruitment of distinctive personalities for the Supreme Court. Whereas, the controversies during the seventies were largely responsible for focusing public attention on the Supreme Court appointments and subjecting them to wider scrutiny, they also contributed significantly to making the Supreme Court more visible to the common man. A perceptible change in outlook in this regard also marks the decade in the sense that the executive, the Bar and the intelligentia (including the press) suddenly became concern as to who should be appointed to the Supreme Court and how such appointments should be made whereas, during the first two decades appointment of Supreme Court Judges remained broadly the concern of the Chief Justice with subtle role played by the executive.

Selection and Background Characteristics

The draft Constitution Article 103 had also made provision for qualifications for the Supreme Court appointees. Accordingly, clause 3 of the draft Article provided that 'a person shall not be qualified for appointment as a judge of the Supreme Court unless he is a citizen of India,[43] and (a) has been for at least five years a judge of a High Court or two or more such courts in succession, or (b) has been for at least ten years an advocate of a High Court or two or more such courts..."[44]

H.V. Kamath seeking to open a wider choice for the President in the matter of selection of judges, moved an important amendment. Introducing his amendment, Kamath said, 'the House will realise that it is desirable, nay it is essential, to have men - or for the matter of that, women - who are possessed of outstanding legal and juristic learning. In my humble judgment, such are not necessarily confined to judges or Advocates'.[45] The proposal was accepted by the Constituent Assembly in principle, however, the choice of appropriate words to be used was left to the drafting Committee.[46]

The Constitution provides for the minimum eligibility requirements for the candidates, in addition to specifying the respective roles of the executive and the Chief Justice in the selection and appointment process. Accordingly, in order to be considered for a Supreme Court judgeship, one must (a) have served for at least five years as a High Court judge, or (b) have been for at least ten years a High Court advocate, or (c) be a distinguished jurist.[47] These requirements are of general nature, and leave a considerable flexibility in the selection process. Of the three categories mentioned above only two have been represented on the Court so far.[48] The governing elite of independent India has yet to find a jurist who could be entrusted with a judgeship on the Supreme Court. Even among the other two, category (a) virtually reigned over the selection process during the past three and a half decades.

Seventy one judges were appointed to the Supreme Court till the end of 1981.[49] An overwhelming majority of sixty nine i.e. 97.1 per cent came from among the High Court judges, the remaining two i.e. 2.9 per cent[50] were recruited from the Bar. According to the Law Commission, members of the Bar were virtually excluded from the field of selection because of the government's view that it will be somewhat hazardous to appoint to the Bench a person straight from the Bar without previous judicial experience.[51] The government while acknowledging that it "desires to appoint those who have much experience", claimed to have offered, even during the first decade Supreme Court judgeships to "at least two advocates", but both refused the appointment because they were reluctant to sacrifice lucrative practice for a less remunerative Supreme Court post.[52]

Table I shows the 69 judges elevated from the High Courts. In addition to depicting the pattern of appointment made during the tenure of each one of the sixteen Chief Justices, it also shows the rank position of all the 69 judges on their respective High Courts at the time of their elevation to the Supreme Court. The table shows that 33 of the 69 judges (including Baharul Islam who was elevated after he had retired as Chief Justice of Gauhati High Court) came from among the High Court Chief Justices and, the remaining 36 (including those who were elevated after they had retired from High Courts as puisne judges) were selected from among the puisne judges of the High Courts. This shows an almost equal proportion of judges coming from the two categories.

Considering that almost all the judges were elevated to the Supreme Court from the High Courts, who have had more or less similar initial groundings, what additional attributes could have influenced their selection for the apex court in the country. The available information on the selection process is extremely inadequate to allow a comprehensive analysis of the attributes considered important in the selection of Supreme Court Judges. Most of the relevant information remains burried in the official records to which a researcher in India can possibly have no access-undoubtedly a most unfortunate aspect of our democratic credentials. At the same time, unlike in some developed countries, their is no tradition of writing memoirs and biographies by the retiring judges in India barring a few exceptions. In view of these limitations and others pointed out earlier in chapter I, what follows here is an attempt to draw certain inferences from the available data on judges' backgrounds.

As per the prevailing practice, whenever a vacancy arises in the court, a search is launched, the list of potential candidates invariably gets narrowed down to the Chief Justices and the senior most judges of 22 odd High Courts in the country. In the absence of any institutional framework to evaluate merit of the potential appointees, it appears that the choice gets limited to factors like High Court rank, experience, age, regional and other considerations. These factors have been analysed below with a view to ascertain the extent to which they have influenced the selection process. (The background characteristics of the 39 judges covered by the study are given in the Appendix in a tabular form.)

(i) *High Court Chief Justices appointed to the Supreme Court*: Quite a few Chief Justices who were elevated to the Supreme Court had much less experience in the High Court than many of the puisne judges who were elevated to the Supreme Court. This was so because many judges who had held much lower ranks among the puisne judges of the High Court where they were originally appointed, were appointed Chief Justices of other High Courts where they served in that capacity for some time, before being selected for a judgeship in the Supreme Court.

For instance, Wanchoo was originally appointed a judge of the Allahabad High Court in 1947. Within four years he was appointed as the Chief Justice of Rajasthan High Court. Similarly Justice Beg had hardly put in four years in Allahabad High Court when he was appointed as the Chief Justice of the newly created Himachal Pradesh High Court.[53]

Table I : Chief Justices and High Court Ranking of Judges elevated to the Supreme Court during their terms 1950-81

Sl. No.	Chief Justice	Retd.	Rank position of judges in the High Court at the time of Elevation						
			CJs	PJ1	PJ2	PJ3	PJ4	PJ5	PJ6-9
1.	Kania (1950-51)	N.C. Aiyar	Das S.R. Bose S. Fazal Ali	Kania Mahajan B.K. Mukherjea	-	-	Sastri	-	-
2.	Sastri (1951-54)	Hassan T.L.V. Ayyar	Jagannathas	-	-	N.H. Bhagwati	-	-	-
3.	Mahajan (1954)	-	Sinha	-	-	-	-	-	-
4.	B.K. Mukherjea (1954-56)	-	Imam	-	-	-	-	-	-
5.	S.R. Das (1956-59)	-	S.K. Das Subbarao Wanchoo Hidayatullah Das Gupta	Menon	-	Gajendra gadkar	Kapur	-	Sarkar
6.	Sinha (1959-64)	N.R. Ayyangar	- -	Shah Dayal Mudholkar	-	-	-	-	-
7.	Gajendra-gadkar (1964-66)	-	Ramaswami Raju Shelat	-	Bachawat	-		-	
8.	Sarkar (1966)	-	-	-	-	-	-	-	-
9.	Subbarao (1966-67)	-	Bhargava	-	Vaidialingam	-	Mitter	-	-

contd. . . .

Sl. No.	Chief Justice	Retd.	Rank position of judges in the High Court at the time of Elevation: CJs	PJ1	PJ2	PJ3	PJ4	PJ5	PJ6-9
10.	Wanchoo (1967-68)	-	Hegde	-	Grover	-	-	-	-
11.	Hidayatullah (1968-70)	-	P.J.Reddy Dua	-	-	A.N.Ray	-	-	-
12.	Shah (1970-71)	-	-	-	-	-	-	-	-
13.	Sikri (1971-73)	-	Khanna Beg	-	Mathew Dwivedi Chandrachud	A.K. Mukherjea	-	Palekar Aliagiriswami	-
14.	Ray (1973-77)	-	Bhagwati Goswami Untwalia M.Fazal Ali Singhal Jaswant Singh Kailasam	-	-	Gupta	Sarkaria	-	Krishna Iyer
15.	Beg (1977-78)	-	Pathak	Tulzapurkar	-	Desai	-	-	-
16.	Chandra chud (1978-81)	Baharul Islam	Koshal A.P.Sen Eradi A.N. Sen	-	R.B. Misra	Chinappa-reddy	Venkat-ramiah	Vardha-rajan	-
Total:		5	32	8	7	7	5	3	2

Another notable feature of the High Court Justices who accepted puisne judgeships in the Supreme Court was that no Chief Justice of Bombay High Court[54] and none from Madras till 1977,[55] was among them. However, K.C.Das Gupta was the first Chief Justice of Calcutta to have accepted puisne judgeship in the Supreme Court in 1959, and thereafter A.N.Sen was to follow after a long gap in 1980.[56] Could this absence of Chief Justices from these High Courts be attributed to the fact that Bombay, Madras and Calcutta being the oldest and the most prestigious High Courts in the country, their Chief Justices regarded their positions in their respective High Courts as more important than puisne judgeship in the Supreme Court ? Such suggestions have been made in the past.[57] However, there is little one can say with confidence whether Chief Justices of these High Courts declined themselves or an offer was never extended to them. Among the High Court Chief Justices, one had already retired when appointed to the Supreme Court.[58]

(ii) *Puisne Judges appointed to the Court*: Of the 36 puisne judges who were selected, four had[59] already retired from the High Courts when offered judgeship in the Supreme Court, and the remaining 32 judges held rank positions ranging between the seniormost down to the 6th position in their respective High Courts at the time of their elevation. Table I shows the number of judges appointed under each one of the six positions. Krishna Iyer's location in the 6th position is approximate as he served on Kerala High Court for roughly about two years effectively and later he was with the Law Commission for three years before his elevation to the Supreme Court in 1973. At the time of joining the Law Commission Krishna Iyer's position was 9th among the puisne judges in the High Court. A.K.Sarkar was the only other judge atleast till 1981 to be selected from amongst the juniormost ranks considering the average High Courts strength during the period.

A significant feature of the selections from various ranks indicates an upward trend in the recruitment of High Court Chief Justices in the post 1973 period with Ray's assumption of Chief Justiceship. For instance, seven (70.00%) of the ten appointments during his tenure went to the High Court Chief Justices. Similarly of the fourteen appointments made during Chandrachud's tenure as Chief Justice ten (71.40%) were offered to the Chief Justices.[60] On the contrary, the pre Ray period had a much lower percentage of selections made from among the Chief Justices. In fact, seventy five per cent judges appointed during Sikri's tenure revolved around the puisne judges, and only twenty five per cent went to the Chief Justices. Even if one compares the post 1973 figures with the pre 1973 period, the change appears to be perceptible.[61]

All this goes to show that the trends in the selection process in the Seventies and the Eighties had undergone changes and Supreme Court judgeship more often came to be offered to the Chief Justices. Although no particular reason can be cited for this change, it appears that supersessions in the appointment of Chief Justice in the Supreme Court in 1973 and early 1978 coupled with the controversy surrounding the appointment of Justice Desai from the Gujarat High Court may have had their repercussion in building an opinion against the supersession be it in the Supreme Court or, in the selection of Supreme Court judges from the High Courts.

(iii) *Experience in the High Court*: The conception of seniority in the High Court does not seem to be necessarily related to the experience in the sense of number of years put in by a judge in the High Court since his appointment. There have been large variations in the actual High Court experience of those judges who were elevated from various High Courts to the Supreme Court. The High Court experience of judges appointed to the Supreme Court varied from a minimum of two (T.L.V. Iyyar and Krishna Iyer) to a maximum of nineteen years (S. Fazal Ali). Between these two extremes, there are at least 25 judges who have had less than 10 years standing in the High Court, and on the other hand, 11 judges had put in fifteen and more years of service in the High Court before they were appointed to the Supreme Court. The remaining 33 judges had put in 10 to 15 years of service before they were considered for judgeship in the Supreme Court. In fact some of the High Court Chief Justices had far less standing in the High Court than many puisne judges who came to occupy positions in the Supreme Court. Jagannadhas had put in only five years in Orissa High Court and Goswami's total service in Gauhati High Court did not exceed six years before they were elevated to the Supreme Court in 1953 and 1973 respectively.

Thus, it is quite obvious that in selecting High Court judges for appointments to the Supreme Court, the length of service in the

High Court has not been one of the important considerations. Since there is no all India High Court seniority sometimes judges with little service in the High Court get elevated to Chief Justiceship because of factors like, small sized courts, quick retirements or transfers to other High Courts with promotion to the Chief Justiceship.[62] Some judges were appointed very young and therefore had long years of service in the High Court. The average actual experience of such judges in the High Court was approximately 14 years as compared to those who joined the High Court in their late years. In such cases, as will be seen, the judges had already put in more number of years either in practice at the Bar, or in judicial service. This will be illustrated in the next section dealing with the pre High Court experience of judges.

(iv) *Pre High Court Experience*: While considering professional experience in relation to the selection and appointment process, one may as well take into account the pre-High Court experience and the career patterns of judges of the Supreme Court. The judges appointed from the High Courts came from three different career backgrounds i.e. from the Indian Civil Service, The Judicial Service, and the Bar. In all, seven judges with ICS background were appointed to the Supreme Court, S.K. Das being the first to be appointed in 1956. His name was initially mentioned to Chief Justice Patanjali Sastri, "who did not take kindly to the suggestion, as Sastri himself had long practice at the Bar before his elevation to the High Court Bench, and did not think very high of civilian judges".[63] However, S.K. Das did make it to the Supreme Court later when S.R.Das became the Chief.[64] All the ICS judges, except A.K. Mukherjea, had fairly long experience in the civil service and had held judicial positions before they were elevated to the High Court. A.K. Mukherjea, had twelve years standing at the Calcutta High Court Bar in addition to his having served for 13 years in the Indian Civil Service before he was appointed judge of the Calcutta High Court in 1962. Since ICS was abolished in 1950 and was replaced by the Indian Administrative Service, he was the last ICS judge to have served in the Supreme Court.

Thirteen judges came from judicial service background. A distinction is to be made here between the lower and the higher judicial services. Those who were from the lower judicial service had started their career at the lowest rung of the judiciary, obta[illegible] their promotions in due course and served as district and sess[illegible]s

Table II : Pre High Court Career and Experience, 1950-81

Career	Length of Experience								
Patterns	14-16	16-18	18-20	20-22	22-24	24-26	26-28	28-30	30-34
ICS	–	Rama- swami	Bhargava	–	S.K.Das Wanchoo Das Gupta Dayal	A.K. Mukherjea (13 ICS+ 12 Bar)	–	–	–
Bar	Kania S.Fazal Ali Hidayatullah P.N. Bhagwati Untwalia M.Fazal Ali Pathak	Shah Mitter Ray Chandra- chud	Bose Gajendra- gadkar Sarkar Bachawat Gupta O.C. Reddy A.P.Sen A.N. Sen	B.K. Mukherjea Hassan Sinha Imam Subbarao Hegde Grover Beg Dwivedi Kailasam B. Islam R.B.Misra Eradi	S.R.Das N.H. Bhagwati Raju Mathew Goswami Venkat- ramiah	Patanjali Sastri Mahajan Vaidia- lingam Dua Jaswant Singh	Menon Kapur	Jaganna- das Ayyangar Krishna Iyer	T.L.V Iyyar Sikri Roy

contd. . . .

Career Patterns	Length of Experience								
	14-16	16-18	18-20	20-22	22-24	24-26	26-28	28-30	30-34
Higher Judicial Service	P.J. Reddy	–	–	Khanna Tulzapurkar	Mudholkar Shelat Desai	–	–	–	N.C. Aiyar Koshal
Lower Judicial Service	–	–	–	Singhal	–	Sarkaria	Palekar Vardharajan	Aliagiri swami	–
	8	5	9	16	13	7	4	4	5

Note: Sikri and Roy were recruited direct from the Bar and had no judicial experience whatsoever before their elevation to the Supreme Court judges before being elevated to the High Court, and the number of such judges finally making it to the Supreme Court was only five during the past three and a half decades. On the other hand, eight judges came from the higher judicial service background; joined the judicial service at the district and sessions judges' level after having practiced at the Bar for a number of years and were appointed to the High Courts. The selections for the higher judiciary are made normally from among the leading members of the District Bar which presupposes at least ten to twelve years (although seven years is the minimum requirement) of active practice at the Bar. This distinction between the lower judicial service and the higher judicial service serves to illustrate the recruitment patterns in the High Courts as well. For instance, almost 70 to 75 per cent of the total recruitments to the various High Courts take place from among the members of the Bar, and the remaining 25 to 30 per cent are made from the two categories of the judicial service, of which major share goes to the Higher Judicial Service. Lately however, the representation of the Lower Judicial Service in the High Court appointments seems to have improved, and the overall percentage of High Court appointments from the judicial service is also on the increase.[65] Nonetheless, pre High Court career patterns of the Supreme Court judges clearly correspond to the general recruitment patterns at the High Courts.

The pre-High Court career patterns, if further analysed in terms of the length of experience in their respective fields, one would find considerable flexibility in the options exercised in the selection process. Table II shows that the pre-High Court experience of judges appointed to the Supreme Court varied between a minimum of 14 to a maximum of 34 years in their respective fields. This variation is more prominent among those who were raised to the High Courts from the Bar, and the Higher Judicial Service. The wide range in the length of experience of lawyer-judges is partially explained by the fact that a large number of them had taken considerable time in building their practice in the District Courts before they could eventually settle down in the High Court Bar. On the other hand, those who had family support, and someone in the family with a distinguished career as a judge or an advocate, could make it straight to the High Court Bar, and were able to establish themselves in a relatively shorter time span.[66] However, 18 to 22 years experience at the Bar seems to have been considered as ideal for High Court appointments.

The lawyer-judges also depict a variety of other experience besides their usual practice at the Bar. For instance, six judges[67] had taught law in the colleges of their respective states. B.K. Mukherjea had also had the distinction of being a Tagore law lecturer. Another seven judges[68] had served as Advocate Generals mostly in their respective High Courts, and twelve[69] had been on the government pay rolls as its standing counsels.

The pre-High Court experience of judges recruited from the Higher Judicial Service also include the years they spent at the Bar before their appointment to the higher judiciary. Five of the eight judges from this category had 20 to 24 years experience before they were elevated to the High Courts. P.J. Reddy was appointed with a minimum of 15 years of experience whereas, N.C. Aiyar and A.D. Koshal had already put in 31 and 32 years respectively before their elevation to the High Courts. Both Aiyar and Koshal had exceptionally long standing at the Bar before their selections to the Higher Judicial Services.

The ICS and the Lower Judicial Service on the contrary, depict a narrower range of the length of experience within which the selections for High Court appointments were confined. Four of the seven ICS judges were appointed within 22 to 24 years of service, and another two i.e. Ramaswami and Bhargava had 17 to 19 years of standing in the Civil Service. A.K. Mukherjea, however, had only 13 years of service in the ICS, but had also practiced at the Calcutta High Court Bar for almost 12 years before his elevation to the High Court.

Three out of the five judges raised from the Lower Judicial service to the High Courts had 24 to 28 years of service; the fourth had 31 years, and P.N. Singhal, the fifth judge had put in only 21 years before his elevation to the Rajasthan High Court. Singhal, incidentally has been the only judge appointed to the Supreme Court so far, who had no experience at the Bar whatsoever. All other judges in this category had acquired some experience at the Bar whether before joining the judicial service or, after having retired from it, but before their elevation to the High Courts.[70]

(v) ***Age and Standing in the Profession***: In view of the importance of the role which has been assigned to the Court under the scheme of our Constitution, it is necessary that persons of highest calibre should be appointed judges of this Court and no other consideration except that of merit should weigh in the matter of appointment.[71]

The evaluation of the merit of the judges to be appointed is by no means an easy task, especially, when no institutional framework exists for such evaluation. The Chief Justice's personal judgment based on information received from various sources about the calibre of the prospective nominee or, in the alternative the Law Minister's random consultations with judges of the Supreme Court and High Courts, are the only available channels, and none can claim to be in a position to systematically evaluate the merit of the candidate. If at all selections are based on merit evaluation, then such assessments are merely impressionistic and highly subjective in their character.

Nevertheless, since almost all the judges except two, were elevated from the High Courts, and assuming that some experience at the High Court was considered as absolutely necessary in order to be selected for Supreme Court judgeship, majority of the High Court judges would be ipso facto found suited for elevation to the Supreme Court. Yet there could be considerations other than merit which may provide the key to the selection process. Prominent among such factors, appear to be the advanced age and the long professional experience. "Persons appointed as judges of the Supreme Court should not only have legal acumen and sound knowledge of law, but also have within them that great quality which eludes description but which comes with the passage of years and after long contemplation and reflection - the quality imparting maturity".[72]

The data relating to the age and the total professional experience of judges at the time of their appointment to the Supreme Court appears to have assimilated the above ideology to a large extent. Table III classifies all the judges according to the length of their total experience before they were appointed to the Supreme Court. It shows that whereas, A.K. Sarkar and P.N. Bhagwati were appointed with a total of only 27 years standing in the profession, on the other extreme, there were judges like Kailasam and Koshal who had put in 39 and 42 years respectively before their elevation to the Court. It also shows that the maximum number of judges were appointed with 35 to 36 years of professional experience behind them. The average length of total experience of all appointees before their elevation to the Supreme Court works out to about 34 years. The two appointees from the Bar, Sikri and Roy, both conform to this average of 34 years in their standing at

Table III : Range of Total Experience at the time of Elevation, 1950-81

27-28	28-29	29-30	30-31	31-32	32-33	33-34	34-35	35-36	36-37	37-38	38 and above
Sarkar	Hidaya-	Ray	Goswami	Mahajan	Hassan	Imam	Kania	Patanjali	S.Fazal	Palekar	N.C.
P.N.	tullah	Beg	Untwalia	S.R.Das	Sinha	Bachawat	Bose	Shastri	Ali		Aiyer
Bhagwati	-			N.H.	Subba-	Shelat	S.K.Das		T.L.V.		Dayal
	Shah	Chandra-	B.Islam	Bhagwati	rao	Venkat-		B.K.	Ayyar		Kaila-
		chud	-	Gajendra-	Mitter	ramiah	Wanchoo	Mukherjea	Menon		sam
		Gupta		gadkar	Grover	-	Sikri	Jaganna-	Bhargava		Koshal
		Pathak		Hegde	P.J.		Roy	dhas	Dua		
				Khanna	Reddy		Jaswant	Kapur	Vardha-		
				M.Fazal	Mathew	-	Singh	DasGupta	rajan		
				Ali	Sarkaria		A.N.Sen	Ayyangar	Eradi		
				O.C.	Desai			Madholkar			
				Reddy				Ramaswami			
								Raju			
				A.P.Sen				Vaidia-			
								lingam			
								Dwivedi			
								A.K.			
								Mukherjea			
								Aliagiri-			
								swami			
								Krishna			
								Iyer			
								Singhal			
								Tulzapurkar			
								R.B.Misra			
2	2	5	3	9	9	4	8	17	7	1	4

the Bar rather remarkably. At the same time one would notice that almost 89 per cent of the appointees to the Court had a professional standing of more than 30 years which shows that despite large variations, a minimum of at least 30 years of professional experience was regarded as an essential criterion in the selection process, barring of course, a few exceptions.

Age is the next important factor which seem to have influenced the selection process, and the age groups within which appointments to the Supreme Court have been made clearly correspond to the years of professional standing of the appointees. It has been argued that maturity and understanding which are almost indispensable for anyone to hold office on the high Bench are derived from long experience and advanced age. Therefore, the proper age, according to the Law Commission's recommendations, for appointment as a judge of the Supreme Court should be between 54 and 60 years.[73]

On an average judges of the Supreme Court launched their professional career at the age of 25 years, and with the addition of a minimum of 30 years in the profession, the minimum age for appointment to the Supreme Court works out to 55 years. Only 9 of the 69 appointments were made within the age group of 52 and 55 years which exactly correspond to the 9 appointees who had 27 to 30 years of professional experience. But taking into consideration the average length of experience of 34 years, the most opportune age for appointment to the Supreme Court works out to 59 years. The remaining 62 appointments were made within the age group of 55 to 63 years which roughly corresponds to 87 per cent of appointees having professional standing of more than 30 years.

The theory that age and professional experience add to the maturity and understanding of judges seems to have received more than its due in the selection process. In 50 per cent of the appointments made to the Court the appointees had crossed the average age of 59 years. There have been a few instances, particularly, where the age factor seems to have been a predominant consideration in the selection of judges to the Supreme Court. Palekar was appointed in preference to Chandrachud from Bombay High Court in 1971 even though the former was much junior to the latter in the High Court. Palekar was almost approaching his retirement from Bombay High Court, whereas, Chandrachud, on the other hand, was much younger in age. Chandrachud was, however, elevated to the Supreme Court at the very next opportunity that came in 1972. Similarly, Aliagriswami made to the Supreme Court in 1972 on the day he was due to retire from Madras High Court even though he was much junior to Kailasam who had to wait it seems because of his relatively younger age, and was subsequently appointed a judge of the Supreme Court in 1977 when he was about to retire from the High Court. Incidentally, Kailasam held the position of seniormost puine judge in the Madras High Court for a long time and became its Chief Justice only a few months before his elevation to the Supreme Court. Madras High Court also holds the distinction of having provided with judges who were all either approaching, or, had crossed the age of 60 years at the time of their appointments to the Supreme Court. The oldest judge ever appointed to the Court was the retired Chief Justice of Gauhati High Court, Justice Baharul Islam at the age of 62 years and 9 months. The youngest ever to be appointed, on the other hand, was Justice P.N. Bhagwati from Gujarat High Court in 1973 at the age of 51 years and 7 months. The other relatively younger judges were, Chandrachud (52.1) from Bombay High Court in 1972, Hidayatullah (53)[74] from Madhya Pradesh in 1958 and Pathak (53.4) from Himachal Pradesh in 1978. Of these four, three were already serving as Chief Justices of their respective High Courts when they were offered Supreme Court judgeship. These four also happened to be among those exceptionally few who had professional standing of less than 30 years when they were appointed to the Supreme Court.

Thus, the age and the professional standing syndrome has been prominent in the selection process as demonstrated above. The only exception to this was the appointment of Justice Baharul Islam in 1980, who had approximately 30 years of professional standing which did not correspond well with his advanced age at which he was appointed to the Supreme Court. This can be partially explained with reference to his exceptionally late entry into the profession at the age of 33, whereas the average entry age into the profession for Supreme Court judges has been worked out to be 25 years.

(vi) ***Regional and Communal Considerations***: There are other considerations like region and community which appear prominently in the selection of judges for the Supreme Court. 'Regional loyalties, based especially on language, but also on ethnic and caste considerations, long have been strong in India, and have increased in political significance in recent years. Thus it is not surprising that regionalism is important in making appointments to the Supreme Court".[75] These remarks reveal the influence of regional factors in the selection of the first twenty three judges appointed to the Court during the first decade. Twenty five years later, the same can be said with even more confidence. The regional base of 71 judges appointed to the Supreme Court upto 1981 as shown in Table IV is fairly representative in character. While considering the representative character of an appointment, one may wonder whether an appointee represents the High Court from which he is elevated, or he represents the state or, region in which the High Court is located. Ordinarily one would think that the judge represents both, since the judges of the High Court seldom came from outside the state or the region. But there have been a number of instances where the person selected for Supreme Court appointment from a particular High Court, had no ethnic or any other ties with the region or state which the High Court represented. For instance, S.R. Das' appointment from East Punjab High Court in 1950, B.P. Sinha's from Nagpur High Court in 1954, Hegde's from Delhi High Court in 1967, and Beg and Pathak's from Himachal High Court in 1971 and 1978 respectively, are a few examples of this kind which cannot be explained strictly in regional terms.

The reorganisation of states in 1956 on linguistic basis brought in certain changes in the existing composition of the High Courts, and the placement of their judges. Oudh High Court and Nagpur High Court were abolished, Hyderabad and East Punjab High Courts were reconstituted as Andhra Pradesh and Punjab (which later became Punjab and Haryana) High Court. Five more High Courts were established in newly formed states of Gujarat, Kerala, Madhya Pradesh, Mysore and Rajasthan. Eventually, three more High Courts came up, one each for Delhi, Himachal and Sikkim, taking the total strength of High Courts to 18. Table IV accordingly, shows the rearrangement and transfers of those judges of High Courts who were elevated to the Supreme Court which correspond by and large with the above changes barring those transfers made during the emergency. This explains the placement of at least 17 judges in more than one High Court, and counting them twice, the High Court regional representation shows as follows : Bombay (12), Calcutta (10), Madras (10), Punjab (9), Allahabad (8), Patna (6),

Kerala and Andhra Pradesh (4 each), Gujarat, Delhi and Rajasthan (3 each), Jammu & Kashmir, Assam, Himachal Pradesh and Mysore (2 each) and Orissa and Madhya Pradesh (one each). The only High Court which remains unrepresented in the Supreme Court is Sikkim High Court which incidentally also happens to be the youngest of all the High Courts in India. Besides this, two judges from the Bar were recruited one each from Punjab and Calcutta High Court Bars.

The three oldest High Courts, Bomaby, Calcutta and Madras have proportionately contributed more judges than any other High Court. Whereas, Bombay and Calcutta always had at least one judge in the Court, Madras High Court, on the contrary, went unrepresented for five years from 1967 to 1972 and then again for two years from 1975 to 1977. This, however, seems to have been done in order to accommodate the other three High Courts in the South, and thus the region as a whole remained well represented in the Court.

Considering the relative standing of High Courts, one finds that whereas, Assam and Orissa remained neglected for a very long time, Kerala and Gujarat, on the contrary, were relatively better placed especially towards the eighties.[76] Whereas, Gujarat's ascendancy in this respect can partially be attributed to the State's leading role in industrialisation, consumer movement, cooperatives and concept of property ownership in the sphere of trade and commerce, relatively exposing the Gujarat High Court judges to much wider and complex issues that are finally agitated in the Supreme Court these days. No such nexus is easily traceable in the case of Kerala, except for the highest rate of literacy which the state enjoys over the rest of the country. Whether the higher rate of literacy has any thing to do with higher percentage of Kerala High Court judges being appointed to the Supreme Court is a moot question. If at all such considerations as attributed in case of Gujarat have had anything to do with the selection of judges from that Court, it would be a welcome addition to the criteria of selection of judges for the Supreme Court in future too.

The communal considerations too appear to have had their share in the selection process, but such considerations have been mainly restricted to the major religious groupings. Of the 71 judges, 61 have been Hindus, 7 Muslim, 2 Christians, and one Sikh. At least one Muslim judge has always been in the Supreme Court

Table IV: Regional Representation in Supreme Court Appointments, 1950-81

High Court	Judges								
Allahabad/Oudh	Hassan, (1952)	Wanchoo,	Dayal, (1960)	Bhargava, (1966)	Beg,	Dwivedi (1972)	Pathak,	R.B. Misra (1981)	
Andhra Pradesh/ Hyderabad	Subbarao, (1958)	Raju, (1965)	P.J. Reddy, (1969)		Chinnappareddy (1978)				
Assam & Nagaland	Goswami, (1973)	Baharul Islam (1980)							
Delhi	Hegde, (1967)	Dua, (1969)	Khanna (1971)						
Gujarat	Shelat, (1966)	P.N.Bhagwati, (1973)		Desai (1977)					
Himachal Pradesh	Beg, (1971)	Pathak (1978)							
Jammu & Kashmir	M. Fazal Ali, (1975)		Jaswant Singh (1976)						
Kerala	Vaidialingam, (1966)		Mathew, (1971)	Krishna Iyer, (1973)	Eradi (1981)				
Karnataka	Hegde	Venkatramiah (1979)							
Maharashtra/ Nagpur	Kania, (1950)	Bose, (1951)	N.H. Bhagwati, (1952)		Sinha, (1954)	Gajendragadkar, (1957)		Hidayatullah,	Shah, (1959)
	Mudholkar, (1960)	Shelat,	Palekar, (1971)	Chandrachud, (1972)		Tulzapurkar (1977)			
Madhya Pradesh	Hidayatullah, (1958)		A.P. Sen (1978)						

contd. . . .

High Court	Judges								
Orissa	Jagannadhas (1953)								
Bihar	S.Fazal Ali, (1950)		Sinha,	Imam, (1955)	S.K. Das, (1956)		Ramaswami, (1965)		Untwalia (1974)
Rajasthan	Wanchoo, (1958)		Singhal, (1975)	A.P.Sen					
West Bengal	B.K. Mukherjea, (1950)		S.R. Das,	Sarkar, (1957)	Das Gupta (1959)	Bachawat (1964)		Mitter, (1966)	Ray, (1969)
	A.K. Mukherjea, (1972)		Gupta, (1974)		A.N. Sen (1981)				
Tamil Nadu	Shastri, (1950)	N.C. Aiyar, (1950)	T.L.V. Ayyar, (1954)		Menon, (1956)	Subbarao,	N.R. Ayyangar, (1960)		
	Aliagiriswami, (1972)		Kailasam, (1977)		Koshal,	Vardharajan (1980)			
Punjab & Haryana/ East Punjab	Mahajan, (1950)	Kapur, (1957)	S.R. Das, (1950)	Grover, (1968)	Dua,	Khanna,	Sarkaria, (1973)	Koshal, (1978)	
	Chinappareddy								

since 1950. This practice of always having a Muslim in the highest tribunal dates from the colonial period, for the British made certain that there was always a Muslim judge on the Federal Court, which was the predecessor to the Supreme Court.[77] S.Fazal Ali was one of the six original members of the Supreme Court. When he retired in September, 1951. Ghulam Hassan, a retired judge of the Allahabad High Court was appointed in September 1952. Hassan died in late 1954, and the vacancy was filled in January, 1955 by Syed Jaffar Imam, who at the time of his elevation was the Chief Justice of Patna High Court. In December, 1958, Mohammed Hidayatullah was appointed as the Court strength was increased to ten, so there were two Muslim judges on the bench for almost five years till Jaffar Imam had to resign due to ill health in February, 1964. Beg was the fifth Muslim judge to be appointed almost one year after Hidayatullah's retirement. In 1975, M. Fazal Ali, another Muslim judge was added to the Court, and since then there have always been two Muslim judges in the Court; but with a short interlude before Baharul Islam's appointment in 1980.

Apart from Muslims and Hindus, the Court had two Christians, Vivian Bose appointed in 1951 and Mathew in 1971, and one Sikh, appointed in 1973. The caste hierarchy does not seem to have influenced the selections at the Supreme Court level even though the majority among the Hindus appointed during the first decade happened to be Brahmins as they were the ones who by virtue of their better social and economic status were quick to capture the opportunities available for higher education both at home and abroad. The caste differenciations, however, have been quite prominent in appointments to the High Courts over the years, and to that extent they are bound to be reflected in appointments to the Supreme Court as well particularly when the High Courts have virtually monoplised the recruitments to the Supreme Court.

Only one appointment has been made so far from among the Scheduled Castes (Vardharajan in 1980). No woman was appointed to the highest Court until 1981.

(vi) *Social Philosophy of Judges*: Another criterion was sought to be introduced in the selection process when Mohan Kumaramangalam argued that some attention ought to be paid to the social philosophy of judges.[78] This argument was no doubt raised with a view to defend the appointment of Ray as the Chief Justice of India in 1973, at the same time its possible repercussion on the selection process cannot be altogether ruled out in the later appointments. Justice Khanna's supersession in 1977 was clearly an instance of giving effect to this policy. But to what extent this new criterion was used in the appointment of puisne judges to the Court is not very well known. On the basis of the background characteristics of judges appointed during the period under investigation, it will be rather difficult to arrive at any definite conclusion as regards their social philosophies which may have influenced their selections to the Supreme Court. However, it cannot be denied that some judges who were appointed during this period were responsible for giving a new direction and an overall liberal activist orientation to the Court.

The general picture that emerges from the analysis of the background characteristics of the seventy one appointees to the court since its inception is that of a judge who began his career more often as a member of the Bar at about 25 years of age, got elevated to the High Court preferably where he had practiced(this would not be so in the present context in view of the government's policy of appointing one third of the High Court judges from out side the state), and having served in that capacity on an average for about 18-20 years, was elevated to the apex court in his late fiftees or early sixties from amongst the senior most judges in that High Court, provided of course, he also happened to be the right person who fitted into the regional and the communal slots. In other words, for a person to be appointed to the Supreme Court, he ought to be a member of the Bar with some judicial experience at the High Court, should be fairly advanced in age with a minimum of 35 years of total experience, and should fulfil the representative criterion which in all probability is likely to be extended to other categories in the years to come.

What is it that we want in our judges? What should be the criteria of selection? Do we want judges who are value neutrals? Can judges be value neutral? What should be their social philosophy? Who should determine such philosophy and how? Is it relevant to consider their social philosophy, particularly within a system of justice which is fundamentally based on formal notions of justice accordingly to the law? Should we have judges who are experienced, mature, well advanced in age and have the expertise in the formal adjudicatory process or should we insist on judges who are young, active and possess the knowledge and experience in the problems of contemporary Indian society? There are a host of questions which may be asked. The real question remains as to what is our perception of a judge. One possible answer is provided by a judge himself according to whom:

> A judge is a human being who is a bundle of passions and prejudices, likes and dislikes, affection and ill will, hatred and contempt and fear and recklessness. In order to be a successful judge these elements should be curbed and kept under restraint and that is possible only by education, training, continued practice and cultivation of a sense of humility and dedication to duty. These curbs can neither be bought in the market nor injected into human system by the written or unwritten laws ... It is the inner strength of judges alone that can save the judiciary. The life of a judge does not really call for great acts of self sacrifice; but it does insist upon small acts of self denial almost every day.[79]

Notes

1. John R. Schmidhauser, *The Supreme Court: Its Politics, Personalities, And Procedures* 6 (Holt. Rinehard And Winston, New York, 1963).
2. The ad hoc Committee on the Supreme Court had made the following alternative recommendations as regards the method of choosing Supreme Court Judges: the first of these was that the President should nominate puisne judges with the concurrence of the Chief Justice and this nomination would then be subjected to confirmation by a panel composed of High Court Chief Justices, "Some members' of both houses of the Central Legislature, and the Law Officers of the Union. The second scheme was that the panel should submit three names to the President who would choose one of them with the concurrence of the Chief Justice. See, "Ad hoc Committee Report," paras 15-16; Reports, First Series cited in Granaville Austin, *The Indian Constitution: Cornerstone of a Nation* 177 (Clerendon Press, Oxford, 1966).
3. IV *C.A.D.* 887 (1947). The recommendation incorporated in clause 18 of the Union Constitution Committee Report was in fact closer to the Sapru Committee Report wherein it had recommended that "the judges of the Supreme Court should be appointed by the head of the State in consultation with the Chief Justice of the Supreme Court..." *Sapru Report*, Ch.13 pp. xi-xii.
4. *Supra* note 3 at 901.
5. *Id.* at 887.
6. *Id.* at 902.

7. *Ibid.*
8. B. Shiva Rao, *The Framing of India's Constitution : Select Documents*, Vol IV, 142 (1967).
9. *Id.* at 143.
10. B. Shiva Rao, *The Framing of India's Constitution : A Study* 491 (1968).
11. *Supra* note 8, Vol.III at 554.
12. VIII *C.A.D.* 258(1949).
13. The Constitution of India, Art. 124(2).
14. The Government of India Act, 1935, Sec. 200(2).
15. *Id.* Sec. 220(2).
16. M.C. Mahajan, *Looking Back* 191 (Asia Publishing House, New Delhi, 1963).
17. Id. at 192; Similar evidence is available as regards the existence of such practice in the appointment of High Court Judges in M.C. Chagla's autobiography, *Roses in December* 122-124 and 166-168 (Bharatiya Vidya Bhavan, Bombay, 1974) and, in M. Hidayatullah, *My Own Boswell* 131-133 (Arnold-Heinemann. New Delhi, 1984).
18. The first Bench comprised Chief Justice H.J. Kania, Justices Patanjali Shastri, S. Fazal Ali, M.C. Mahajan, B.K. Mukherjea, and S.R. Das (appointed to the Federal Court on January 20, 1950).
19. Seniority Principle in the context of the appointment of the Chief Justice of India refers to the practice of elevating the seniormost judge next in line in the Court to the office of the Chief Justice, and is discussed in the chapter on Appointment of the Chief Justice.
20. B.P. Sinha was the Chief Justice of Nagpur High Court when he was elevated to the Supreme Court in 1954.
21. M.C. Setalvad, *My Life* 428 (Tripathi, Bombay, 1971).
22. Altogether nine judges were appointed during Chief Justice S.R. Das' tenure. For details refer Table I.
23. *Supra* note 21 at 508.
24. The Law Commission of India : *Fourteenth Report* 34 (1958).
25. 28 Lok Sabha *Debates*; Second Series, Col. 7521 (1959).
26. *Ibid.*
27. *Supra* note 16 at 212-213.
28. George Gadbois, "Selection, Background and Voting Behaviour of the Indian Supreme Court Judges", in Shubert and Danelaski (ed.) *Comparative Judicial Behaviour* 222 (Oxford University Press, 1969).
29. *Supra* note 21 at 508.
30. P.B. Gajendragadkar, To *The Best of My Memory* 153-154 (Bharatiya Vidya Bhavan, Bombay, 1983).
31. Rajeev Dhavan, *The Supreme Court of India* 22 (Tripathi, Bombay, 1977).
32. *Supra* note 17 at 242.
33. See Kumaramanglam, *The Judicial Appointments Passim* (1973). A.R. Antulay, *Appointment of a Chief Justice Passim* (1973).
34. Justice Fazal Ali originally came from Patna where he was practising in the Patna High Court, but was appointed a judge of the Jammu & Kashmir High Court in 1958 for the first time from where he was elevated to the Supreme Court. Moreover, Untwalia was elevated from the Patna High Court only six months before Fazal Ali joined the Court.
35. V.D. Tulzapurkar and D.A. Desai, both were appointed on 30.9.1977; R.S. Pathak was appointed on 20.2.78, two days before Chief Justice Beg retired.

36. Northern india Patrika, 13 January, 1977, cited in Rajeev Dhavan & Alice Jacob, *Selection and Appointment of Supreme Court Judges* 124 (Tripathi, Bombay, 1978).
37. *The Statesman*, September 28, 1977.
38. *Supra* note 36 at 21.
39. *Id.* at 26.
40. *Id.* at 27.
41. *Id.* at 21-23.
42. All the three Justices A.D. Koshal, O. Chinnappareddy and A.P. Sen were the victims of the transfers made during the 1975-77 emergency, and it is believed that this factor had considerably influenced their elevation to the Supreme Court.
43. This was proposed by Smt. G. Durgabai through an amendment moved on July 29, 1947, but the amendment was withdrawn by her on N. Gopalaswamy Ayyanger's assurance that it will find its place in the draft, see IV *C.A.D.* 894-904.
44. *Supra* note 8 at 555.
45. H.V. Kamath's amendment No. 1845 read as follows: "That in clause (3) of article 103, the following new sub-clause be added : (c) or is a distinguished jurist," see VIII *C.A.D.* 1241.
46. *Id.* at 257. Article 124(2) (c) of the Constitution says, is, in the opinion of the President, a distinguished jurist.
47. The Constitution of India, Art. 124 (3).
48. Since 1971 untill 1986 at least, all appointments have been made from among the judges of the High Courts.
49. Seven more judges have been appointed since then. Four (Madan, S. Mukherjea, Thakkar and R. Mishra) were appointed in 1983; One (V. Khalid) in 1984, and two (G.J. Oza and B.C. Roy) in 1985. Of the five vacancies created by the retirement of Justice D.A. Desai, Chief Justice Chandrachud, Justice Vardharajan and A.N. Sen, and by the death of Justice Fazal Ali while still in Office, only two were filled up in October, 1985. All these seven judges were elevated from the High Courts. Six of the seven appointees came from among the High Court Chief Justices, and only one i.e. Justice B.C. Roy was appointed from among the puisne judges, Seven High Courts, viz., Bombay, Calcutta, Gujarat, Orissa, Jammu & Kashmir, Kerala and Madhya Pradesh were represented by these seven appointments.
50. The two judges directly recruited from the Bar were: S.M. Sikri (1964), and S.B. Roy (1971).
51. *Supra* note 24 at 35.
52. 43 Lok Sabha *debates*; Second series, Cols. 14, 150-157 (1960).
53. Besides, there are other instances like S.R. Das (1949). M.J. Shelat (1960), K.S. Hegde (1966), and R.S. Pathak (1972).
54. Madan was the first Chief Justice of Bombay High Court to have accepted puisne Judgeship in the Supreme Court in 1983.
55. Justice Kailasam then the Chief Justice of Madras High Court.
56. S. Mukherjea was the next Chief Justice of Calcutta High Court appointed to the Supreme Court in 1983.
57. See, for instance, M.C. Chagla, *Roses in December* 171 (Bharatiya Vidya Bhavan, Bombay, 1975); and Gadbois, *Supra* note 28 at 223.
58. Mr. Justice Baharul Islam had retired as Chief Justice of Gauhati High Court when offered the appointment.

59. N.C. Aiyar (1950), G. Hassan (1952), T.L.V. Iyyar (1954) and N.R. Ayyangar (1960).
60. Five appointments made thereafter between 1981 and 1985 during the remaining tenure of Chief Justice Chandrachud went to the Chief Justices of the High Courts, taking the total to 71.4 per cent.
61. Since 1981, there has been a further increase in the number of High Court Chief Justices being appointed to the Court. At 1985 level the ratio as compared to the pre 1973 period stood at 62 : 42.
62. Beg and Pathak were appointed Chief Justices of Himachal High Court in 1966 and 1971 respectively from Allahabad High Court. Similarly, Hegde was appointed Chief Justice of Delhi High Court in 1966 from Karnataka High Court. Dua and Khanna were brought from Punjab to Delhi High Court, and both became Chief Justices of Delhi High Court in quick succession because their predecessors got elevated to Supreme Court and they were next in line by virtue of seniority in the court which had a small size to begin with.
63. *Supra* note 21 at 343.
64. *Ibid*.
65. See *Judges of the Supreme Court and the High Courts* (as on 1.4.83) published by Ministry of Law, Justice and Company Affairs.
66. For instance, Justice P.N. Bhagwati, M. Fazal Ali, and R.S. Pathak had only 14 to 15 years of total experience at the Bar before they were elevated to their respective High Courts. All the three came from distinguished families of lawyers and judges.
67. B.K. Mukherjea, V. Bose, P.B. Gajendragadkar, M. Hidayatullah, M.H. Beg and Y.V. Chandrachud.
68. Imam (Patna H.C.), Hidayatullah (Central Provinces), Mathew (Kerala), Jaswant Singh (Jammu & Kashmir), Kailasam (Madras), A.P. Sen (Madhya Pradesh) and Venkatramiah (Mysore).
69. B.K. Mukherjea, Bose, Sinha, Menon, Raju, Vaidialingam, Hegde, Dwivedi, Chandrachud, Aliagiriswami, P.J. Reddy and Goswami.
70. Palekar had five years experience at the District Bar before joining the Lower Judicial Service; Aliagiriswami had five years before and six years after retirement from the Lower Judicial Service, Sarkaria had put in 6 years at the Patiala High Court Bar; and, Vardharajan had practiced for 6 years at the Madras High Court Bar before joining the Lower Judicial Service.
71. The Law Commission : *Eightieth Report*, 119 (1979).
72. *Ibid*.
73. *Ibid*.
74. Hidayatullah felt that he was bypassed several times simply because he was too young; see, *Supra* note 17 at 144 and 190-191.
75. *Supra* note 28 at 225.
76. In 1983, with the appointment of Justice Thakkar from Gujarat High Court, the Court had three judges from Gujarat, and with the appointment of Justice R. Ranganath Mishra from Orissa High Court, a long gap of thirty years was filled up after Jagannadhadas was appointed in 1953.
77. *Supra* note 28 at 224.
78. See Kumaramangalam, *Supra* note 33 passim.
79. *S.P. Gupta* V. *Union of India*, 1981 Supp. S.C.C. 87 per Venkatramiah judge at 917.

Part II
Institutional Environment

4

Business of the Court

The work of the Court consists of the normal routine of giving full hearings to cases coming under various jurisdictional categories, admission work where the special leave petitions are posted for admissions, preliminary hearings of original writ petitions and the miscellaneous work. According to the prevailing practice the Court spends two full days i.e. approximately 40 per cent of its total time in disposing of the admission matters every week. The remaining three days are utilised in dealing with the normal work besides, at times, taking up some important admission matters. In addition to this a fair amount of time and judge power is spent in dealing with the miscellaneous work.

The quantum and the nature of the work in the Supreme Court constitute the immediate institutional environment for the judges within which they have to function besides the formal and informal rules regulating the practice and procedure in the Court. An attempt is made here to explain the nature and character of the business of the Court in terms of factors like the access channels, geographic spread out of the appellate work, the court's response to the appeals under different jurisdictional channels, the composition of the parties before the court and the subject matter areas often litigated at the portals of the highest tribunal of the land.

Jurisdiction

Jurisdiction is simply the authority by which judges take cognizance of and decide matters brought to their attention.[1] The Indian Supreme Court's jurisdiction is perhaps uncomparable to any apex court in the world today, and is largely determined by the Constitutional provisions, and the legislative enactments in so far as the Constitution empowers the Parliament to enlarge the jurisdiction of the Court as and when it is necessary.

The Court has an original jurisdiction in federal matters,[2] the original writ jurisdiction in the protection of fundamental rights,[3] and has a special jurisdiction to ensure that the removal of a member of the Public Service Commission is made in accordance with the procedure prescribed by the Constitution.[4] The Court also has jurisdiction conferred upon it by Parliament under Article 71 of the Constitution to decide disputes arising out of the election of the President and the Vice-President.[5]

The appellate jurisdiction of the Court can be classified into four categories, viz., (1) where the High Court certifies that the case is fit for the consideration of the Supreme Court,[6] (2) where the Supreme Court may in its discretion grant special leave to appeal,[7] (3) where an appeal may lie to the Court as a matter of right,[8] and (4) where Parliament by law may have conferred additional appellate jurisdiction on the Court.[9]

Under the first category an appeal may lie to the Court in Constitutional matters,[10] civil[11] as well as criminal matters.[12] This jurisdiction can be availed in Constitutional matters even from judgment of a single judge of the High Court where he certifies that the matter is fit for the consideration of the Supreme Court, but not in the case of civil matters, where appeal against judgment of one judge of a High Court is not appealable directly to the Court.[13] The Court's discretionary jurisdiction under article 136 is very wide whereunder, it may allow appeal from any judgment, decree, determination, sentence or order in any cause or matter passed or made by any court or tribunal in the territory of India.[14] The right of appeal to the Supreme Court is given in criminal matters where a High Court on appeal has reversed an order of acquittal, or has withdrawn for trial before itself any case from a subordinate court, and has sentenced the accused person to death. The Court's criminal jurisdiction was further expanded by Parliament in 1970.[15] The fourth category of jurisdiction was added to the Supreme Court by Parliament from time to time. Some examples of this type of jurisdiction are to be found in section 116-A of the Representation of people's Act (1951), section 257 of the Income Tax Act (1961) and section 55 of the Monopolies and Restrictive Trade Practices Act, 1969.

In addition to the original and appellate jurisdiction, the Court has an advisory jurisdiction,[16] a power to review its decisions,[17] and the power to transfer cases.[18] Besides these channels which allow access to the Court, there are number of other factors which determine the nature and quantum of work inflow to the Court, directly or otherwise. For instance, in 1956 the Labour Appellate Tribunal was abolished and no provision was made for an appeal to the High Court with the result that most of the labour matters started going in appeal to the Supreme Court under its discretionary jurisdiction.[19] Similarly, "when the Constitution (Forty-Second Amendment) Act, 1976 diminished the powers of the High Courts to superintend the work of tribunal et al these "High Court" cases came to the Supreme Court.[20]

The docket of the Court thus comprises cases coming through various jurisdictional channels. Considering the nature of jurisdiction conferred upon the Court by the Constitutional provisions and the legislative enactments, some part of the docket is such over which it has no control. But there is, at the same time, considerable amount of freedom which the Court enjoys over the remaining part of its docket. Depending upon what view the Court takes of its own jurisdiction where it has the discretion to decide whether the case needs to be admitted or, reviewed or not, to that extent, the Court determines its own environment.The decisional output of the court spread over a decade is analysed below with a view to ascertain the extent to which different access channels influence the docket of the court.

Decisional Output, 1973-1981

Table I shows the decisional output of the Supreme Court by jurisdiction and by the year reported[21] in the All India Reporter (Supreme Court). The table depicts six jurisdictional categories, viz, the original writ jurisdiction, special leave civil, special leave criminal, certificate civil, certificate criminal, and 'others'. The last category consists of a variety of cases falling under different jurisdictions and includes, among others, the original jurisdiction matters under article 131, review petitions under article 137, and direct appeals from Ministries and tribunals.

The reported data will generally be subject to various constraints. Firstly, the judges exercise some amount of discretion in the matter of whether their judgments should be reported or not. Secondly, all judgments of the Court are not reported in any one single report. Even the official Supreme Court Reporter which reports the decisions chronologically, does not include all the cases decided by the Court.[24] For instance, the official Supreme Court Reports published 4244 decisions during the period 1967-81,[25] whereas the All India Reporter (Supreme Court) published 4033 decisions during a shorter time span between 1973-81. Thirdly, the editors of these Reports exercise considerable discretion in selecting the cases to be reported. And fourthly, the number of cases to be reported in each volume would also depend upon the availability of space in it.

Table I : Yearwise Frequency of Decisions by Jurisdiction, 1973-81

		Special Leav		Certificate			
Year	Writ Petns.	Civ.	Crim.	Civ.	Crim.	others	Total
1973	48	158	124	129	8	28	495
1974	86	133	131	88	8	16	462
1975	87	171	84	85	4	24	455
1976	11	205	118	118	6	24	482
1977	6	227	139	120	4	24	520
1978	9	121	85	46	4	·25	290
1979	16	122	184	67	11	23	423
1980	38	170	108	80	2	21	419
1981	79	186	143	35	1	35	479
Total	380	1493	1116	768	48	220	4025
(%)	(9.5)	(37.0)	(27.7)	(19.1)	(1.2)	(5.5)	(100.0)

(i) ***Original Writ Petitions***: The original writ petition cases dealt with by the Court under article 32 of the Constitution were about 9.5 per cent of the total number of 4025 cases. The year wise frequency of disposals in this category show considerable fluctuations. For instance, the disposal of writ petition cases appears to be maximum in the years 1974 and 1975. The disposal of writ petitions during the next four years registered a sharp decline according to the reported data. A steady increase is recorded in 1980, and in 1981 the frequency of disposals again went up sharply.

A sudden fall in the disposal of writ petitions during the year 1976-77 may have been brought about by the fact that the remedy under article 32 of the Constitution was suspended during the 1975-77 emergency.[22] It is also possible to argue that the low disposal rate continued in the subsequent years immediately following the restoration of civil liberties as it would take sometime before the process could be re-vitalised after it was suddenly snapped with the imposition of the national emergency. Another possible factor which may account for a lower disposal rate during 1978-79 can be explained in terms of the Constitution (42nd Amendment) Act, 1976 which among other things, had brought about certain changes in the Supreme Court's powers and its manner of functioning. A seven judge bench requirement for the disposal of any matter raising the issue of Constitutional validity of any central or state law could have imposed serious limitations on its manpower consequently affecting its total output as is clearly borne out by the table. There were only 290 cases reported in the year 1978 which shows the total output of the Court during the time the amendment remained in operation.[23] Accordingly, the number of writ petitions disposed off by the Court during this period may also have been affected.

Of the 380 writ petition cases, the Supreme Court allowed the claim of the petitioner in 166 (43.7 per cent) cases. This is a considerable increase over the figures collected and analysed for the first seventeen years (1950-67) of the Court where the petitioner succeeded only in 33.5 per cent of the 310 writ petition cases.[24] The ten per cent increase registered in the third decade over the previous years in the court's response to civil liberty issues being quite significant prompted further investigations. It was discovered that a large number of detentions challenged under the writ petitions during this period were set aside thus allowing the claim of the petitioner in about 54 per cent of such claims. This figure was quite high as compared to other claims agitated under writ petitions where the court responded favourably only in about 24 per cent of total number of such claims.

(ii) *Special Leave Jurisdiction*: The special leave jurisdiction under article 136 of the Constitution is very wide, and it appears that the Court has made an extensive use of its prerogative under this category. Table I clearly shows that majority (64.7 per cent) of the cases dealt with by the Court during the period 1973-81 belonged to the special leave jurisdiction category. This pattern has been consistent all throughout which strongly suggests that the Court's docket has been dominated by appeals through the special leave channel.[25]

The Court's appellate jurisdiction in civil and criminal matters is fairly wide. At the same time one would notice that both the civil and criminal appeals under the special leave jurisdiction far exceeded in number than under the normal channel of appeals on certificates issued by the High Courts. According to the reported data analysed in table I, almost 65 per cent of the total disposal consisted of appeals under the special leave category.

Within the special leave category, it will be further noticed that the disposal of civil special leaves (37.0 per cent) have exceeded those of the criminal special appeals throughout the nine years period except in the year 1979. Special leave criminal, on the other hand, account for 27.7 per cent of the total number of cases disposed of by the Court, thus forming the second largest category.

(iii) *Certificate Appeals*: The third major source, and the second largest feeder to the Supreme Court docket appear to be the certified appeals from the High Courts. Almost 20 per cent of the total number of cases decided by the Court during the this period came from this jurisdictional source. Of these at least 19 per cent belonged to the civil certified appeal category and only about one per cent comprised the criminal certified appeals. From the disposal rate it is quite evident that very few criminal appeals lie to the Supreme Court under this jurisdiction, and invariably it has been a channel for the civil appeals. But even the civil appeals which go to the Supreme Court through this channel are far less in number than those admitted by the Court under its special leave jurisdiction. All this goes to show that the Supreme Court maintains its vigilance over the High Courts primarily through its special leave jurisdiction, and does not depend upon the manner in which the High Courts exercise their power to issue certificate of fitness for appeal to the Supreme Court.

(iv) *Others*: The last category comprises a variety of other jurisdictional avenues. The figures from 1973 to 1981 show that there has not been any significant change in the character of workload of the Court under this head. The disposal rate has been more or less constant, and they add only about 5 per cent on an average to the Court's annual docket.

The above analysis of the court's disposals under different jurisdictional heads spread over a period of almost a decade not only reveals the recurrent patterns in its major preoccupations but also helps in understanding how external factors sometimes intervene and influence the docket of the court. One of the important areas with which the court has been kept busy is in the protection of Rights guaranteed by the Constitution where its response has registered a significant change over the years. But it is in the area of appallete work that its disposals at least in quantitative terms stand out prominently particularly under its special leave jurisdiction. Almost 85 per cent of its total work output consists of nothing but appeals from various High Courts an aspect which would require further scrutiny.

Geographic Spread Out of the Appallete Work

The distribution of the geographic origin of the appeals from the High Courts decided by the Supreme Court is shown in Table II. The term geographic origin refers here mainly to the State High Court from which the case travelled to the Supreme Court by way

Table II : Regional Distribution of Appeals from the High Courts

State* Ranked by Population	Total Number of appeals Spl. from the High Court	Civ. Spl. Leave	Crim. Cert. Leave	Civ. Cert.	Crim.
U.P.	557	42.5	34.3	21.2	2.0
Bihar	171	35.7	34.5	29.2	0.6
Maharashtra	378	39.4	41.3	18.0	1.3
A.P.	201	47.3	26.9	24.9	1.0
West Bengal	183	38.8	13.7	42.6	4.9
Tamil Nadu	211	50.2	19.9	28.9	1.0
Karnataka	151	58.3	17.2	24.5	0.0
M.P.	213	43.7	35.7	18.8	1.9
Gujarat	211	41.7	30.3	26.1	1.9
P&H.	466	38.6	42.3	18.9	0.2
Rajasthan	103	40.8	42.7	15.5	1.0
Orissa	78	46.2	43.6	7.7	2.6
Kerala	139	51.8	23.0	25.2	0.0
Gauhati	49	63.3	14.3	20.4	2.0
J&K	22	63.6	22.7	13.6	0.0
H.P.	16	43.7	43.7	12.5	0.0
Sikhim	0	0.0	0.0	0.0	0.0
Delhi	254	43.3	36.6	18.5	1.6
U.Ts.	22	59.1	22.7	18.2	0.0
Total	3425	47.6	30.3	21.3	1.2

* Population ranking of states is in accordance with 1981 census.
Note : All figures except total appeals are in per cents.

of appeal. The table shows a fair spread out of the Supreme Court's work in geographical terms. All the states and the union territories in the country barring the state of Sikkim until 1981 resorted to the Court for dispute resolution. Although, the size of the state in terms of population may not necessarily lead to a high rate in litigation, yet a correlation does exist between the two and, the table reveals such a relationship to a considerable extent. Punjab and Haryana, Delhi, and Bihar are the only major exceptions from where the number of appeals flowing to the Supreme Court every year appear to be greatly disproportionate to their population.

Delhi, being the seat of power and its close proximity with the Court's location explains the large number of cases going to the Supreme Court. In case of Punjab and Haryana majority of the litigation is land based and, the relative affluence of the farmer in these two states coupled with certain economic and cultural factors can be correlated with long and enduring litigation which finally end up in the highest tribunal. In both these cases proximity in terms of distance from the seat of the Supreme Court can be considered as an important factor from another point of view as well. There is a possibility that a large number of advocates coming from these areas find it relatively easier to maintain their liaison with their colleagues in the lower courts which facilitates the inflow of cases from these areas to the Supreme Court.

On the other hand, a lower proportion of inflow from Bihar which happens to be the second largest state in terms of population, may be due to the relative poverty and backwardness both of which are not conducive to sustained litigation. Population, however, is not the only index to measure the litigation rate. Population may generate litigation at the lower levels, but it is not necessary that the litigation rate at the lower levels would always determine the number of cases going to the Supreme Court from a particular state. There may be other contributing factors such as the efficiency and experience with which litigation is dealt with by the lower courts and also by the High Courts, the nature of litigational activity which predominates the area, the social attitudes, the reverence attached to the decisions of the courts below, accessibility in terms of distance and financial stability of the litigants, are a few among them. The role of the Bar at the lower levels is an equally important factor in this regard. Their professional competence, knowledge of law and the current decisions of the higher courts, their attitudes towards their clients and the trust they enjoy with the litigants are some of the factors which would need to be explored in a systematic manner.

The regional distribution of appeals from the High Courts has been further analysed in terms of jurisdictional categories .This was done in order to find out whether any correlation exists between the frequency with which a High Court issues certificate of fitness to appeal and the tendency of the Supreme Court to grant special leave to appeal. It may be clarified in this context that no suggestion is being made that there exists such a relationship, nor that the Court has followed any such policy. However, the state-wise pattern of disposals under the two jurisdictional heads, show that the incidence of special leave disposals have been exceptionally high in case of appeals from almost all the High Courts. Accordingly, the disposal of certificate appeals has been consistently on the lower side, except in the case of civil certified appeals from West Bengal High Court. The pattern of disposals do not suggest any correlation between the two factors as hypothesised above. The table merely confirms that the Supreme Court primarily maintains its surveillance over all the geographical regions through its discretionary power under article 136 of the Constitution.

Disposition of the High Court Appeals

A total of 3425 decisions i.e., almost 85 per cent of the decisional output of the Supreme Court consists of the determination of appeals from High Courts. Only 24 per cent of such appeals reach the Court through the channel of certificate of fitness granted by the High Courts whereas, the remaining 76 per cent are added to the docket of the Supreme Court by the Court itself under its special leave jurisdiction. In other words, in the Court's opinion a much larger per centage of cases decided by the High Courts require a review.

Table III shows the disposition of High Court appeals both in the special leave as well as certificate categories in terms of their affirmation ratio. All the state High Courts and the Union territories are arranged in descending order according to their affirmation ratio. The table reveals that the range of total affirmations of High Court appeals by the Supreme Court has been between 58.9 per cent on the upper side and 36.3 per cent on the lower side. In other words, one may say that the High Court decisions have been overruled from a minimum of 42 per cent to a maximum of 64 per cent cases which were subjected to a review by the Supreme Court. The average affirmation ratio of all High Court appeals is about 51 per cent which means almost 49 per cent of such decisions were overruled by the court.

Table III : Disposition of appeals from the High Courts and their Affirmation ratio, 1973-81

High Court	Per cent Affirmed by Jurisdiction		Total No. of Appeals	Affirmation ratio all Appeals
	Special leave	Certificate Appeals		
Orissa	58.5	62.5	78	58.9
Rajasthan	55.8	70.5	103	58.2
Kerala	51.9	65.7	139	56.1
Uttar Pradesh	52.1	60.5	557	53.3
P&H.	49.8	65.1	466	52.7
West Bengal	47.9	59.7	183	52.4
Karnataka	51.7	54.0	151	52.3
A.P.	51.0	53.8	201	51.7
Bihar	45.0	62.7	171	51.4
Delhi	52.2	50.9	254	50.7
H.P.	42.8	100.0	16	50.0
M.P.	47.9	54.5	213	49.3
Gauhati	50.0	45.4	49	48.3
Maharashtra	47.2	60.2	378	48.6
Gujarat	49.3	40.6	211	46.9
Tamilnadu	36.5	58.7	211	44.0
U.Ts.	38.8	25.0	22	36.3
J&K.	33.3	0.0	22	27.2
Total Average	47.8	54.9	3425	51.1

These figures indicate that the Supreme Court has not been simply putting a stamp of approval on the High Court decisions. It has in fact discharged its appellate functions in a rather significant manner. The highest affirmations are scored by Orissa and Rajasthan High Courts which stand well above the average affirmation rate. On the other hand, Gujarat, Tamil Nadu, the Union Territories and Jammu & Kashmir High Courts have recorded affirmations much below the average ratio. Two of the three oldest and prestigious High Courts in India, viz., Maharashtra and Tamil Nadu, formerly known as Bombay and Madras High Courts respectively, find their place almost towards the bottom in the order. This shows that irrespective of standing and reputation for which some High Courts are renowned, they have fared no better than others which are not so well renowned.

How does then one explain almost 50 per cent reversals of all those High Court decisions which are contested before the Supreme Court particularly in view of the fact that almost all the judges of the Supreme Court have been elevated from these very High Courts? To say that High Court judges lack the necessary skill or ability to perceive the issues in their right perspective and determine them accordingly would not be fair as these very judges occupy Supreme Court bench in due course of time. This phenomena can perhaps be explained in terms of differences which flow from their respective institutional hierarchy to which they belong.

The pattern of affirmations and overrulling of High Court appeals by the Supreme Court throws further light on the institutional relationship between the two higher appellate courts. As indicated above, the High Courts appear to be extremely reticent in granting certificates of fitness which would enable the litigants to challenge their decisions in the Supreme Court. At the same time the apex court seems to have taken a rather skeptical view of the High Court's powers and their ability to finally determine the issues which are contested before them. This is borne out by the fact that 76 per cent of appeals from the High Courts are reviewed by the Supreme Court under its special leave jurisdiction. Looking at the pattern of disposals in terms of affirmations and overrulings of the appeals coming from the two channels, one would find that the affirmation ratio of appeals coming through the certificate jurisdiction is much higher than those which the Supreme Court admits under its special leave jurisdiction. For instance the Court has affirmed on an average 54.9 per cent of the certified appeals as against 47.8 per cent of the appeals admitted through the special leave jurisdiction. By lesser number of overruling of cases coming through certificates the Supreme Court seems to be indirectly hinting at the High Courts that they should exercise more restraint and carefully scrutinise the matters before granting such certificates. On the other hand, a relatively much higher per centage of cases undertaken for review under its special leave jurisdiction are reversed as indicated above leading to inevitable inference that in the Court's opinion High Courts are making many more errors in arriving at their judgments assailed before the Supreme Court. This, in other words, provides adequate institutional justification for the Supreme Court judges to liberally grant special leave to appeal even in such cases where High Courts have already considered and rejected an application for the issue of certificate of fitness to appeal to the Supreme Court.

The Supreme Court's perception of its role and its responsibilities under the Constitution has prompted it time and again to spread its wings far beyond its institutional resources. The Court is conscious of its expanding docket but at the same time, it seems to be anxious to maintain its wide jurisdiction,[26] and for that reason perhaps, it has not been able to evolve self discipline in order to channelise its own discretion under article 136 of the Constitution. This may provide a partial explanation to the apparent contradiction in its attitude towards the High Courts.

Crisis of Arears in the Court

The docket of the Court has been increasing steadily since the early fifties. It is for this reason that the strength of the Court was first increased to ten in 1956 and then to thirteen (excluding the Chief Justice) in 1960. Despite these two increases, the arrears in the Court which stood at 2,319 cases in 1960, had gone upto 7,104 by the end of 1970.[27] By the time the third increase in the strength of judges was made in 1977, the arrears had gone upto 14,109, and by April, 1978, the number had already shot up to 23,092.[28] The arears in the court went up to monumental proportions by the Ninties where they were estimated to over two lacs despite a further increase in the strength of the court to 26 in 1986. These figures do not include the miscellaneous workload of the Court.

(i) ***The Inadequacy of Judges:*** The problem of arrears in the Supreme Court thus, is not a recent phenomenon. It has been there with the Court since its very inception. The inadequate strength of judges in the Court was perceived as one of the factors contributing to this institutional dilemma and the number of judges was increased on five different occasions. But one may ask did the Court ever normally function with the full sanctioned strength? This aspect is analysed in Table IV which shows the yearwise pattern of vacancies and the appointments made to the Court upto 1984.

Table IV : Yearwise Pattern of Vacancies and Appointments,* 1950-84

Year	Vacant	Filled	Outstanding	Year	Vacant	Filled	Outstanding
1951	3	1	2	1968	4	1	3
1952	2	2	Nil	1969	5	3	2
1953	1	1	Nil	1970	3	Nil	3
1954	3	2	1	1971	7	5	2
1955	1	1	Nil	1972	4	4	Nil
1956a	2	2	Nil	1973	5	4	1
1957	4	3	1	1974	3	2	1
1958	3	3	Nil	1975	3	2	1
1959	2	2	Nil	1976	2	1	1
1960b	3	3	Nil	1977c	3	3	Nil
1961	Nil	Nil	Nil	1978	6	4	2
1962	1	Nil	1	1979	3	1	2
1963	2	Nil	2	1980	6	2	4
1964	5	2	3	1981	5	3	2
1965	5	2	3	1982	4	Nil	4
1966	7	4	3	1983	5	4	1
1967	4	1	3	1984	1	1	Nil

(a) The Court strength was increased to ten excluding the Chief Justice.
(b) Strength of judges increased to thirteen.
(c) Strength of judges increased to seventeen.
* All the vacancies and appointments are on annual basis, and do not project the actual court strength during the working session within a particular year.
Note: Since 1986, the court strength has been increased to twenty six.

The first decade witnessed upto the end of 1959 a turnover of 24 judges and 5 Chief Justices in the Court. The second decade shows a slight fall in the frequency of appointments as only 16 judges were appointed during this period, but, at the same time, the Court had no fewer than 6 Chief Justices. The third decade had the maximum turnover of 26 judges while maintaining the frequency of change in the Chief Justiceship at 6. The fourth decade had already had 12 judges appointed, and considering that of the 18 sitting judges (including the Chief Justice), at least 14 were to retire before December, 1989, the frequency of change in the Court's membership was very likely to be maintained at its previous levels. The only distinctive feature of the first half of the 1980's was in the relative stability in the office of the Chief Justice which did not undergo any change since Chief Justice Chandrachud who had taken over in February 1978 continued in office till the middle of 1985.

The average frequency of appointments to the Supreme Court every year worked out to approximately 2.2, and accordingly, the frequency of change in the Court's membership on the basis of its total sanctioned strength varied from 12 to 27 per cent during different intervals. On an average 19 per cent of the Court's membership has been changing almost every year since 1950. This per centage of change would be much higher if it is calculated on the basis of actual rather than sanctioned strength at particular interval because the Court seldom functioned with its full sanctioned strength. The above calculations, however, do not take into account the usual leave of absence of judges and some other factors like, short and long term of absence of judges from the bench in order to enable them to attend to conferences, seminars in India and abroad, or attend to assignments like commissions of enquiry, boundary disputes and arbitration matters which take them away from their normal court work and consequently affect the Court's institutional output.

The rapid turnover of judges caused vacancies in the middle of the working sessions of the Court which were invariably filled up after considerable delays. The table clearly reveals that the Court was working with less than the sanctioned strength particularly between 1962 and 1971 and then again from 1973 upto the middle of 1984. In 1977 too, the Court acquired its full strength only in the month of September when Justices Tulzapurkar and Desai were appointed. All this shows that the Supreme Court has been working for most of the time with short-strength and this constitutes one of the factors contributing to the arrears in the Court.

The quick succession of judges and the Chief Justices in the Court have also caused fluctuations in its membership as well as its leadership. The reason underlying this malady has been the appointment of judges in their fairly advanced age, which because of the mandatory retirement at the age of 65 years, leaves them with exceedingly short tenures on the Bench. Although, there were few exceptions where judges were appointed with a tenure of ten years or more, yet the Court has by and large suffered from institutional instability. Judges with short tenures apparently found themselves close to their impending retirements even before they could adapt to the new institutional environment. This kind of situation, therefore, hardly leaves much scope for many judges to grasp the institutional needs of the Court and respond accordingly.

(ii) ***Liberal Use of Special Leave Jurisdiction***: Another factor which appears to have contributed significantly to the appellate docket of the Court is the manner in which the Supreme Court has exercised its discretion under article 136 of the Constitution. As pointed out above, the court has been unable to evolve an institutional criterion for allowing appeals under its special leave jurisdiction consequently opening a flood gate of litigation in the court over the years. The data on jurisdictional origin of disposals by the Court and analysed in the previous sections shows that cases under this jurisdiction alone constituted 65 per cent of the total number of cases decided by the Court during the nine years period. This was neither contemplated by the Constitution makers nor in conformity with the conceptual orientation of the apex court which was structurally designed to cater to 'breach of certain principles which strike at the very root of administration of justice as between man and man'. Considering the Federal principle underlying the Indian polity, the state High Courts ought to have been in a position to determine and give finality to majority of the issues that are agitated in appeals with extremely rare cases requiring the intervention under the special leave jurisdiction of the Supreme Court. However, the facts and figures speak for themselves and the court has not only contributed significantly to the deepening crises of institutional adaptability to the rising demands and expectations from the highest seat of justice, but also in the process created a crises of credibility for the High Courts.

(iii) ***Fragmented Benches:*** An equally important factor in this context, and one which is often overlooked, is the fragmented bench structure of the Court which performs its decision-making functions. In admission matters too, the policy with regard to determining the inflow of cases under its discretionary jurisdiction is likely to vary depending upon the manner in which different judges constituting different panels approach the problem. The concept of the Court as an entity whose functional unity is presupposed, tends to break down at this level, and acts as a major constraint in the evolution of an institutional discipline in channelising discretion in this area.

These factors seem to have had important bearing on the docket of the Court in terms of institutional constraints. They partly explain why the Court within the existing frame work could not effectively deal with the increasing workload, and why it failed to develop a unified approach to the admission of special leave petitions resulting in heavy backlogs in the apex court. Two other aspects i.e, the composition of the litigants and the subject matter litigated before the court, have been dealt with briefly hereafter in order to understand who have been the major constituents for the court and what kind of issues keep the court busy most of the time.

Who Keeps the Court Busy

An attempt was made on the basis of available information to classify the litigants in certain broad categories in order to find out what kind of groups and sections of the Indian society mostly find access to the court. It has been pointed out above that people from all the geographical regions of India have come to the Court for resolving their disputes. Although, this statement here only applies to the appeals from the High Courts since the geographical origin of other categories like original writ petitions, original suits and the like was not ascertained, yet it is significant because they constitute 85 per cent of the total decisional output. But in determining the access to the Court it is far more important to ascertain factors like economic, political and social status of the litigants involved. This information, however, was not always easily available in the reported decisions. One had to rely invariably upon the case titles and, quite often had to draw inferences as regards the identity of the litigants involved from either the subject matter in dispute, or from the text of the judgment itself. Broad categories were chosen in order to avoid, as far as possible, the analyst's subjective discretion in classifying a litigant under one or the other category. These broad categories were formed by grouping together characteristics which were found to be common in certain types of litigants. For instance, all levels of government appearing in any capacity, including that of an employer, as one of the parties to the disputes was regarded as a class backed by the state power. Similarly, all types of business, both big and small was considered to comprise relatively economically advantageous section of society and clubbed together to form one large category for the purpose of approximate identification.

Although one is fully aware of the dangers involved in this kind of generalisation and equalising the otherwise unequals yet, given the nature of information available a further break up of this category into small, medium and large business would have been rather arbitrary and would only result into distortions in the frequency with which each component of the business community had approached the Court. The employing capacity of the business is only second to that of the government and, accordingly, business as an employer has been counted in the business category itself.

Table V : Composition of Litigants

Litigant	No. of Times a litigant	Per cent of Total (N = 8050) (N = 4025)	Petitioner/ Appellant	Defendant/ Respondent
Business/ Employer	753	9.36	475 (11.80)	278 (6.91)
Worker/ Union	164	2.03	43 (1.07)	121 (3.01)
All levels of Government	3028	37.62	811 (20.15)	2217 (55.07)
Private Party (Other than Government)	3842	47.73	2564 (63.70)	1278 (31.75)
Political Party	251	3.12	128 (3.18)	123 (3.06)
Others	12	0.14	4 (0.10)	8 (0.20)
Totals	8050	100.00	4025 (100.00)	4025 (100.00)

Table V shows the frequency with which a party appeared as a litigant before the Supreme Court and, the number of times it did so in the capacity of either petitioner/appellant or, defendant/respondent. Businessmen, who not only form one of the largest single litigant category, but also carried their disputes to the threshold of the highest Court for final determination more often than any other single identifiable private party (i.e. non-government), were among the easiest to identify. They appeared before the Court almost invariably either as employers in disputes with their workers, as private entrepreneurs aggrieved by government regulations, as parties in dispute with other businessmen, or as assessee under variety of tax laws.

Private party which accounts for 47.73 per cent of the 8050 litigants consists of a variety of individuals and groups staking their claims as against another individual or group, or against the businessman employer, or against the government. The most numerous in this category were the individuals prosecuted for offences against the state praying for the Court intervention. These individuals came from different socio-economic backgrounds with different motivations for committing crimes which could not be easily classified under one separate category. For instance, socio-economic offences like smuggling, corruption, adulteration and a host of others likewise are very different kind of offences than those of murder, robbery or dacoity cases, and the individuals involved may not have any thing in common to form respectively a distinct class. For this reason all such litigants were treated as private individuals under private party category.

Similarly large number of individuals contesting their claims as landlords and tenants too were treated as private party. In addition to this, private individual litigants comprised mostly rural landlords, debtors, mortgagors, mortagees, professionals like doctors, lawyers, teachers, judges, executives, students, ex-rulers of the princely states, etc. Among the private groups which appeared as litigants in the Supreme Court were the religious groups, trusts and, the associations. Since the number of such litigant groups was too small, they were merged with the 'private party' category. This single largest category thus, comprised a broad spectrum of litigants who came from different walks of life to get their disputes finally resolved in the Court of last resort.

Another single largest category which accounts for 37.62 per cent of the total number of litigants is the government. All levels of government like the Central, State, Union Territory, Municipal, District and other government levels are included in this category. It is, however, interesting to note that the major share of litigation in the Supreme Court is claimed by the state governments which along with union territories account for 32.30 per cent of the litigants out of 37.62 per cent in the government category. Among others, 4.34 per cent is claimed by the central government and only 0.98 per cent is shared by the municipal governments.

Two other categories of litigants identified are, workers/unions involved in labour disputes accounting for 2.03 per cent of litigants and, the political parties or candidates locked in election disputes appeared 2.12 per cents in the court.

The above composition of litigants suggests that a fairly wide section of the Indian society has had access to the apex court. But two significant features of this composition stand out prominently. First, there appears to be a middle, or upper middle class bias in the character of the various litigants which suggests that the socially and economically weaker sections of society did not get the opportunity to have their grievances heard by the highest Court in the land. Second, the table shows that the Business/Employer appeared in the Court as petitioner/appellant much more frequently than it did in the capacity of defendant/respondent. This means that business being, relatively, an economically stable group was in a better position to exploit its resources to have their disputes resolved at the highest forum. Worker/Union, on the contrary, approached the Court in much less number of times than they were proceeded against. However, in the case of private party, the inflated figures shown under petitioner/appellant capacity were mainly due to preponderance of criminal cases where the accused convicted for serious offences approached the Court for relief.

From the general picture of the composition of litigants in the Supreme Court which emerge from the analysis it is quite clear that the Court has been kept busy for most of the time by the government and the businessmen. The figures shown in Table V adequately substantiate this proposition as the two categories by themselves account for 46.9 per cent of the total number of litigants before the court during the period under study.

Nature of Business of the Court

Table VI presents the data on subject matter areas with which the Supreme Court was preoccupied most of the times. The thirteen categories listed in the table are broad generalised categories and, do not reveal the entire landscape of the business of the Court. For instance all type of tax matters were lumped together to form one single category to show the total preoccupation of the Court with taxes as such. Tax matters were the subject matter of litigation in the Supreme Court in 12.72 per cent of all decisions and, as is clear from the table, the third largest category accounting for the business of the Court.

The disputes among private parties although span over wide range of issues touching a variety of subject matter like rent, lease, contract, inheritance, succession, divorce and the like, were kept together in the category designating private disputes. These disputes together accounted for 15.93 per cent. Similarly, criminal offences of all types under the Indian Penal Code as well as those created under local and special laws sought the Court's intervention in 28.77 per cent cases constituting the largest number of decisions falling under a single category. It was noticed that within this category the largest number of decisions pertained to the offence of murder. Similarly, prevention of corruption was the Court's concern in a large number of decisions rendered in this category. The Court's preoccupation with such a large number of criminal decisions can partly be explained in view of the enhancement in its criminal jurisdiction by Parliament in 1970 besides those admitted by the court under its special leave jurisdiction.

Table VI : Nature of the Business of the Court

	Subject Matter	Frequency	Percentage
1.	Taxes	512	12.72
2.	Regulations	187	4.65
3.	Rights of Public Servants	355	8.82
4.	Industrial Disputes	222	5.52
5.	Election Disputes	132	3.28
6.	Civil Liberty Claims	277	6.88
7.	Criminal Offences	1158	28.77
8.	Private Party Disputes	641	15.93
9.	Land Reform Non-Agrarian Acq, Contract, Lease, etc.	378	9.39
10.	Others	163	4.04
Total		4025	100.00

The Court seems to have played an important role in some of the other classified areas too. For instance, regulation of business and economy engaged the Court in 4.65 per cent of decisions; tenures and rights of public servants were the subject matter for the Court's consideration in as many as 8.82 per cent decisions; election disputes occupied the Court's attention in 3.28 per cent decisions;[29] and, religion where individual had some grievance against the state, sought the court's intervention in seventeen 0.42 per cent decision.

Of special significance has been the court's contribution in the areas of land reforms and acquisition of property of an individual for public purpose by the state. Land reform decisions accounted for 4.20 per cent and, acquisition of non-agrarian property was challenged in 1.81 per cent decisions in the court. Another area in which the court significantly intervened between the individual and the state concerned government contracts and leases which alone was the subject matter of litigation before the court in 2.96 per cent of decisions.

Civil liberties, symbol of all free and civilized people, demanded constant and vigorous surveillance by the court. The court, having exclusive original jurisdiction to enforce fundamental rights under article 32 of the Constitution, was called upon by the injured party in 6.88 per cent decisions to provide the healing touch.

All those decisions which either could not be classified under any one of the above categories or, where subject matter area could not be identified, were combined in 'others' category and such decisions accounted for 4.04 per cent of the total numbers. Some of the important subject matters which were included in this category were : federalism, reorganisation of states and, defining powers and jurisdictions for the lower courts and tribunals.

The nature of subject matter areas emerging out of the above description shows that the Court's business in terms of subject matter is almost infinite. But, quite evidently, there has been large concentration of areas like Tax matters, rights of public servants, labour disputes, offences and the original writ petitions under article 32 of the Constitution engaging the attention of the Court most of the time.

Thus, the business of the court which sets the tone and the tenor for decision making activity is the primary stimulus to which judges respond in their decisions and, therefore, essential to any understanding of the court's decision making process besides the formal and informal arrangements within which the process operates.

Notes

1. Harold Jr. Spaeth, *Supreme Court Policy Making* 35 (W.H. Freemen and Company, San Francisco 1979).
2. The Constitution of India, Art. 131.
3. *Id.*, Art. 32 .
4. *Id.* Art. 317 .
5. The Presidential and Vice Presidential Election Act, 1952.
6. The Constitution, Arts. 132, 133, and 134(c).

7. *Id*. Art. 136.
8. *Id*. Art. 134 (a) and (b).
9. *Id*. Art. 138.
10. *Id*. Art. 132(1) & (2).
11. *Id*. Art. 133(1).
12. *Id*. Art. 134(c)
13. *Id*. Art. 133(3)
14. Except in the case of a tribunal set up for the Armed Forces.
15. See Sec. 2(i) (a) of the Supreme Court (Enlargement of Criminal Jurisdiction) Act, 1970, where the Court was also given jurisdiction not just in capital punishment and life imprisonment cases but also in cases where a sentence of ten years and more was imposed by way of punishment. In civil matters too, the pecuniary limits as regards the subject matter of litigation was done away with in 1972 by the Constitution (Thirtieth Amendment) Act.
16. The Constitution, Art. 143.
17. *Id*. Art. 137.
18. See Sec. 406 of the Code of Criminal Procedure(1973).
19. See VII L.S.D. Col. 3804 (1956). Also see Law Commission of India : *Fourteenth Report* 55 (1958).
20. Rajeev Dhavan, *The Supreme Court under Strain: The Challenge of Arrears* 21 (Tripathi, Bombay, 1978). See also TADA (1985) which provides for direct appeal to the Supreme Court from the orders of Designated Court.
21. The year of reporting in many cases is not the same as the year in which the case was decided. This is so because the AIR has not been reporting the decisions of the court in strictly chronological order, and many a time cases decided in the previous year are reported in the subsequent year. All such cases were included in the year in which they were actually reported.
22. The writ petitions dealt with during 1975-77 period were in fact pending before the court and some of them were disposed off during this period or even earlier but were reported by the AIR in these years
23. The requirement of seven judges bench was done away with by the Constitution (45th Amendment) Act. 1977.
24. George Gadbois, "The Supreme Court of India - A preliminary report of an Empirical Study", 4 *Journal of Constitutional And Parliamentary Studies* 36 (1970); see also, Gadbois, "Selection, Background Characteristics, and Voting Behaviour of Indian Supreme Court Judges, 1950-59" in Schubert and Danelski (ed). *Comparative Judicial Behaviour* 237 (Oxford University Press, 1969).
25. See also Rajeev Dhavan, *Supra* note 20 at 54-55.
26. *Supra* note 20 at 43
27. *Ibid*.
28. *Ibid*.
29. In some election disputes the Government was one of the parties to the dispute, which explains the difference in figures provided in Table V from the one appearing in Table VI.

5

Structure of Decision Making

The structural arrangements of the Supreme Court's decision making process constitute as significant an input as the nature of its work discussed in the previous chapter. The term structural arrangement here refers to the manner in which the Court is organised in terms of bench compositions and assignment of work to various panels of judges comprising the division benches. The division of the Court into various panels of judges for all practical purposes conceptually amounts to creation of more than one court within the institutional frame work and, implies the induction of an important variable in the Court's decision making process. All the judges do not sit en banc and decide every case that is brought before the Court for its determination. Neither can the judges choose cases for themselves which they would decided. Just as the process of appointment and selection of Supreme Court judges, as discussed in chapter 3 is an important but an external factor which determines the composition of the Court, bench assignments likewise determine the participation of judges and in this sense is an internal variable but equally significant to the decision making process of the court.

At the outset, therefore, it has to be understood that the decision making function in the Supreme Court is performed by various panels of judges and not by the Court sitting en banc. The decisions made by these panels of judges are known as the decisions of the Court and they can not be challenged in any other court of law in the country. These decisions cannot be assailed either before a larger bench or, even before the full Court in appeal. A review of any decision of the Court is within the discretion of the Court,[1] but such a review is normally undertaken by judges who had initially decided the case, save where the review is entertained after the retirement of the original judges.[2] In law, therefore, there is no distinction between the finality of the decision of a division bench and that of the full Court. In order to understand the institutional fabric of the Court's decision making process it is thus, essential to analyse the bench assignments and study the small sub-sets of the Court than studying the Court as a single decision making entity.

The practice of employing division benches for the purpose of decision making in the Supreme Court was adopted in the very early years of the Court's inception. The Supreme Court began functioning in 1950 with six judges including the Chief Justice, and many of the decisions of the first few months were given by the full Court, i.e. all judges participating in such decisions. Before the year ended, however, the division bench system was being employed, with the Court's work divided among panels of judges.

Among the formal rules regulating the practice and procedure in the Court are a few which provide certain guidelines as regards the constitution and composition of division benches. Order VII of the Supreme Court rules which provides for the constitution of division courts lays down that every cause, appeal or matter shall be heard by a bench consisting of not less than two judges nominated by the Chief Justice.[3] And, where in the course of hearing of any cause, appeal or other proceeding, the bench considers that the matter should be dealt with by a larger bench, it shall refer the matter to the Chief Justice, who shall thereupon constitute such a bench for the hearing.[4]

Similarly, in matters involving a substantial question of law as to the interpretation of the Constitution or, for the purpose of hearing any reference under article 143 of the Constitution the minimum number of judges who are to sit and decide a case is fixed at five.[5] In addition to these a seven judge bench requirement was introduced by the Constitution. (42nd Amendment) Act, 1976 to decide matters involving Constitutional validity of Central and State laws, but the provision was later repealed by the Constitution (45th Amendment) Act, 1977.[6] Before the amendment and after it was repealed, the constitution of larger benches has been entirely the prerogative of the Chief Justice.

According to the rules, therefore, the Chief Justice has the power to constitute benches, nominate judges and assign cases to them. This power is constrained by two formal requirements, viz., a minimum of two judges would sit and decide a case and, where a matter involves the interpretation of the Constitution the quorum shall not be less than five. These provisions clearly show that bench assignments in the Supreme Court are the exclusive prerogative of the Chief Justice and he enjoys considerable discretion in these matters. How this discretion has been exercised by the successive Chief Justices; what are the considerations which may have influenced their bench assignment behaviour; how and to what extent this gets reflected in judges' participation in the court's decision making activity; are some of the important institutional factors examined hereafter.

The data concerning the bench assignments are easily located in the reported decisions, because each decision indicates who the participating judges are. The date of decision indicated in each case was relied upon to ascertain the Chief Justice who constituted the bench. For the purpose of computing the total number of bench assignments, each reported case was treated as an index for one distinct assignment. It was assumed for the purpose of analyses that each assignment is in itself an independent and conscious exercise of discretion by the Chief Justice to appoint a panel of judges to hear a particular matter. Although, considering the number of benches to be constituted, the amount and nature of work to be assigned to each of them, it would be almost impossible for any Chief Justice to undertake such a rigorous exercise by himself. As per the normal practice in the Supreme Court the Registrar (Judicial) prepares the roster for the Court's business and, with the approval of the Chief Justice, cause lists are prepared showing matters assigned to various panels of judges. Since the Chief Justice can modify or change the cause list if he so desires, the ultimate discretion is his and he is always free to exercise it.

The division benches are constituted to hear and dispose of a number of matters and, sometimes the same panel may continue to function for considerable length of time. Judges may also be rotated from one to another division bench for longer or shorter durations or, for the purpose of hearing a particular matter only.

There are a number of factors which may be relevant in making bench assignments. For instance, the size and the nature of the docket to be dealt with, the number of division benches to be constituted, the strength of each division bench to be fixed, the total number of judges available for assignments, which judges are to be assigned which matters and how to adjust them on various division benches. Besides these factors, there would be a number of other considerations which are likely to influence the discretion of the Chief Justice in making bench assignments. These would possibly include, the utilization of judges strength with a view to maximise the decisional output of the court, effort to minimise overt dissent in the Court where unanimity is a preferred value with the Chief Justice, and consideration like subject matter specialisation of judges or their interest in a particular area of the law. It is also quite likely that the Chief Justice takes to account the judges' ideological preferences and their probable voting response atleast in important controversies. In addition to all this, one may perhaps also take into account the possibility of judges being accommodated according to their choice, particularly, in view of the fact that acute differences among some judges have not only existed but such differences have been openly expressed by the judges themselves several times in the past.[7] Last, but not the least, the senior lawyers too may contribute although discretly to the bench assignments.[8]

It will require more comprehensive and in-depth studies with more reliable data to examine all these aspects in order to fully understand the institutional implications of the decision making function of the Court. It is not the aim of this study either to prove or disprove any one of the specific assumptions. The data on bench assignments has been analysed mainly with a view to explore several possibilities which would enhance our understanding of the decision making process in the Supreme Court as well as furnish a basis for further investigations.

Constitution of Division Benches

Four Chief Justices led the Court during the nine year's period under investigation. Although Chief Justice Sikri retired in April 1973 the year with which the study begins, a considerable number of cases decided during 1972 were also included as they were reported by the All India Reporter (Supreme Court) in its 1973 volume.[9] It may be mentioned, however, that the All India Reporter recorded 442 decisions made during Chief Justice Sikri's tenure in its report appearing in 1973 onward but his own participation as a judge in the decision making process was recorded in only thirty nine decisions. Consequently, the data on Sikri's role as the Chief

Justice was found to be adequate for the purpose of a comparative analysis but, his participation as a judge was too inadequate for a statistical analysis of his judicial behaviour.

Presented in Table I are the comparative figures on the bench assignments made by each one of the four successive Chief Justices and the approximate tenure in months covered as shown against them.

Table I : Bench Formations By Four Chief Justices, 1973-81

Chief Justice	Tenure* in mts.	Bench Formations							
		1&2	3	4	5	7	9	13	Total
Sikri	10	165 (37.33)	223 (50.45)	15 (3.39)	34 (7.69)	4 (0.90)	Nil (0.0)	1 (0.23)	442 (10.98)
Ray	45	817 (46.39)	785 (44.58)	79 (4.49)	74 (4.20)	5 (0.28)	1 (0.06)	Nil (0.0)	1761 (43.75)
Beg	13	223 (62.29)	116 (32.40)	Nil (0.0)	4 (1.12)	15 (4.19)	Nil (0.0)	Nil (0.0)	358 (8.89)
Chand-rachud	46	939 (64.14)	473 (32.31)	1 (0.07)	48 (3.28)	3 (0.29)	Nil (0.0)	Nil (0.0)	1464 (36.37)
Total (%)		2122 (53.27)	1597 (39.68)	95 (2.36)	160 (3.98)	27 (0.67)	1 (0.02)	1 (0.02)	4025 (100.00)

* Tenure of each Chief Justice is as approximately covered by decisions in the reported volumes of AIR (SC) 1973-81.

Note: The above figures include 22(0.55%) single judge assignments made by the four C.Js. during vacation periods clubbed with two judge panels.

The figures show that Chief Justice Sikri made 442 assignments in approximately 10 months time; Ray 1761 in 45 months of his tenure as Chief Justice; Beg, 358 in about 13 months; and, Chandrachud made a total of 1464 assignments in about 46 months period covered upto the end of the reported year 1981. It was noticed that the frequency of assignments made during each successive Chief Justice has shown a consistent decline. On an equalised time scale with one month as an index, each Chief Justice's bench assignment output was computed on an average to be: Sikri 44 ; Ray 39 ; Beg 28 and, Chandrachud 32. This shows that Sikri recorded the highest turnover of monthly assignments whereas, Beg recorded the lowest. These variations can be partly explained in terms of judge strength available to each Chief Justice. For instance, Chief Justice Sikri had 16 judges as against the then sanctioned strength of 14 during the period covered by the data.[10] On the contrary, Ray worked with less than the sanctioned strength almost all throughout, Beg did not have the full strength for most part of the year 1977, and Chandrachud despite the increase in the number of judges in the Supreme Court in 1978, managed with sixteen or even less number of judges atleast upto 1981.[11] But this can only be a part explanation of the decline in the rate of bench assignments. In other words the frequency of bench assignments is not only dependent upon the number of judges at the disposal of the Chief Justice, but there may at the same time be other controlling factors which determine this output. One such factor appears to be the number and nature of bench formations.

(i) *Division Bench Formations:* According to the rules noted above a division bench can function with a minimum of two judges participating in it. The Supreme Court rules also provide for the sitting of a single judge during vacation times who may, in addition to exercising all the powers of a judge in chambers,[12] exercise the powers of the Court in relation to certain matters specified in the rules.[13] Even here there is in one sense, an area of discretion open to the Chief Justice which enables him to request anyone of the sitting judges to function as vacation judge for the entire vacation period or, a part thereof. But his discretion is limited to the extent that all the cases coming during the vacation period will have to be dealt with by the vacation judge subject to the rules, and in this regard the Chief Justice cannot be said to have exercised discretion in assigning particular matters to the Judge who functions as vacation judge. Given the minimum requirement of two judges, a Chief Justice could constitute 7 to 9 division benches functioning simultaneously depending upon whether the Court had 14 or 18 judges including the Chief Justice. There being an additional requirement that a Constitution bench must have a minimum of five judges one would expect that such benches as also a few larger benches and three judge benches were constituted by all the four Chief Justices.

During the period 1973-81, the division benches which were constituted comprised two, three, four, five, seven, nine and thirteen judges besides a single judge sitting as vacation judge. The data relating to these bench formations is shown in Table I above depicting the frequency of each type of formations under the four successive Chief Justices.

The table shows four distinct features of the bench formations under the four successive Chief Justices. First, the frequency of two judge benches shows a continuous upward trend from Sikri to Chandrachud. Second, the number of three judge benches registered a decline. Third, the four judge panels became almost extinct under Beg and Chandrachud. And, fourth, the Constitutional benches too recorded an overall decline from 1973 onwards. It was also noticed that the larger benches generally came down from Sikri to Chandrachud with the only exception of a large number of seven judge benches constituted by Beg. This was so because of the mandatory requirement introduced by the Constitution (42nd Amendment) Act, which remained in operation during Beg's tenure as Chief Justice.[14] This also partly explains why during Beg's tenure the five judge Constitutional panels touched an ever low figure of 1.12 per cent of the total number of benches constituted by him. A brief discussion of the various bench formations will be in order before we go into the factors which possibly influence the wide discretion vested in the Chief Justice in relation to the bench assignments.

The largest number of judges ever participating in a decision and comprising a bench of the Court came up only once i.e. in 1973. Thirteen of a total of fourteen judges constituted the bench in *Kesavananda Bharati*[15] to review *Golak Nath* decision.[16] Chief Justice Sikri had included the first twelve judges in order of seniority in the Court leaving out the then juniormost judge, Aliagiriswami from the bench. This apparently may have been done in order to avoid a deadlock in case there was an equal split among the judges as to the outcome of the decision. Considering the importance of the case and the high stakes involved, one can argue that the Chief Justice knowing the composition of the Court, had some hunch about a possible split and, therefore, may have opted to play safe. This tendency not to have even number of judges on the bench except of course, in case of smaller benches comprising two and four judges, is quite evident from the virtual absence of even number of judges being nominated on the division benches in course of time. The division bench comprising four judges was extensively employed by Chief Justice Ray and to some extent by Chief Justice Sikri also. The practice, however, was almost abandoned by their successor Chief Justices Beg and Chandrachud.

After the thirteen judges bench, there was only one other occasion when another large bench was constituted. This was in the first quarter of the year 1974 when Chief Justice Ray constituted a bench of nine judges with himself and eight of his seniormost colleagues in the Court to hear a writ petition under article 32 concerning the rights of the minority institutions.[17]

Seven and five judge panels were constituted by all the four Chief Justices. An examination of the five and seven panel compositions under Sikri, Ray, Beg and Chandrachud reveals more or less similar pattern. Judges nominated on these benches are almost evenly represented from the seniormost to the juniormost in order of seniority in the court. It is also true that every Chief regarded his own presence on the larger benches as important and, invariably,[18] it was noticed that the Chief Justice, as far as possible would lead the bench himself rather than nominating one of the senior colleagues to do so.

Constitutional benches which must have minimum of five judges, appear to have dwindled with the passing years as mentioned earlier. Their frequency declined from 7.69 per cent under Sikri to the lowest of 1.12 per cent in Beg's time, but recovered to 3.28 per cent during Chandrachud's period. The lowest per centage of five judge panels during Beg's time is partially explained by the highest per centage of seven judge panels constituted by him because of the mandatory requirement introduced by the 42nd Amendment to the Constitution[19] and, also explains to some extent a shortfall in the overall frequency of bench assignments made by him. It is quite evident that when majority of the membership of the Court is tied up with larger panels, they will not be available for that duration for assignments on the smaller panels which will consequently affect the overall output. On the other hand, even a 2.26 per cent increase over Beg in five-judge panels during Chandrachud's time when compared to Ray and Sikri maintains consistently a declining trend in the formation of such panels.

The overall decline in the formation of five judge constitutional benches may perhaps suggest that fewer constitutional issues were agitated before the Court during this period than they were in the past.[20] Both the Constitution as well as the Supreme Court rules clearly provide for a bench consisting of a minimum of five judges to hear any matter which involves the interpretation of the

Constitution. In this respect the Chief Justice has no option but to constitute a bench of a minimum of five judges, although he can refer any such matter to be decided by a larger bench as well. The data on larger benches consisting of seven and more judges however clearly rules out the possibility of a large scale diversion of Constitutional matters to larger benches by the successive Chief Justices. This is also corroborated by the decline in number of such benches from Sikri's 1.13 per cent to Ray's 0.34 per cent, and with the only exception under Beg when it stood at 4.19 per cent, the frequency of larger benches touched upon the lowest of 0.20 per cent[21] under Chandrachud's tenure upto the end of 1981.

Of the 95 four judge panel assignments, 15 were made by Sikri and 79 by Ray. The sole four judge assignment shown under Chandrachud in fact was made during his short leave of absence by Bhagwati who was acting as Chief Justice. This bench comprised Fazal Ali as the presiding judge along with Singhal, Desai and A.P. Sen and, there was a 3-1 split with three of the four judges writing separate opinions in a matter relating to prevention of corruption.[22] Ray's largest number of four judge panel assignments all went off smoothly with Ray himself presiding over in as many as 75 of them.

As regards the smaller panels, figures shown in the table clearly establish the overwhelming presence of such formations during the tenure of all the four Chief Justices. Two and three judge panels together account for 92.40 per cent of all the bench assignments. These panels obviously handle bulk of the workload and, at least, in quantitative terms overshadow the work output of all the larger panels put together. On a closer scrutiny of the figures relating to these two types of bench formations one would notice that the three judge panels have recorded a consistent decline from Sikri's 50.45 per cent to Chandrachud's 32.31 per cent. On the other hand, the two judge panels have registered an enormous increase from Sikri's 37.33 per cent to Chandrachud's 64.14 per cent(both the figures include assignments made during vacation periods). This suggests that the successive Chief Justices have treated even three judge panels in the Court as a luxury and, hence, shown more and more dependence upon the two judge panels.

The increasing number of two judge panels in the court in the successive years suggest that their increase was brought about by sheer compulsion of mounting arrears. If the maximum utilization of the manpower has been at the root of the increasing fragmentation of the Court into two judge decision making panels, this approach may as well explain the virtual disappearance of the four judge panels during Beg and Chandrachud's tenures. But this correlation falls short of explaining Ray's bench assignment behaviour. The two judge panels during Ray's tenure had registered approximately 10 per cent increase over that of Sikri, yet the former resorted to a large number of four judge formations which were quite unnecessary in view of the increasing arrears in the Court. Instead, Chief Justice Ray preferred to have one two judge panel less than what would have been available to him if he had dispensed with the four judge panels. This can perhaps be explained by the fact that whereas the Chief Justice may have been fully aware of the need for speedier disposal of cases, the pressure of arrears had not yet reached the breaking point so as to deprive him of a little liberty. The figures[23] relating to the institutions, disposals and the pendency of cases during Ray's period partly substantiate the above impression. The total pendency during his entire tenure went up by 3263 which was far below the rate of increase registered in the post Ray period. For instance, the pendency had gone up by over 8000 cases from January 1977 to April, 1978. The institutions had gone up by 6000 in 1977 over 1976.24 These figures indicate the phenomenal increase in the workload of the Court in the year that immediately proceeded Chief Justice Ray's tenure and thereafter. The steep rise in the two judge panels during Beg and Chandrachud's tenures thus supports the view that the bench making activity by the successive Chief Justices was considerably influenced by the increasing pressure of workload.

(ii) ***Participation of Judges in Panel Formations***: It was assumed in the beginning of this chapter that participation of judges in the decision making process of the court depends upon the extent to which they are assigned benches . The Chief Justice as the leader of the Court manages the bench assignments exclusively in his own discretion which includes the nomination of judges to different panels. The participation of thirty nine judges (including those of the four Chief Justices) as recorded in Table II are the manifestations of the bench assignment behaviour of the four successive Chief Justices. The table also shows the tenure of each judge, court decisions reported during his tenure, and the participation rate of each judge in the decisions of the court. For the purposes of analysis every single nomination of a judge to a panel is considered as a

Table II : Judges' Participations in the Bench Formations

Judge	Bench Size					Total Participations	Tenure yrs.-mts.	Total court decisions	Participation rate
	1&2	3	4	5	7-13				
Sikri	2	5	X	28	4	39	0-10	442	8.82
Shelat	21	33	X	6	4	65	0-10	442	14.17
V.Lingam	32	82	X	2	X	116	0-6	442	26.24
Mitter	8	13	X	2	X	23	0-4	176	13.07
Hegde	32	76	6	X	2	116	0-10	442	26.24
Grover	47	54	X	4	1	106	0-10	442	23.98
Ray	56	199	75	99	11	440	4-7	2204	19.96
J.Reddy	62	112	19	9	4	206	2-6	1154	17.85
Palekar	39	50	9	41	8	147	2-1	843	17.44
Khanna	199	169	17	21	7	413	4-8	2268	18.21
Mathew	114	154	22	48	7	345	3-5	1646	20.96
Beg	125	233	42	46	23	469	5-7	2561	18.31
Dwivedi	37	37	7	28	5	114	2-5	1002	11.38
Mukherjea	11	41	X	8	2	62	1-2	507	12.23
Chandrachud	192	272	5	77	20	566	9-6	3935	14.38
Al.Swami	118	181	3	36	3	341	3-0	1315	25.93
Bhagwati	184	263	9	58	19	533	8-5	3538	15.06
Krishna Iyer	319	341	22	40	18	740	7-4	3227	22.93
Goswami	135	225	15	17	1	393	4-3	1963	20.02
Sarkaria	340	235	47	41	3	666	7-4	3221	20.68
Gupta	180	207	10	12	3	412	7-4	3124	13.19
Untwalia	191	233	X	33	11	468	5-10	2562	18.27
Fazal Ali	407	195	19	18	14	653	6-8	2756	23.69
Singhal	149	137	37	23	8	354	4-11	2219	15.95
J.Singh	122	184	6	14	8	334	3-0	1401	23.84
Kailasam	149	126	X	8	9	292	3-8	1650	17.70
Tulzapurkar	77	75	X	11	6	169	4-3	1604	10.54
Desai	111	102	1	8	4	226	4-3	1604	14.09
Pathak	139	125	X	8	X	272	3-10	1474	18.45
Koshal	172	125	X	21	X	318	3-6	1375	23.13
O.C.Reddy	209	123	X	6	1	339	3-6	1375	24.65
A.P. Sen	80	115	1	19	X	215	3-6	1375	15.64
V.Ramiah	74	42	X	3	1	120	2-10	1009	11.89
B.Islam	43	42	X	X	X	85	1-1	306	27.60
Vardharajan	25	29	X	X	X	54	1-1	306	17.53
A.N.Sen	8	20	X	1	X	29	0-11	254	11.42
V.B.Eradi	9	22	X	X	X	31	0-11	247	12.55
R.B.Mishra	8	21	X	X	X	29	0-11	247	11.74
							(Total Averages)		
Total	2144	1597	95	160	49	10448	(3-09	1464	18.29)

distinct response resulting in the participation of a judge in the decision making process of the Court. The seven judges who are underlined in the table completed their entire tenure during the period covered by the study. As such, there are 10,448 such participations recorded through which the table seeks to project the bench assignment behaviour of Sikri, Ray, Beg and Chandrachud during whose tenures as Chief Justice these judges participated in various panels.

All the judges, including the four Chief Justices were nominated on the two and three judge panels. The participation of judges in these two most frequently used panels vary considerably. It was noticed that mostly a junior judge is nominated with a senior judge on a two judge panel. On the other hand in nominating judges to a three judge panel, the presiding judge is invariably one of the senior judges. The four Chief Justices' own participation on these panels, has been relatively lower although they do not depict the same pattern. Sikri's 39 participations indicate roughly his involvement on various panels while he was the Chief Justice.

Ray, on the other hand, recorded only 66 participations under Sikri's leadership and, the remaining 374 participations were registered by him during his own tenure as Chief Justice which shows that the frequency of his own participation considerably increased during the latter period. His participations on various panels show that he concentrated more on three and four judge panels apart from heading almost all the Constitution benches and larger benches constituted by him.

Beg's participation increased on the larger benches especially after he became Chief Justice as most of the time he was involved in seven judge panels constituted by him during his 13 months tenure as Chief Justice. The over all frequency of participation recorded by Beg on two and three judge panels is, however, more than that of Ray. This is explained by the fact that Beg during his own term recorded only 60 participations out of a total of 469 appearances on the bench majority of them under Chief Justice Ray.

Chandrachud's participation on two judge panels show a significant increase over Beg, Ray as well as Sikri consequently registering a slight fall in his participation on three judge benches over Beg and Ray. Chandrachud also registers significantly lower participations on the five judge Constitution panels.

Among other judges too, significant variations in their participations have been recorded. For instance Fazal Ali, Chinnappareddy and Venkatramiah figure prominently among those who had higher participations on two judge panels during their respective tenures in the court. On the other hand, Vaidialingam, Hegde, Dua, Mukherjea, Goswami, Jaswant Singh were engaged most of the time with the three judge panels. All these judges who have recorded high participations on two or three judge panels in turn appeared much less frequently on five judge Constitutional panels. The judges who participated more often on five judge panels such as Ray, Palekar, Mathew, Dwivedi, Aliagiriswami and Bhagwati accordingly appeared much less on the two and three judge panels. There are also significant differences in their total involvement in the decision making activity while they were on the Bench. Normally one would expect that decision making activity in the apex court is an equally shared responsibility and that all the judges more or less participate in it in the same manner. But this assumption appears to be empirically unsustainable once the judges' total participations are subjected to further scrutiny in the light of variables like: length of tenure in the court, their involvement in different bench formations, and change in the leadership of the court.

(iii) ***Tenure and Participations:*** Table II also indicates the tenure of each judge on the Court covered by the study period. Fourteen judges[25] joined the Court before 1973 and in their case the approximate tenure was computed on the basis of their involvement in cases reported during the last six months of the preceding year. An approximate six months were therefore added to their tenure in the Court from July 1972 onwards, except in case of Chandrachud and Aliagiriswami who joined the Court in July and October 1972 respectively and such period was accordingly adjusted from their date of appointment. Two judges[26] were re-appointed as adhoc judges of the Court during this period and, therefore, their participations were also included. Among those judges who were appointed in the year 1973 and onwards seven[27] completed their full term on the Court within the study period. Another three, Aliagiriswami, Gupta and Koshal almost had their entire period covered, and Beg, Chandrachud, Bhagwati and Fazal Ali were there on the Court for substantial period of their total tenure. Judges appointed between 1977 and 1979 too had significant participations in the decision making process of the Court.[28] Whereas, five judges appointed during 1980-81, had too little time on the Court and for that reason record low participations.

A comparison of the participation rate of a few judges who were contemporaries and who spent more or less the same time on the Court will show that length of time for which a judge happened to be there by itself does not determine his participation in the decision making process of the court. For instance, Krishna Iyer, Bhagwati, Sarkaria and Gupta each spent over seven years in the Court during almost the same time period but their rate of participation in the decision making process records large variations. Krishna Iyer and Sarkaria both record much above the average participations (18.29 per cent). On the other hand, both Bhagwati and Gupta have a low profile in the number of times they participated in the decision making activity of the court while they were on the bench.

Similarly, such differences can be seen among Tulzapurkar and Desai both of whom joined the same day and, were together in the Court for the same duration but their participation in the decision making process widely vary. Koshal, Chinnappa Reddy and A.P. Sen who also joined on the same day provide another instance of variations in the participation rate of judges in the Court's decision making process.

Thus, the table adequately demonstrates that variations in the participation rate of judges do exist despite their length of service in the Court being the same.

(iv) *Participation in Panel Formations and Participation Rate*: One reason which may account for the variations in the participation rate of judges perhaps would be in the fact that some of them may have participatod more often in larger bench formations which normally consume more time, and are less productive in quantitative terms. In order to see how far participation in larger benches affects the participation rate of judges, seven judges who had completed their tenure during the study period and underlined in the table above furnish good example. The table depicts the participation of seven judges in different panel formations, their total participation, their tenure, Court decision during tenure, and their participation rate. The comparisons between Krishna Iyer and Sarkaria, and Jaswant Singh and Kailasam clearly demonstrate that there may not be a necessary relationship between participation rate and participations in bench size. Krishna Iyer's participation rate was higher than Sarkaria's even though the former had more participations on larger bench formations. The same was the case with Jaswant Singh when compared with Kailasam.

(v) *Change in Leadership of the Court*: The difference in the participation rate of judges may have something to do with the change in the leadership of the Court. This aspect has been dealt with in table III which shows the participations of judges under the leadership of different Chief justices.

Table III : Participations* under four Chief Justices, 1973-81

Judge	Chief Justices				Total Participations
	Sikri	Ray	Beg	Chandra-chud	
Ray	66	374	-	-	440
P.J.Reddy	100	106	-	-	206
Palekar	68	79	-	-	147
Khanna	118	295	-	-	413
Mathew	72	273	-	-	345
Beg	49	360	60	-	469
Dwivedi	44	70	-	-	114
Mukherjea	48	14	-	-	62
Chandrachud	53	315	68	130	566
Aliagiriswami	76	265	-	-	341
Bhagwati	-	335	67	131	533
Kr.Iyer	-	394	98	248	740
Goswami	-	315	78	-	393
Sarkaria	-	397	27	242	666
Gupta	-	280	55	77	412
Untwalia	-	263	69	136	468
Fazal Ali	-	208	92	353	653
Singhal	-	156	78	120	354
Jaswant Singh	-	154	88	92	334
Kailasam	-	17	83	192	292
Tulzapurkar	-	-	21	148	169
Desai	-	-	29	197	226
Pathak	-	-	2	270	272

Sixteen Judges who recorded all their participations under one Chief Justice are excluded from this table.

The table excludes from comparison the first seven judges excluding Justice Jagmohan Reddy but including Justices Vaidiạlingam, Mitter and Dua who had participated as ad hoc judges during Sikri's Chief Justiceship and the last nine judges. The remaining twenty three judges had served under the leadership of two or more Chief Justices. In fact, Chandrachud had the rare distinction of functioning under four Chief Justices including that of his own. The participation of ten judges from Ray to Aliagiriswami under Sikri's leadership is only representative in character as the data covers approximately about ten months of Sikri's tenure as Chief Justice. Chief Justice Sikri seems to have relied considerably upon Hegde, Grover and Jagmohan Reddy besides the two adhoc judges Vaidialingam and Dua during this period of his tenure. Khanna, among the 1971 appointees and, Aliagiriswami who was last to be appointed in October 1972, in addition, record relatively high participation under Sikri.

A comparative participation rate of judges computed on a monthly index basis shows that Jagmohan Reddy, Palekar, Khanna, Mukherjea and Aliagiriswami had participated more often under Sikri than their frequency of participations under Chief Justice Ray. On the other hand, Mathew, Beg and Chandrachud seem to have improved their participation rate under Chief Justice Ray than what it was under Sikri. Under Beg's leadership, Sarkaria's participations show a sharp decline over his participations under Ray. During Beg's thirteen months tenure as Chief Justice the overall rate of bench assignments was very low as compared to what it was under Chief Justice Ray. Considering the low rate of decisional output during his time the participations recorded by the other judges also show an overall low in their total participations. However, from the figures it appears that Chief Justice Beg relied heavily on Krishna Iyer, Fazal Ali, Goswami, Singhal, Jaswant Singh and Kailasam. On the other hand, Chandrachud and Bhagwati were apparently less often on the bench despite their preoccupation with seven judge benches. Krishna Iyer, Jaswant Singh and Kailasam too had participated frequently in the seven judges panels, but their overall participations remained higher than their counter parts.

During Chandrachud's tenure, however, the decisional output had shown a significant increase over Beg and, accordingly the judges participation too had gone up. The table however, reveals that with Chandrachud's assumption of the office of Chief Justice, the frequency of participations of some of the seniormost judges in the Court diminished to an ever low. For example, Bhagwati records only 131 participations and A.C. Gupta shows only 77 of them. Gupta's low participations can be accounted for by his absense from the Court when he was heading the Maruti Commission set up by the Government of India in 1979. But this factor only partly explains his overall low participations. However no explicit reason is available in case of Bhagwati which would explain a significant fall in his frequency of participations.[30]

On the contrary, Justices Krishna Iyer, Sarkaria and Fazal Ali amongst the senior judges, and Justices Pathak, Koshal and Chinnappa Reddy from among the lower order in seniority recorded much higher number of participations under Chief Justice Chandrachud. Justice Koshal's 318 participations had 21 involvements in five and seven judge panels. These variations do indicate that there is a possibility that change in leadership may bring about significant changes in the extent of involvement of judges in the decision making process of the court. It may, however, be added that the judges' participation rate under the respective Chief Justices would have furnished more scientific basis for comparison which could not be attempted here. Table III simply makes use of the bifurcated figures of the total participation of each judge under different Chief Justices and therefore, shows the relative frequency of participations and not the participation rate of each judge under the respective Chief Justice.

Thus, it would appear that the rate of participation of judges may vary despite their length of service in the Court being the same; that their involvement in the larger benches may not necessarily affect their total participations within a given time period; and, the change in the leadership of the Court may bring about substantial changes in the frequency with which they participate in the decision making process.

The nominating discretion of the Chief Justice is not constrained by any formal rules whatsoever. How does he go about nominating judges to different panels? In this regard, data on two aspects, viz., (a) frequency of participation among pairs of judges, and (b) each judge's involvement with different subject matter areas was examined with a view to ascertain what kind of judges frequently get nominated together on the bench, and whether there is any plausible correlation between their area of interest and their nomination to the bench.

(a) ***Frequency of Participation among pairs of judges***: The data on bench assignments was analysed in terms of the number of times each judge participated with the other judges in the Court in order to find out the nature of alignments on the bench.

The analyses revealed certain prominent groupings among the judges. For instance Ray's associations with Mathew and Beg on the bench far exceeded his participations with any other judge who was his contemporary in the Court. Similarly, one could not help noticing Ray's large number of participations with Singhal and Jaswant Singh considering that these two judges joined the Court during 1975-76, i.e. towards the concluding period of his tenure as Chief Justice. Ray's participation with Khanna on the other hand was significantly low considering that both of them were together in the Court for almost five years covered by the data. The other judges who revealed relatively large number of participations with Ray, were, Palekar, Chandrachud, Krishna Iyer and Sarkaria.

Among those who were senior to Ray, his participation with Chief Justice Sikri appeared to be significant. Although Sikri's total number of participations were only 39, Ray appeared with him on the bench as many as 35 times. The other judges with whom Sikri participated most often on the bench were Palekar, Beg and Dwivedi. Incidentally, all the four judges Ray, Beg, Palekar, and Dwivedi were opposed to the stand taken by the Chief Justice in *Kesavananda Bharati's* case. On the other hand, all those[31] who stood by the Chief Justice in this monumental decision had shown very little interaction with him on the bench. This would have some relevance to the theory which was floated particularly, in the heat of 1973 supersessions controversy that judges in the Supreme Court are divided on ideological grounds and, by implication it may also affect their interaction in the decision making process.

In this context, Khanna and Beg's participations, considering that the two judges were in the Court almost during the same period, till Khanna resigned in protest against his supersession by Beg in early 1977, seem to be quite relevant as they appeared together on the bench on rare occasions. Khanna's association with Mathew equally appears to be abnormally low although they spent a considerable time together in the Court. However, Khanna's participations with Hedge and Jagmohan Reddy were quite significant as he was most often seen on the bench with both or one of the two judges on a three or two judge panel. Among those judges who were appointed in 1973 and thereafter, Khanna participated more often with Chandrachud, Aliagiriswami, Krishna Iyer and Goswami.

Beg, on the other hand, besides his long drawn partnership with Ray paired more frequently with Chandrachud, Sarkaria, Singhal and Jaswant Singh. Noticeable among those who had very little interaction with Beg on the bench were Goswami, Untwalia and Fazal Ali. It may be recalled that Justice Goswami in his opinion in *Dissolution Case*[32] had questioned the propriety of the then Chief Justice Beg and had remarked that the Chief Justice went beyond the limits of judicial propriety when he met privately with the Acting President before the judgment was announced in that case.

Chandrachud too revealed certain fixed alignment patterns. His number of associations with the few judges like Bhagwati, Krishna Iyer, Goswami, Sarkaria and Gupta far exceeded his total participations with the remaining judges. However, it is important to note that Chandrachud's participations with Bhagwati, Krishna Iyer, Sarkaria and Gupta were spread over a period of more than seven years. Chandrachud's participations with Aliagiriswami and Jaswant Singh, however, were only 11 and 6 respectively when both these judges were together with him for not less than three years though, at different intervals.

Bhagwati and Krishna Iyer joined the Court on the same day and, recorded a total of 84 participations over a period of almost seven and a half years whereas, Bhagwati participated with Fazal Ali more often (141) than he did with Krishna Iyer (84) in a shorter span of time. This would be a matter of concern to an analyst who might wish to make certain predictions about Bhagwati's alignments on the bench on the basis of controversies that appeared during those years about groupism and factions[33] amongst the judges in the Court.. Similarly, Tulzapurkar and Desai both of them were together with Bhagwati in the Court for the same duration. Tulzapurkar's open criticism of Bhagwati and Desai is a matter of record[34] and, one would perhaps expect Bhagwati to have aligned with Desai more often than he would with Tulzapurkar. However, alignments on the bench revealed otherwise. Bhagwati sat on the bench with Tulzapurkar 57 times whereas, his total alignments with Desai amounted to a paltry 16. But, when one looks at Krishna

Iyer's low participation with Tulzapurkar one may not help attributing the same to the widening differences among the two judges due to the latter's open criticism of the former.[35]

About the same time as Krishna Iyer was due to retire, Baxi commenting upon the then composition of the Court, its source of energy and dynamism observed:

> "...If upon the retirement of Justices like Krishna Iyer, attempts are made to obtain his functional equivalents (for, who, alas, can ever replace Krishna Iyer) on the bench, the Court will continue to sustain its infectious activism. Already, we have in Justice D.A. Desai, an activist with a frankly socialistic predisposition, which augurs well for the Court. The Court's craftsmanship, too, is on the whole going to be sustained; with Justices Chandrachud and Bhagwati to continue on the Bench till 1985-86 and with the induction of "Younger" Justices like Justices Pathak, Chinnappa Reddy, A.P. Sen, and Venkatramiah. Some loss of "legalism" on the Court would be occasioned by the retirement of Justices Untwalia (1 August, 1980) Kailasam (12 September, 1980), Singhal (15 November, 1980), and Sarkaria (16 January, 1981). But Justice Fazal Ali would continue on the Bench till nearly the end of 1985."[36]

Most unfortunately, Justice Fazal Ali died in office much before the completion of his term. Assuming that the judges in the Court are ideologically different and divided one would expect such differences to show more prominently either in the alignment patterns or then perhaps, in the form of sustained dissent in the Court. Some such evidence seems to be there in the few alignment patterns examined above such as in the case of very high frequency of participations among Ray, Beg and Mathew. On the other hand Justice Khanna, who was one of the seniormost judges during Chief Justice Ray's tenure records significantly low frequency of participations with each one of these three judges. Ideologically, perhaps these judges were different as it would also appear from the nature of their response in a few important decisions from *Kesevananda Bharati* to the famous *Habeas Corpus* case[37] decided during the emergency period. Moreover, since Chief Justice Ray was at the helm of affairs during this period it can be safely assumed in view of the alignment patterns, that the Chief Justice may have arranged the composition of benches so as to minimise interaction with Justice Khanna in the decision making panels. One may perhaps also rely upon instances[38] like Beg and Goswami, and Krishna Iyer and Tulzapurkar to further substantiate the argument that differences of one or the other kind among the judges do affect their coming together on the decision making panels. At the same time, one cannot ignore Bhagwati-Fazal Ali type of alignments where the two judges were believed to have pursued dogmatically opposite styles of decisions making.[39]

Thus, the evidence although not conclusive would suggest that there is a likelihood that the differences among the judges either ideological or inter-personal may affect their alignments on the bench. In other words it may be argued that the nominating discretion of the Chief Justice operates within the group environment and such factors are likely to influence his bench making activity. However, this aspect of the decision making process would require an in-depth study which will also take into account the decisional response as well as their off the bench behaviour over a given time period.

(b) *Subject matter assignment to Judges*: It may be true that in view of the Chief Justice's role in bench assignments, little choice is left to the judges to determine their own participation in the decision making process. One would therefore, assume that just as judges cannot decide for themselves the benches they will participate in and who they will participate with, they are likely to have little choice in the kind of cases which they would hear and decide. The data on subject matter assignment to judges as presented in Table IV adequately bears it out.

A cursory glance through the table will reveal that all the 39 judges included in it have dealt with the major subject matter areas shown therein. But, the individual variations among the judges in the frequency with which they dealt with various subject matters are also quite prominent. For instance, Hegde's overwhelming participation in tax matters which accounts for 75.86 per cent of his total participations shows that most of the time he was occupied with tax matters alone. Jagmohan Reddy and Khanna too seem to have had considerable participation in tax matters during the period Hegde was in the Court and, the three judges frequently appeared together on the bench.

Table IV : Frequency of Participation in Subject Matter Areas

Judge	Taxe	Regu-lation	Serv-ice	Ind dispt	Elect-ions	Civ lib	Offen-ces	Pvt dispt.	Land reform	Other	Total
Sikri	4	2	6	1	-	8	4	2	3	9	39
Shelat	2	3	3	1	-	19	21	8	6	2	65
V.Lingam	2	1	8	39	-	7	34	13	7	5	116
Mitter	1	2	1	1	1	1	7	5	1	3	23
Hegde	88	1	1	1	2	3	-	9	5	5	116
Grover	10	6	6	28	6	2	12	18	8	10	106
Ray	62	49	80	5	5	28	21	75	74	41	440
P.J. Reddy	76	12	7	18	10	19	21	26	9	8	206
Palekar	5	8	23	3	8	28	8	34	18	12	147
Khanna	157	12	19	12	14	30	100	29	29	11	413
Mathew	32	33	40	9	9	35	38	64	65	20	345
Beg	54	26	58	8	13	33	95	88	59	35	469
Dwivedi	4	6	10	16	8	16	17	19	9	9	114
Chandra-chud	55	28	60	25	22	46	186	80	38	26	566
Aliag. Swami	22	23	30	32	32	24	78	63	25	12	341
Bhagwati	106	28	33	19	19	70	152	48	43	15	533
Kri. Iyer	51	59	79	74	32	67	133	126	79	40	740
Goswami	32	27	40	45	21	32	81	65	32	18	393
Sarkaria	68	26	50	8	31	60	248	110	40	25	666
Gupta	68	19	39	22	23	13	85	84	39	20	412
Untwalia	67	33	41	35	20	33	94	87	39	19	468
Fazal Ali	54	21	47	12	15	30	314	82	56	22	653
Singhal	33	15	43	8	6	6	126	61	38	18	354
J. Singh	49	14	44	30	10	5	66	58	44	14	334
Kailasam	31	9	15	13	9	11	98	72	22	12	292
Tulzapur-kar	49	11	14	9	7	4	27	25	21	2	169
Desai	18	20	24	18	3	6	50	57	20	10	226
Pathak	79	16	34	18	4	15	36	40	22	8	272
Koshal	15	9	20	13	5	16	163	36	29	12	318
O.C. Reddy	10	23	42	12	1	24	146	50	21	10	339
A.P.Sen	22	20	27	9	4	18	45	32	27	11	215
V.Ramiah	50	4	13	2	6	5	13	14	10	3	120
B.Islam	4	4	6	1	-	19	40	7	4	-	85
Vardha-rajan	1	1	8	1	1	7	19	7	6	3	54
A.N.Sen	3	2	8	-	1	-	2	6	3	4	29
V.B.Eradi	2	2	5	-	1	1	7	6	5	2	31
R.B. Mishra	1	4	3	2	-	-	5	7	5	2	29

Similarly, Fazal Ali, Koshal, Chinnappa Reddy, Sarkaria, Chandrachud and Bhagwati have shown more participations in criminal matters than their preoccupation with any other subject matter. Desai's maximum participation in private matters which deal with, among others, a large number of rent control matters suggest his involvement in rent cases more than in any other subject matter. How does one explain these variations particularly in view of the fact that these matters are assigned to them by the Chief Justice and they may not be free to choose the cases which they will decide according to their individual interests and areas of specialisations, if any? One plausible explanation may be that the Chief Justice takes into consideration, as far as possible, such factors while allocating subject matter to judges for their determination. Whereas, this explanation may hold true in a few cases like those of Pathak and Desai to some extent both of whom are known to have special interest in their respective areas of taxes and rent control matters, the others may not necessarily fall in line with this explanation. It is also quite possible that benches consisting of two or three judges may sometime continue to function over long stretches and assigned among others, mostly cases falling under a particular subject matter head. For instance a division bench consisting of Vaidialingam, Dua and Aliagiriswami regularly met during 1972-73 and dealt with mostly criminal cases. This is reinforced by the number of times the three judges paired with each other.

Fazal Ali and Koshal on a two judge bench appeared quite regularly during 1979-81 and together dealt with a large number of criminal matters. This is evident from both their frequency of pairing as well as Table IV which records their participations in the subject matter. There are some judges who have shown a close proximity among themselves and have not only been appearing together on the bench consistently but show the same consistency in the frequency with which they participated in various subject matter areas. Noticeable among them are Aliagiriswami and Goswami who were together in the Court for almost two years during 1973-75 and appeared together no less than 80 times. Their frequency of participation under all the subject matter heads approximates to one another. However, the same cannot be said about Bhagwati and Krishna Iyer who seem to have maintained close affinity in many respects for over seven years in the Court but, show only 84 participations among themselves which is proportionately much less than what one would expect. The two judges' overall participation rate in the decisions of the Court as shown in Table II earlier as well as their frequency of participation under different subject matter heads also vary widely.

Despite a wide spread over of judges on various subject matter areas which was inevitable in view of the large amount of disposals by smaller benches in which they most frequently participate the above data reveals a certain correlation between bench composition and subject-matter areas. To what extent judges' specialization or interest in particular area may have motivated the Chief Justices to assign particular cases to them can be roughly ascertained by examining the background characteristics of some judges with special reference to their area of specilisation or special interest, pursued by them at any stage before they were elevated to the High Court.

From the available evidence it appears that most of the judges while at the Bar had undertaken general civil and criminal practice. There are a few who seem to have worked in specific areas such as Pathak and Sikri who both handled majority of Income Tax cases. Grover and Bhagwati were engaged in a larger number of commercial and Company Law cases; and, Desai had a large practice of tenancy, land revenue and labour matters.[40] Perhaps, some judges continue to maintain close affinity with their areas of interest, despite the fact that they had possibly dealt with all type of matters in the High Courts.

Pathak and Desai do provide such instances, and it appears that both the judges have had their largest participations in their respective areas of interest. This is, only possible if the Chief Justice takes into account the special subject matter interest or expertise of judges in making bench assignments either in order to accommodate the judges having such interest or, where he feels that such expertise is needed.

Thus the judges' participation in the decision making process gets subjected to both the formal and informal rules and practices adopted in the bench assignment activity which, as it appears from the above analysis, is a complex phenomenon and involves the interaction of multiple factors. Although the Chief Justice makes bench assignments in his own discretion, his choice, at least in determining the number and nature of bench formations, gets subjected to a variety of institutional factors like the judge strength available in the court, the requirement of five judge Constitutional benches, number and nature of important issues coming before the Court which may require in the opinion of the Chief Justice consideration by a larger bench, and the like. In addition to these, the nominating discretion of the Chief Justice is further likely to be influenced by ideological or interpersonal differences among the judges as well as their personal attributes like area of subject-mattor interest or expertise to handle particular kind of cases. Subject to these constraints, how do the judges go about performing their decision making functions and what is the nature of their response in terms of their voting behaviour, are some of the important aspects which will be examined in the next part.

Notes

1. See, e.g., the Supreme Court Rules, 1966, Order XL, rule 1.
2. *Id.*, order XL, rule 3.
3. Initially in 1950, the Supreme Court rules provided that at least three judges had to participate in every decision. The rules were amended later in 1957 to enable the Chief Justice to constitute a bench of two judges.
4. See Order VII, rule 2, *supra* note 1.
5. The Constitution of India, Art. 145(3); also see, order XXXV, rule 1, *supra* note 1.
6. For comments on the repeal of this provision, see, Upendra Baxi, *The Indian Supreme Court and Politics* 15 (Eastern Book Company, Lucknow, 1980).
7. See, Justice V.D. Tulzarpurkar's Criticism of Justice Krishna Iyer in *Manohar* Vs. *Marotrao*, A.I.R. 1979 S.C. 1084; also see, Justice Goswami in *State of Rajasthan* Vs. *Union of India*, A.I.R. 1977 S.C. 136; A.I.R. 1983 Journal 9-18; Also see Chaitanya Kalbag, "A Battle Supreme", in *India Today* 118-120 (December 15, 1982).
8. Upendra Baxi, *Courage, Craft and Contention: The Indian Supreme Court in the Eighties* 31 (Tripathi, Bombay, 1985).
9. An examination of the AIR's reporting of the Supreme Court decisions in its 1973 volume revealed that it covered approximately six to seven months of Chief Justice Sikri's tenure in 1972 in addition to the cases decided in the first four months of the year 1973 before Chief Justice Ray took over from him. Accordingly, Chief Justice Sikri has been allotted 10 months on the basis of the approximate time period covered by the reported decisions.
10. Besides the full quota of 14 judges (including the Chief Justice), two adhoc judges were also appointed during this period, Justices Vaidialingam and Dua along with whom the total court strength had gone upto 16.
11. See, Table IV in chapter 4.
12. See, Order VI, rules 2, 3 and 4, *supra*, note 1.
13. Order VII, rule 4 in *ibid.*

14. The Act had received President's assent on December 18, 1976. Beg's tenure as Chief Justice coincides substantially with the time period during which this provision remained in operation because he took over as Chief Justice on January 30, 1977 and retired in February 22, 1978. The provision was repealed by the Constitution (45th Amendment) Act, 1977.
15. A.I.R. 1973 S.C. 1461.
16. A.I.R. 1967 S.C. 1643.
17. *St. Xavier's College* Vs. *State of Gujarat*, A.I.R. 1974 S.C. 1389; The four junior most judges who were in the Court but none was included were; Bhagwati, Krishna Iyer, Goswami and Sarkaria.
18. All, except one were headed by the respective Chief Justices, One bench was presided over by Shelat as acting Chief Justice during Sikri's tenure in his absence.
19. See *supra* foot-note 12.
20. See George Gadbois, "The Decline of Dissent on the Supreme Court, 1950-81", in Ram Avtar Sharma (ed.), *Justice and Social Order in India* 261-79 (Intellectual Publishing House, New Delhi, 1984).
21. *In re-special Court's Bill*, A.I.R. 1978 S.C. 478; V. *Dhanpal Chettiar* Vs. *Yesodbi Ammal*, A.I.R. 1979 S.C. 1745; *Tara Prasad Singh* Vs. *Union of India*; A.I.R. 1980 S.C. 1682. All three benches were presided over by the Chief Justice and all the three judgments were unanimous.
22. *V.C. Shukla* Vs. *State*, A.I.R. 1980 S.C. 962. Justice Singhal wrote the dissent.
23. Rajeev Dhavan, *The Supreme Court under Strain : The Challenge of Arrears*, (Tripathi, Bombay 1978). See statement 21, showing the arrear figures on the normal workload at 51
24. *Ibid.*
25. Sikri, Shelat, Hegde, Grover, Ray, P.J. Reddy, Palekar, Khanna, Mathew, Beg, Dwivedi, A.K. Mukherjea, Chandrachud and Aliagiriswami.
26. Vaidialingam and Dua.
27. Krishna Iyer, Goswami, Sarkaria, Untwalia, Singhal, Jaswant Singh and Kailasam.
28. Eight Judges appointed during this period were: Kailasam, Tulzapurkar, Desai, Pathak, Koshal, Chinnappareddy, A.P. Sen and Venkatramiah.
29. Baharul Islam, Vardharajan, A.N. Sen, V.B. Eradi and R.B. Misra.
30. Unless, Bhagwati's low frequency of participations are explained in terms of a possible strained relationship between himself and Chief Justice Chandrachud; See *Minerva Mills Ltd.*, Vs. *Union of India*, A.I.R. 1980 S.C. 1789; see also Upendra Baxi, *supra*, Note 8 at 105-106.
31. Justices Shelat, Hegde, Grover, Jagmohan Reddy and A.K. Mukherjea.
32. *State of Rajasthan* Vs. *Union of India*, A.I.R. 1977 S.C. 1361
33. See *supra* notes 7 and 30
34. Tulzapurkar, *supra* note 7 at 9-18.
35. *Manohar* Vs. *Marotrao* A.I.R. 1979 S.C. 1084; See also Krishna Iyer's report in *Organo Chemical Industries* Vs. *Union of India*. A.I.R. 1979 S.C. 1803-4.
36. *Supra*, note 6 at 125
37. *A.D.M. Jabalpur* Vs. *Shiv Kant Shukla* A.I.R. 1976 S.C. 1207 (Justice Mathew had retired then). See also, for instance, *Indira Nehru Gandhi* Vs. *Raj Narain* A.I.R. 1975 S.C. 2299.
38. The differences between Chandrachud and Bhagwati as pointed out earlier would also fall under this category, although such differences cannot be clearly

made out from the figures because they represent participations over a long stretch of time.

39. *Supra* note 6 at 125.
40. For professional background and the nature of experience of Judges, see Appendix.

Part III
Voting Behaviour

6

Nature of Participation: Dissent Concurrence and Unanimity

The decision-making behaviour of the judges is reflected in the manner in which they participate in the decisional output of the Court. The data so far presented in the two preceding chapters dealt with the quantam and nature of work of the Court and the structural arrangements of the decision making process both of which act as institutional parameters within which judges participate in the decisions of the Court. Since both these factors operate upon judges in the extent to which they participate in the the decision making activity of the court, the nature of their response in terms of oral votes, written opinions, dissent and concurrence too is likely to be influenced and get reflected in their decisions in addition to differences which may be the product of their personal attributes.

What is the extent to which judges do vary, if at all, in the manner in which they record their participations in the decisional output of the Court, and how far these variations can be explained in terms of norms and practices of the court? How is opinion assignment activity carried out in a fragmented bench structure? How often do the judges dissent, and what is the character of their dissent? What is the nature of their written concurrence, and how can unanimity among the judges as projected by the total decisional output of the Court be characterised? How do the judges vote in the cases heard by them for the purpose of deciding their outcome? Some of these questions dealt with here have a direct bearing on the decision making behaviour of the judges reflected in their voting response.

Opinion Assignment

In view of the division bench system adopted by the Court in its decision making process and, the distinctive position held by the Chief Justice in making bench assignments, it would also be useful to look into the manner in which, the responsibility for writing 'opinions for the Court' is shared amongst the judges who participate in decision making on these panels. There are two ways in which the judges may record their responses in the decisional output, i.e., in the form of a written opinion and, by casting a simple vote in favour of judgment written by one of their colleagues on the bench. A written opinion may be in the form of an 'opinion of the Court' (the opinion of a unanimous bench or, if the decision was a divided one, of the majority), a separate opinion concurring with the outcome or, a dissenting opinion (solo, non-solo or a dissenting opinion concurring with another dissenting opinion). Similarly, when a judge casts a simple vote it may represent his agreement with the 'opinion of the Court' (with the majority or as a member of a unanimous bench), with concurring opinion or, with the minority in a divided decision in which some other member of the minority wrote the minority opinion.

Whereas judges are free to write concurring opinions and dissents, the writing of the majority or the opinion of the Court may not be accessible to every judge according to his own preference. Once a majority (in case of a split decision), or all the justices participating have agreed upon the outcome of a case, one of them will be assigned the task of writing the majority or the 'opinion of the Court'.

The past practice in this regard has revealed that the opinion writing may be assigned in any one of the two alternative courses adopted by the Court. In the normal Course, it is the Chief Justice who has the prerogative of writing an opinion himself in a case in which he participates or, he may assign it to any one of the justices participating in the decision of a case and, if it is a split decision, to any one of the judges voting with the majority assuming that the Chief Justice himself voted with the majority. But, given the bifurcated bench structure with different division benches functioning simultaneously, it would not be possible for the Chief Justice to preside over all the benches. Moreover, majority of the division benches consist of very small panels of frequently two or three judges participating in them. In the absence of the Chief Justice, it is the seniormost judge amongst those participating on the division bench who carries the option either to write an opinion himself or assign it to one of his colleagues. The other method resorted to most often on the smaller division benches is, that judges would write opinions by rotation. The principle of rotation may work smoothly with the division benches consisting of two or three judges, particularly, considering that these benches have to cope with heavy work schedule and therefore writing of opinions by rotation agures well with equitable division of labour amongst themselves.

But in both these alternatives, the judge's choice of writing an opinion of the Court is restricted and, is subject to, either the option exercised by the senior judge, or the rotation principle. Thus, every judge participating on the smaller division benches possibly gets an opportunity to write an opinion of the Court in every second or, every third case that is decided by the bench. Whereas, in the larger division benches consisting of five or more judges this opportunity gets further reduced to one fifth of even lesser assuming that the principle of rotation is also followed by them.

The larger benches are, however, different in many respects from the regular two and three judge benches which function normally. Apart from the five judge constitution bench which functions depending upon the need to constitute it, the seven and more judges participate on rare occasions as is evident from the data. These benches are specially constituted for the purpose of hearing matters of relative importance and, are invariably presided over by the Chief Justice. These benches have also resulted in bulky judgments, proliferation of opinions and relatively more dissents amongst the judges as depicted below:

Bench size	No. of decisions	Average length	Multi-opinion decisions	Split Decisions
7-13	29	55 pages	17	5

Taking all these factors into account one would not expect the value-neutral rotation principle to govern the opinion assignments on these benches and, mostly, it is the Chief Justice if he finds himself in majority (very rarely the Chief Justice will find himself in minority), who would choose to write an opinion of the Court or, he may assign the task to one of the justices voting for the majority. Therefore, some judges participating on these bigger benches may rarely get an opportunity to speak for the Court unless, of course, they choose to express themselves through a separate concurrence, or dissenting opinion. The opinions of the Court, as is shown in the data presented in Table I, account for almost 97 per cent of the total number of written opinions and, thus, constitute the single most important category of written decisional response of the judges of the Indian Supreme Court. The extent to which every judge participated in this category would be significantly determined by the opportunities available to him within the constraint of opinion assignment practice followed by different benches apart from other factors examined in the subsequent sections.

Nature of Voting Response

The data on the nature of participation is given in Table I below, showing the extent to which judges wrote opinions of the Court, separate opinions concurring with the opinion of the Court (of the majority or minority, in case of a split decision), or with the minority. Figures in columns one to five are percentages of the total participations of each judge shown in column 6. Column 7 shows the total written participation of the judges obtained by adding the frequencies in columns 1, 2 and 3. The written opinions concurring with minority are included under the written dissents in column 3 as their number was too small. The percentage of total participation in column 6 with total written participation of judges in column 7 are shown in column 8.

Before examining the nature of participation of judges a few limitations of the quantitative analysis of the judges' behaviour will need to be re-emphasized here. One such limitation arises from the fact that its major concern is related to what judges do rather than to what they say. It is not so much concerned with the justifications, the ratio or the obiter dicta of a decision as its focus is simply to elicit the voting response of judges in terms of their overt behaviour. The behaviour of judges is recorded as their agreement or disagreement with the final outcome of a decision which may have been expressed in oral or in any one of the written forms. Hence the nature of participation recorded here would only reveal the patterns and variations in quantitative terms.

Another drawback of this method is that since its focus is on the voting response of judges in the final outcome of a decision, it fails to take into account the possibility of multiple issues being raised and answered in a decision some of which may have been decided favourably while others may have not, and yet the decision goes in favour of the petitioner or respondent as the case may be. The data, therefore, reflects only the final outcome of each decision and not the issue based response.

1. *Opinions of the Court*: The judges' written expression is to be found mostly in the form of opinions of the Court. Usually, an opinion of the Court speaks for all the judges participating in the decision and, occasionally, in case of a split, speaks for the majority. Opinions of the Court represent almost 35 per cent of the total participation and account for about 98 per cent of the written participation of judges. This means that whenever a judge expressed himself in writing he almost invariably spoke for the Court and rarely on his own individual behalf. It is evident from column 1 that speaking on behalf of the Court is a task which every judge has performed while he was on the bench. The figures also show that all the judges do not equally share the responsibility of writing opinions of the Court. 34.77 per cent of the average judge's participation was in the form of an opinion of the Court. However, there are large variations among the judges in the extent to which they wrote opinions of the Court.

Hegde wrote Court's opinions in 86 of the 116 decisions in which he had participated in about ten months of his term covered here. At the other extreme, there is Vardharajan who wrote the Court's opinions in only 6 of the 54 decisions reported during thirteen months after he assumed office. Hegde's frequency of writing opinions of the Court recorded here is much higher than his earlier figures compiled by Dhavan upto the end of 1970 which reveals that he had written court's opinions in about 36.5 per cent of the cases in which he had participated.[1] Hegde's phenomenal increase in writing opinions of the Court towards the concluding part of his tenure may partly be explained by the fact that he invariably presided over a three judge bench or occasionally over a two judge bench mostly dealing with tax matters. It is possible that he being the seniormost judge may have opted to write opinions of the Court himself rather than assigning this task to one of his junior colleagues. It is interesting to note that Hegde never

Table I : Nature of Participation of Judges, 1973-81

Judge	Wrote courts' opinions	Wrote concur-ence	Wrote dissent	Voted with majority	Voted with minority	Total Parti-cipations	Total written opinions	% of Partici-pation	Partici-pation rate	% of all court decisions
Sikri	33.33	2.56	2.56	56.41	2.56	39	16	41.02	8.82	3.62
Shelat	40.00	0.00	0.00	58.46	0.00	65	26	40.00	14.71	5.88
Mitter	13.04	0.00	0.00	86.96	0.00	23	3	13.04	13.07	1.70
V.Lingam	42.24	0.00	0.00	57.76	0.00	116	49	42.24	26.24	1.08
Hegde	74.13	0.00	1.72	24.13	0.00	116	88	75.86	26.24	19.91
Grover	42.45	0.94	0.00	56.60	0.00	106	46	43.39	23.98	10.41
Ray	39.55	0.00	0.23	60.23	0.00	440	175	39.77	9.96	7.94
P.J.Reddy	30.10	0.49	0.49	68.93	0.00	206	64	31.06	17.85	5.54
Dua	37.16	0.00	0.68	62.16	0.00	148	56	37.83	33.04	12.67
Palekár	29.93	0.68	0.00	69.39	0.00	147	45	30.6	7.44	5.34
Khanna	45.24	1.21	0.97	52.30	0.24	413	196	47.45	18.21	8.64
Mathew	29.86	2.61	2.03	65.22	0.29	345	119	34.49	20.96	7.23
Beg	32.62	4.26	1.28	61.83	0.00	469	79	38.16	18.31	6.99
Dwivedi	33.33	1.75	0.88	64.04	0.00	114	41	35.96	11.38	4.09
Mukherjea	27.42	0.00	0.00	70.97	0.00	62	7	27.4	12.23	3.35
Chandrachud	45.58	1.59	0.18	52.65	0.18	566	267	47.17	14.38	6.78
Aliagiriswami	36.66	1.17	0.88	61.29	0.00	341	132	38.70	25.93	10.04
Bhagwati	46.34	2.06	0.94	50.66	0.19	533	263	49.34	5.06	7.43
Krishna Iyer	53.11	3.65	0.00	43.24	0.00	740	420	56.75	22.93	13.01
Goswami	37.40	1.02	0.51	61.07	0.00	393	153	38.93	20.02	7.79
Šarkaria	43.09	0.15	0.15	56.46	0.00	666	290	43.54	20.68	9.00
Gupta	35.68	0.73	0.97	62.62	0.00	412	154	37.37	13.19	4.93
Untwalia	39.32	1.28	0.21	59.19	0.00	468	191	40.81	18.27	7.45

contd. . . .

Judge	Wrote courts' opinions	Wrote concur-ence	Wrote dissent	Voted with majority	Voted with minority	Total Parti-cipations	Total written opinions	% of Partici-pation	Partici-pation rate	% of all court decisions
Fazal Ali	57.12	1.38	0.31	41.19	0.00	653	385	58.95	23.69	13.97
Singhal	28.53	1.13	0.56	69.77	0.00	354	107	30.22	15.95	4.82
J.Singh	26.65	0.60	0.00	72.75	0.00	334	91	27.24	23.84	6.49
Kailasam	29.11	2.05	1.37	67.47	0.00	292	95	32.53	17.40	5.76
Tulzapurkar	34.91	0.00	1.18	63.91	0.00	169	61	36.09	10.54	3.80
Desai	40.7	0.88	0.88	57.52	0.00	226	96	42.47	14.09	5.98
Pathak	27.94	9.56	1.10	61.40	0.00	272	105	38.60	18.45	7.12
Koshal	19.18	1.57	0.31	78.30	0.63	318	67	21.06	23.13	4.57
O.C.Reddy	36.87	1.18	0.29	61.65	0.00	339	130	38.34	24.65	9.45
A.P.Sen	21.86	0.93	2.80	74.42	0.00	215	55	25.58	15.64	4.00
Venkatramiah	26.67	0.83	0.83	71.67	0.00	120	34	28.33	11.89	3.37
B.Islam	18.82	0.00	1.18	80.00	0.00	85	17	20.00	27.60	5.55
Vardharajan	11.11	0.00	0.00	88.89	0.00	54	6	1.11	7.55	1.96
A.N.Sen	17.24	6.90	0.00	75.86	0.00	29	7	24.13	11.42	2.75
Eradi	16.13	0.00	0.00	83.87	0.00	31	5	16.13	12.55	2.02
R.B.Mishra	27.59	0.00	0.00	72.41	0.00	29	8	27.59	11.74	3.24
Total Average(%)	34.77	1.33	0.73	62.99	0.18	268	109	36.13	18.29	6.82

appeared on a five judge bench, and only once participated on a seven judge bench headed by the then acting Chief Justice Shelat during this period even though he was one of the seniormost judges in the Court. This would also mean that Hegde had relatively more opportunity to write opinions of the Court and he seems to have made good use of it.

If it is true that the presiding judge may exercise his option despite the rotation principle which one would have reasons to believe normally regulates the opinion assignment on the smaller panels, the same argument can be applied to explain fewer participations in the opinions of the Court by some of the juniormost judges. For example, some of the judges in the early eighties like Baharul Islam, Vardharajan, A.N. Sen and Eradi had written Court's opinions in less than 20 per cent of the decisions reported till the end of 1981. Mitter on the other hand, who had retired in 1971, but re-appointed as ad hoc judge by Chief Justice Sikri during the first quarter of 1972 also records one of the lowest as he wrote the Court's opinions in only 3 of the 23 decisions in which he participated.[2] His 13.04 per cent was found consistent with his earlier performance till 1970 where he had written the Court's opinions in about 15.63 per cent of the decisions in which he had participated.[3] While Hegde and Mitter represent two extremes, their contemporaries in the Court during that period Chief Justice Sikri, Shelat, Vaidialingam, Grover and Dua maintained fairly close proximity with the total average.

Among the seniormost judges during Ray's tenure as Chief Justice, Khanna's participation in the opinions of the Court is well above the average and Mathew's participations at the other end are the lowest. Khanna's one year stay beyond Mathew in the Court may be partly responsible for the former writing more opinions but is hardly enough to explain over 15 per cent difference among them in the extent to which they wrote opinions of the Court.

In the latter years, one finds among those who wrote opinions of the Court much above the average were Fazal Ali, Krishna Iyer, Bhagwati and Chandrachud. During the same period there were others like Singhal, Jaswant Singh and Kailasam who had relatively much less to say on behalf of the Court. Those who joined the Court in 1977 and thereafter, three judges, Desai, Chinnappa Reddy and Tulzapurkar wrote the opinions of the Court more often than their contemporaries Kailasam, Pathak, Koshal, A.P. Sen and

Venkatramiah. These comparisons which are spread over judges who were contemporaries in the Court during different periods, show that writing opinions of the Court has not been an equally shared responsibility.

2. ***Concurring Opinions***: Although few in number, concurring opinions form the second largest category of written participation of judges. There were in all 110 decisions in which concurring opinions were written by one or more judges and a total of 167 such participations constituting 1.60 per cent of the total number of participations. Thirteen judges did not write a concurring opinion at all, and of the twenty six who chose to state their reasons separately on various occasions, three, Krishna Iyer, Pathak, and Beg account for 43.71 per cent of all such participations. Among others, the only judges with noteworthy disposition to write such opinions were Mathew, Chandrachud, Bhagwati and M.Fazal Ali.

3. ***Dissenting Opinions***: The dissenting opinions were less common but slightly more widely spread out among the judges than concurring opinions. There were in all 68 of such participations in which twenty eight judges had written dissenting opinions in 63 decisions. The judges who wrote the maximum dissenting opinions were Mathew, Beg, Bhagwati and A.P. Sen. Others who had written slighly less often than these three were Khanna, Gupta and Kailasam followed by Aliagiriswami and Pathak. Six judges (Ray, Goswami, Fazal Ali, Singhal, Tulzapurkar and Desai) had two dissenting opinions each to their credit and, the remaining thirteen wrote one dissent each. There were 52 solo dissents and seven opinions concurring with minority

4. ***Voted with Majority***: The figures in column 4 reveal that the most common form of judges' participation in the decisions of the Court was a simple vote in support of the majority view characterised invariably by an opinion of the Court. A simple vote is a silent expression of an agreement with the opinion written by another judge. This kind of silent acquiscence seems to be the most common form of participation as 63 per cent of the average judge's participation was in this form. Only in the case of Hegde, Krishna Iyer and Fazal Ali, their written expressions had exceeded their silent votes. At least four judges, Mitter, Baharul Islam, Vardharajan and Eradi had over 80 per cent participations in the form of oral votes. On the other hand, Sikri, Shelat, Grover, Khanna, Chandrachud, Bhagwati, Sarkaria, Untwalia and Desai besides

Hegde, Krishna Iyer and Fazal Ali expressed more often in writing than casting their votes without stating their reasons explicitly.

5. ***Voted with Minority***: A silent acquiescence in the minority opinion in a non-unanimous decision is the most uncommon form of behaviour to be found among the Indian Supreme Court judges. As shown in column 5, only seven expressions of this nature were recorded in 10,448 participations. This means that a judge would exceptionally dissent without stating his reasons himself in case he decides to do so. Three judges, Khanna, Chandrachud and Bhagwati joined Mathew in his minority opinions written by him in three different cases. Mathew reciprocated by joining Bhagwati in one of the minority opinions written by him. Koshal acquisced in Pathak and Kailasam once each in their minority opinions. And Sikri voted with Ray in a minority opinion written by him.

6. ***Written Participation***: There are 4262 written opinions in the 4025 decisions an average of 1.06 opinions per Court ruling. Thus, 94.43 per cent of all opinions written by these judges were in the nature of opinions of the Court. The typical Court ruling was not only unanimous, but was un-encumbered by concurring opinions as well. The thirty nine judges averaged 109 written opinions, but individually the scores ranged all the way from Mitter's three opinions to Krishna Iyer's 420. A comparison of these figures with those compiled for the first thirty five judges (1950-67) will show that the frequency of writing any opinion other than the opinion of the Court has decline over the years from 1.17 to 1.06 per cent on an average per court ruling.[4] Accordingly, the tendency to write in any form other than the opinion of the Court seems to have lost ground over the years.

7. ***Per cent Participation with Written Opinions***: Column 8 shows the frequency with which each judge's participation was accompanied by a written opinion. Almost four opinions on an average can be assigned to every 10 participations, which shows a six per cent increase when compared with figures compiled in an earlier study carried out by Gadbois of the first 35 judges in the Court.[5] This increase however has to be seen in the context of substantial increase in disposals by the two and three judge panels in the seventies which obviously provided more opportunity to judges to write more opinions of the Court. It will be noticed that the average frequency with which a judge wrote opinions of the court in column 1 has also registered a considerable increase over

the one computed by Gadbois for earlier judges. At the same time the present set of 39 judges show a decline in their tendency to write any opinion other than the opinion of the Court over their predecessors. As against 1.9 and 2.4 per cent concurring and dissenting opinions respectively written by the earlier judges, their successors record 1.33 and 0.73 per cent concurrence and dissent. This clearly shows that over the years whereas, the frequency of writing opinions of the Court registered an increase, the frequency of writing dissent and concurrence have considerably declined.

It is for this reason that one would find that there is a marginal difference between the frequency of writing opinions of the Court recorded under column I which shows the percentage of participation in the opinions of the Court and that of total written expressions of each judge under column 8. The total written opinions in case of some judges, however, show a significant increase over their frequency with which they had written opinions of the Court. This is evident in the case of those judges who had written concurring and dissenting opinions most frequently such as Mathew, Beg, Bhagwati, Krishna Iyer, Pathak and A.P. Sen. Thus, during the period under investigation, one finds that the prototype judge's participation in the written form has been mainly in the form of writing opinions of the Court.

8. *Written Opinions as Per cent of all Court decisions*: On an average a judge wrote 6.82 per cent opinions of those decided during his tenure. This figure would be slightly on the higher side if those cases which were decided during a judge's leave of absence for short or long durations from the Court were excluded from the total number of cases decided during his tenure. The Court decisions during the tenure of each judge were counted from the date on which he joined till the date of h is retirement, resignation or departure from the Court. The overall written participation of judges as per cent of the decisions of the Court during tenure when compared with Gadbois' average (10.3 per cent) for the first thirty five judges, shows a 3.48 per cent decline. The declining trend in the overall written participation over the years is accounted for by a substantial increase in the decisional output of the Court since the late sixties which was achieved by the subsequent Chief Justices by increasing the number of small division benches on the Court hence widening the gap between a judge's total participations and the total decisions rendered during his years on the Court.

Accordingly it will be noticed that the overall rate of participation of the present set of judges in the decisions of the Court during their tenure also registered a sharp decline from 33.49 per cent recorded for the first thirty five judges to 18.30 per cent.[6] Therefore, 15 per cent decline in the participation rate of judges in the decisions of the Court during their tenure is bound to affect the percentage of their written participation too. This is reflected in the low percentage (6.82 per cent) of their written opinions to the Court decisions during tenure.

Despite the macro changes that have taken place over the years at the institutional level affecting the overall response pattern of the judges in the court, it has been observed that individual variations among the judges considering the number of years each one of them spent in the Court, at least, in some cases, are considerable. Chandrachud, Bhagwati and Krishna Iyer provide such examples. Both Chandrachud and Bhagwati spent more time in the Court than Krishna Iyer, but their frequency of written opinions is much less than that of the latter. Similarly, Chinnappa Reddy and A.P. Sen despite their being together in the Court for equal number of years record large variation in the frequency with which they wrote opinions of the Court. A.C. Gupta who had a tenure of almost seven and a half years, records only 4.93 per cent written response which is far below the number of opinions written by his contemporaries who spent either an equal time in the Court or were there on the court for less than one half of his tenure, such as Aliagiriswami and Chinnappa Reddy. Twenty two of the thirty nine judges record below the average (6.82 per cent) of written opinions and only seventeen wrote more frequently than the average for the prototype judge.

How does one explain these variations among the judges? This question can be considered from two different perspectives namely, the individual and the institutional. The individual perspective would take into account the personal attributes of judges such as their skill, proficiency in expression and language, style, inclination, perception, outlook and the like.[7] These characteristics will not only affect their nature of participation in purely quantitative terms, but are also likely to influence the form and the content of their individual written responses. Moreover, the frequency with which a judge expresses himself in writing may not necessarily reflect the quality of his written response. The extent to which the personal attributes of judges influence their written behaviour largely remain intutive, and can possibly be brought out by a systematic and detailed analysis of the background characteristics of judges. Unfortunately, however, such information on the Indian Supreme Court judges has not been sufficiently documented and whatever little exists in the official records, remains inaccessible to a researcher except in the form of a brief career outline. But some of the institutional factors like the role of the Chief Justice in bench assignments and the opinion assignment practice in the Court can be further examined as possible constraints on the opinion writing behaviour of the judges.

The extent to which judges may participate in the decision making process is determined by the Chief Justice as discussed earlier, and hence there is a possibility that the rate of participation of judges may also affect their written participation. Similarly, since the opinions of the Court constitute almost 97 per cent of the total written participation much would depend upon how often a judge had the opportunity to write opinions of the Court in the decisions in which he participated during his tenure in the Court. The option to assign opinion writing in such cases is most likely to be exercised by the senior judge who presides over the division bench, although at times it may be regulated by the rotation principle as mentioned above.

Columns 9 and 10 in Table I show a relationship between the rate of participation and the written response as per cent of all court decisions during the tenure of each judge. It appears that there is a very viable correlation between the rate of participation and the ratio of written opinions of the judges. But, one would also notice that there are some very prominent deviations from this pattern as well. For instance, Khanna's rate of participation was lower than that of Mathew but his ratio of written participation was higher than the latter. Similarly, Aliagiriswami records a very high rate of participation but his written participation is relatively much lower than many of the judges who had much lower rate of participations. Pathak and Koshal provide another such instance where the rate of participation does not correspond to the ratio of written opinions. The majority of the cases, however, do indicate that the written participation of judges closely correspond to their rate of participations. The Chief Justice's role may thus be an important institutional variable which is likely to affect the extent to which a judge may participate and consequently write opinions in the decisions of the Court.

The other factor which may possibly account for variations in the written behaviour of judges is the opinion assignment option exercised by the senior judges who preside over the division benches. Although, judges are free to write separate opinions in the form of concurrence or dissent such opinions only account for a little over two per cent of the total written opinions as is shown in columns 2 and 3. On the contrary, column 1 records approximately 98 per cent opinions of judges which were written as opinions of the Court. Much, therefore, would depend upon the opportunity each judge had to write opinions of the Court in the decisions in which he participated. This may perhaps explain why some judges wrote more opinions of the Court despite lower rate of participations than their counterparts who had higher rate of particiations. Even in the case of judges who were particularly active in writing concurring and dissenting opinions like Beg, Bhagwati, Krishna Iyer and Pathak, the high ratio in total written opinions seem to have been achieved essentially because of the high percentage of their opinions shown in column 1.

One logical consequence of this correlation may seem to be that the junior judges in the Court will have lesser opportunity to write opinions of the Court because there is always a senior judge who may wish to write the opinion himself rather than assign it to one of his junior colleagues. During the period 1980-81 five juniormost judges in the Court were: Baharul Islam, Vardharajan, A.N. Sen, Eradi and R.B. Misra. Despite variations among themselves, on an average they wrote opinions of the Court in 3.10 per cent of the decisions in which they participated which is much lower than 6.82 per cent average for all the 39 judges. It may also be mentioned that out of these five judges, only A.N. Sen had once participated in a five judge bench. The average for the five judges is also lower than the written opinions of any other judge except that of Mitter. These figures, may suggest a possible correlation between the rank of a judge and his written opinions, but the same set of judges perhaps would reveal a different pattern as they move up in the seniority with other judges joining the court in the course of time. Since majority of the judges enjoy a tenure of not more than 3-5 years, the court's membership has a very high turnover at any given point of time. At any cut off point there will be atleast some judges who have either just joined the court or, are about to complete their tenure and, therefore, the cycle keeps moving.

Another possible reason for variations in written opinions of judges may lie in their involvement with division benches of different sizes. This aspect has been examined earlier in relation to its possible effect on the participation rate of judges in the decisions of the Court. The larger benches where the decision is unanimous would provide lesser opportunity to judges to write opinions of the Court as only one of the five or more judges can write an opinion in such a case. Considering that most of the Constitutional and larger benches are presided over by the Chief Justice, it is more likely that some judges on these benches will possibly get fewer opportunities to write opinions of the Court. This may consequently affect their frequency of writing opinions of the Court. While this may hold true in case of majority, there are notable exceptions like Bhagwati, Krishna Iyer, Sarkaria, Tulzapurkar, Desai and Chinnappa Reddy all of whom have recorded relatively higher participation on larger benches as well as high percentage of written opinions.

The nature of participation discussed thus far makes it clear that 63 per cent of the total decisional response consists of oral votes cast by the judges and the remaining 37 per cent is to be found in the form of written opinions. Of the total written participations 98 per cent are opinions of the Court and only about 2 per cent are in the form of separate concurring and dissenting opinions. Whereas the oral votes may indicate the direction of a judge's response, they are essentially a silent manifestation of behaviour. On the contrary, written opinions through the medium of language and expression are likely to convey more about judges' decision making behaviour. An opinion of the Court written by one of the participating judges on the decision making panel represents the views of all the judges, and to that extent may not be a very useful tool in understanding their individual behaviour. Although in terms of language, style and expression even a unanimous opinion may make significant contribution in this, as one may say in the context of the opinions of Justice Krishna Iyer which stand apart from every other judge's opinions either in the past or present. Dissenting opinions however have been generally treated as providing better measure of the individuality of judges and have been relied upon in order to ascertain the attitudinal differences among them.[8] In the case of the

Indian Supreme Court Judges, even the separate concurring opinions would perhaps require a closer scrutiny as they provide an alternate medium of individual expression. Particularly, in view of the meager dissent in the court, separate concurring opinions may provide an additional tool for behavioural analysis.

Dissent in the Court

Dissent connotes a disagreement with the outcome agreed upon by the majority of the judges participating in a decision. In view of the fragmented bench structure a dissent normally does not signify a disagreement among all the judges on the Court regarding how an issue may be resolved in a case. The disagreement is confined to a few judges who participate in the decision in which one or more judges may not agree with the majority opinion. Thus, whenever one speaks about dissent in the Indian Supreme Court, the reference is to a disagreement among a few judges and not amongst all the members of the Court. In fact such occasions have been rare in the history of the Indian Supreme Court when one could possibly say that the Court was divided over a particular issue. *Golaknath* and *Kesavananda* are two instances of this kind where almost the entire Court was divided over the scope of fundamental rights and the majority in each case prevailed over the minority by a narrow margin of one vote. Therefore, dissent in the Supreme Court has to be understood as essentially a disagreement among a fraction of the membership of the Court at any given point of time over how the matter before them ought to be resolved.

An overt dissent which causes a split in the decision may not be the only form in which judges express their disagreement among themselves. It is true that a divided decision is the most categorical statement of their differences over how an issue ought to be resolved and for that reason can be easily identified for the purpose of ascertaining attitudinal differences among the judges. But there might be other ways in which judges may express their differences among themselves in the opinions which they write without causing a split in the final outcome of the decision. One possibility is where a unanimous decision may have been the result of a compromise arrived at among the judges.[9] The unanimous opinion under such circumstances is most likely to reflect the views of different judges in order to accommodate their view points. The differences in this way get subsumed within a unanimous opinion.

Another possibility of such differences being expressed by the judges lies in their separate opinions which may concur in the final outcome of the decision but for reasons different from those adopted in the opinion of the Court.[10] A third possibility would be where a judge may have disagreed with his own views expressed in an opinion in the past which has been termed as 'retroactive dissent'.[11] All these types of disagreements would not reflect in the data on non-unanimous decisions, and, therefore, would not surface in what is technically known as dissent in the Court.

In addition to all this, there may be other factors which perhaps counteract surfacing of the actual disagreement among the judges in their opinions. For instance, substantial increase in two judge decision making panels over the years which handle bulk of the docket of the Court may not only give the judges less time and opportunity to write dissenting opinions,[12] it may also neutralise to some extent their differences as a result of close and continuous interaction on the bench. There is also a possibility that relative decline in the number of Constitutional and larger benches over the years may have actually brought down overt dissent in the court. Some would perhaps argue that the number of contentious issues before the court during this period were not sufficiently large to have given more opportunity to judges to dissent or that, there were no great dissenters in the court during the seventies as compared to fifties and sixties. Some of these propositions have been examined below along with the nature and character of dissent in the court.

(i) ***Two judge panel as a device to eliminate dissent:*** It may be appropriate to test the hypothesis whether bench size has any correlation with the rate of dissent in the Court. Table II presents the data on bench size and dissent in the court. It is quite clear from the figures that the larger benches have produced higher dissent than the smaller panels. One would also notice that in 53.27 per cent of the decisions there was no opportunity for the judges to dissent. The two judge benches alone constituting 52.72 per cent of the decision making panels, a dissent on such panels by one of the participating judges would of necessity rule out a decision as in case of split on such a panel the case would be heard by another panel designated by the Chief Justice. Which means that dissent was possible only in about 46.73 per cent cases. Of these, 39.68 per cent decisions were given by three judge panels which produced 33 (2.06 per cent) dissent. The remaining 7.05 per cent cases were decided by benches consisting of four to thirteen judges contributing to a much higher dissent. The increase in dissent has been proportionate to the size of benches thereby indicating that the larger benches have produced more dissent. As a necessary corollary, therefore, the decline in the frequency of larger benches is expected to produce less dissent in the Court.

Table II : Bench size and Dissent, 1973-81

Bench Size	Total decisions	% of all decisions	No. of dissents	Dissent (%)
1&2.	2144	53.27	0	0.00
3.	1597	39.68	33	2.06
4.	95	2.36	2	2.10
5.	160	3.98	23	14.37
7-13	29	0.71	5	17.20
Total	4045	100.00	63	1.56

One would draw more or less the same inference from Table III below which shows the relationship between bench size and dissent under four Chief Justices. It appears that whereas in Sikri's time the opportunity to dissent existed in 62.67 per cent cases, the same had come down to 35.86 per cent during Chandrachud's tenure. The opportunity to dissent depending upon the number of two judge panels constituted by each Chief Justice thus shows substantial decline. Therefore, the dissent from Sikri to Chandrachud should have registered a substantial fall. But, contrary to this expectation, as one would notice, dissent during the successive Chief Justices varied within a very narrow range and fails to establish the necessary correlation that the decline in the frequency of larger benches should ipso facto lead to a lower rate of dissent. The fact that dissent in the Court has remained more or less unchanged, although there have been lesser number of larger benches in the succeeding years, may also indicate that in quantitative terms dissent in larger benches has not really affected the overall dissent in the court. For example, there were in all 5 benches consisting of seven to thirteen judges which produced non-unanimous decisions contributing to 7.93 per cent of the total dissent in the Court during the study period. The remaining 92.7 per cent dissenting opinions were produced by benches consisting of 3 to 5 judge panels. The number of benches consisting of three and five judges being still large as compared to benches consisting of seven and more judges, the overall dissent in the Court would very substantially depend upon the frequency with which judges dissent on these panels.

Table III : Rate of Dissent Under Four Chief Justices, 1973-81

Chief Justice	Total Decisions	Dissenting opinions	Rate of dissent
Sikri	442	8	1.81
Ray	1761	26	1.48
Beg	358	5	1.40
Chandrachud	1464	24	1.64
Total	4025	63	1.56

Assuming, therefore, that the successive Chief Justices consciously pursued a policy of obtaining maximum unanimity in the decision making panels, and, hence they resorted more and more to the smaller panel formations, one would wonder if they could have achieved the preferred goal simply through this mechanism. In view of the figures presented in the tables above, it is very unlikely that they could succeed substantially in this. The five judge Constitutional benches which produced 36.50 per cent of dissent cannot be dispensed with being mendatory and will continue to remain susceptible to dissent, as also the three judge panels which despite diminishing numbers, may not be done away with altogether. This explains why despite a substantial decline in the number of larger benches, dissent in the court has remained more or less static.

(ii) ***Year wise dissent***: There are in all 63 decisions in which this kind of disagreement was found among the judges. The 63 non-unanimous decisions are spread over a period of nine years which means seven decisions on an average per year revealed some kind of disagreement among the judges deciding cases on different division benches. The year-wise breakup of the dissenting opinions and their percentage to the total number of cases decided every year is shown in Table IV.

Table IV : Yearwise Dissent 1973-81

Year	No. of written dissents	Oral+ Written dissents	Total Decisions	% of total dissent
1973	8	12	495	1.61
1974	9	12	462	1.94
1975	10	12	455	2.19
1976	6	7	482	1.24
1977	1	1	520	0.19
1978	5	5	290	1.72
1979	7	9	423	1.65
1980	9	10	419	2.14
1981	8	9	479	1.67
Total	63	77	4025	1.56

The frequency of dissent every year has varied from a minimum of one in 1977 to a maximum of ten in 1975 according to the reported data. The three years following Ray's assumption of the office of Chief Justice apparently shows a consistent, although marginal, increase in the frequency of dissent among the judges. This does not seem to show much significance as it will be noticed that after a pause of three years during which the dissent had relatively gone down, it shows again a steady increase with Chandrachud taking over as the Chief Justice in 1978. It must, however, be clarified here that the figures indicated against the years do not necessarily correspond with the number of dissents given within the tenure of a Chief Justice who led the Court during that year which has been shown separately in Table III above.

If at all, the low rate of dissent during the tenure of a Chief Justice has any correlation with his ability to procure unanimity[13] in the Court then Beg no doubt would emerge as the most successful of all the four Chief Justices and Sikri the least of all in procuring unanimous Court decisions. Both Ray and Beg became Chief Justices by superseding their senior colleagues in the Court in 1973 and 1977 respectively. Their tenures as Chief Justices have been described as equally 'eventful'. It has been observed that "the Court as an institution was cribbed and crippled by the quiescent personality of the Chief Justice (Ray)"[14] and, that "there were clear indications that brother justices did not accept the leadership of Chief Justice Beg."[15]

Assuming that procuring unanimity is an attribute of leadership and that all the four Chief Justices equally cared to obtain maximum consensus among the judges in the Court, how does one explain the low rate of dissent under Ray and Beg in view of their controversial leadership? It may be noted that earlier above it was shown that in view of the fragmented bench structure, the Chief Justice may not be able to achieve much success in obtaining unanimous court decisions. The figures given in the chart above in a way substantiate the earlier proposition that there is no necessary relationship between dissent and the ability of the Chief Justice to procure unanimity among the judges on the decision making panels. The overall rate of dissent under the successive Chief Justices since 1973 does not reveal significant variations, and by and large has remained constant.

(iii) *Dissent and Participation*: It is also argued sometimes that some Chief Justices so value consensus that they would tend to exclude from benches judges who have demonstrated a tendency towards dissenting behaviour. Thus, assumption is that judges with high dissent ratios will have low participation rate and conversely, that infrequent dissenters will be appointed by the Chief Justices to panels more often than those who have demonstrated a propensity to dissent.[16] An examination of data on dissent and participation, however, did not establish a systematic correlation between dissent and participation rate. For instance, Mathew and Beg dissented more often than Khanna but their participation rate was relatively higher than that of Khanna. Aliagiriswami participated more often than his contemporary Chandrachud during the years they were together in the Court, but the former had registered more dissents than the latter. A.P. Sen, similarly, had a much higher participation than that of Tulzapurkar even though the former revealed more propensity to dissent than the latter. These instances clearly show that there may not necessarily exist a relationship between dissent and participation in the form in which it has been proposed. At least, the data pertaining to the period under investigation does not sustain this proposition. Moreover, it seems too improbable for the Chief Justices to consciously eliminate dissent and increase consensus generally in the Court by reducing participation of judges who are more prone to dissent, particularly, when there were not great dissenters during this period comparable to Subbarao, Sarkar, Hidayatullah and Dayal in the earlier period.[17] However, one does not rule out the possibility in case of important controversies for which larger benches are normally constituted and are invariably presided over by the Chief Justice. The Chief Justice may in such cases include or exclude certain judges from the bench with the object of obtaining a unanimous court decision.

(iv) *Voting Split*: The 63 non-unanimous decisions revealed in all 77 disagreements accounting for 1.22 disagreements per decision. Besides the 63 minority opinions, there were seven opinions concurring with the minority and seven votes cast in favour of the minority. This shows that the dissent in the form of a written concurrence with minority or a simple casting of vote in favour of minority has been most uncommon among the judges. The voting pattern in the non-unanimous decisions reveals that the dissenting judge was usually unsupported. 82.54 per cent of the dissents are one judge dissents whereas only 15.87 per cent of the cases record a voting pattern of two judge dissents. Thus the dissent in the Indian Supreme Court has been by and large a solitary effort put in by an individual judge. It has not only been extremely individual in character but also sporadic and disconnected as illustrated in the next section.

(v) *Voting Pattern in Non Unanimous Decisions*: An examination of the voting pattern of judges in all the non unanimous decisions revealed that there was virtually no pattern in the manner in which judges had recorded their dissent. For instance, Mathew registered the largest number of dissents spread over a variety of issues like freedom of press, regulation of business, taxes, civil liberties, rent control and eviction, minority rights and adoption and maintenance. Similarly, Bhagwati who recorded the second largest number of dissents shows more or less similar pattern. His dissents related to issues like civil liberties, rent control and eviction, regulation of business and economy and validity of the imposition of death penalty. The three seniormost judges Khanna, Mathew and Beg (excluding Palekar who retired in 1974), dissented most of all and they together accounted for one third of the total dissent. There were eleven split decisions[18] in which all the three or, at least, two of the three senior most judges appeared together with Ray.

It was noticed that Ray and Beg who were together in eight of the eleven non-unanimous decisions, never disagreed with one another. On the other hand each one of the other judges disagreed as well as agreed with the others in almost a random manner. For instance, Ray and Khanna disagreed in five of the ten cases in which they participated together; Ray and Mathew disagreed in six of the ten decisions; Khanna and Mathew disagreed in seven of the nine cases; and Khanna and Beg differed from one another in five of the seven cases in which they were together. It is difficult to say whether their differences were issue based or inter personal in nature but one failed to establish any ideological linkage between the issues over which they had recorded their dissent.

Among the judges who joined the Court between 1973 and 1981, Bhagwati and A.P. Sen figured as major dissenters. Bhagwati's seven dissents were spread over a period of almost nine years whereas, Sen wrote six dissents within a relatively shorter span of little over three years. The two judges were together in only three non-unanimous decisions,[19] and in all the three they disagreed with one another. A.P. Sen's disagreement with Krishna Iyer and Desai also appeared quite prominent in the decisions in which the three participated together.[20] Koshal and Krishna Iyer equally revealed their disagreement with one another in all the three non-unanimous decisions in which they were together.[21] And, finally, Chandrachud and Bhagwati were in opposite camps[22] in two of the four non-unanimous decisions in which they participated during the period 1980-81. Bhagwati's dissent in *Minerva Mills*[23] brought to the surface differences between the Chief Justice and the seniormost judge in the Court. Justice Bhagwati apparently did not like the manner in which decisions in *Minerva*[24] and *Wamanrao*[25] were announced by short order without reasons the information concerning which was given to him on the day the orders were read out in the Court. His opinion in these cases reflects an important aspect of the Court's decision making process when he makes a pointed reference to the absence of "judicial collectivism" in the Court.[26] The data on voting split adequately substantiates this proposition. Justice Chandrachud (as he then was) in *Kesavananda* had complained of lack of time `for an exchange of draft judgments' and had written his opinion without `the benefit of knowing' the views of majority of other colleagues who participated in the decision.[27] Twelve years later, Justice Thakkar in *Tulsi Ram Patel*[28] vindicated Chandrachud in *Kesavananda* and Bhagwati in *Minerva Mills* on this score when he launched a similar protest but much more strongly worded in his dissent note. These instances do furnish atleast some evidence which would suggest that differences among judges of the Indian Supreme Court in the form of overt dissent have not always stemmed from pronounced ideological convictions.

Dissent in the Indian Supreme Court, therefore, has been too little, solitary in character and ideologically devoid of any consistent pattern. This, however, does not mean that judges in the Supreme Court are ideologically neutral, or that they hold consensus as a preferred norm, or in the alternative, because of more or less homogeneous backgrounds that they possess their outlook, inclinations and perceptions too are similar. It has been pointed out earlier that overt dissent which causes a split in a decision is only one of the various ways in which judges may project their differences. A fair amount of differences among the judges are, therefore, not likely to emerge in the data on non-unanmious decisions. Such differences can perhaps be brought out by a systematic content analysis of opinions written over a specified time period in different subject matter areas. This kind of analysis is likely to be helpful in obtaining a better perspective of the differences which possibly remain under cover of unanimous decisions. However, dissent in disguise is not the only reason why the overt dissent in the court has remained low. Other factors such as fragmented bench structure of decision making process, quick rotation of judges on different panels, heavy workload, and possibly a decline in contentious issues particularly in Constitutional interpretation over the years have played an important role in shaping the overt dissent in the Court. A high mobility in the decision making panels gets further subjected to the frequent changes in the membership of the Court. Above all this, the composition and character of the decision making panels alters substantially with the changing leadership in the Court which has been equally volatile.

Despite these constraints the data on dissent in the Indian Supreme Court reveals at least two recurrent patterns: First, that the judges tend to dissent more often in larger benches than they would in the smaller benches and second, that they dissent individually rather than in groups or collectively. The second feature is more prominent irrespective of whether the dissent occurs in larger or smaller panels.

Concurrence

A concurrence here signifies a separate opinion which concurs in the outcome of the opinion of the Court (in a unanimous decision where all judges agree to the outcome) or, of the majority (in a non-unanimous decision where one or more judges disagree as to the ultimate result) more often for reasons different from those put forth in the opinion with which the judge concurs. Concurrence in the Indian Supreme Court is not always easy to define as its character would largely depend upon the judge who decides to write a separate opinion for himself. A judge may decide to write a separate opinion with a view to merely agree with all that has already been said but wish to re-state in his own words considering the importance of the matter under consideration. For instance, Justice Chandrachud (as he was then) in *Kesavananda* by way of providing justification for writing a separate opinion says, "the importance of the matter under consideration would justify a personal reflection and it is so much more satisfactory in a matter ridden, albeit wrongly, with political overtones to state one's opinion firmly and frankly so that one can stand one's ground without fear or favour."[29]

It is also quite possible that the judge writing a separate concurring opinion expresses his divergence of outlook while agreeing with the outcome proposed by the opinion with which he decides to concur. This form of concurrence may conveniently be termed as dissent in disguise. Here the judge makes known his disagreement in principle but abstains from casting a negative vote.

Separate concurring opinions provide maximum latitude to judges within the frame-work of a unanimous decision to diversify their exposition and enunciation of the law, and from this perspective they have contributed significantly in the decision making process of the Court. At the same time proliferation of views expressed in the multiple opinion judgment may have certain disadvantages too in the sense that they are likely to cause uncertainty in the law and at times may be incomprehensible too.

For instance, separate concurring opinions of Hidayatullah and Mudholkar in *Sajjan Singh*[30] were largely responsible for giving a powerful jerk to the well established norm of parliamentary supremacy, and shaping the views of majorities in *Golak Nath*[31] and

Keshavananda.[32] The eleven opinions in *Kesavananda* irrespective of whether they sided with majority or minority, were a classic example of the vitality and strength of concurrence as such. The two judges who seem to have particularly distinguished themselves in terms of style outlook and impact on judicial decision making, were Bhagwati and Krishna Iyer. Bhagwati's separate concurring opinion in *Menaka Gandhi*[33] was the most powerful enunciation of the right to personal liberty under article 21 of the Constitution. Similarly, Krishna Iyer leaves his indelible mark on prison justice in *Sunil Batra*[34] in his separate concurring opinion.

On the other hand, the disadvantage of separate concurring opinions is best illustrated in the *Judge's* case.[35] A bench of seven judges presided by Bhagwati and comprising of A.C. Gupta, Fazal Ali, Tulzapurkar, Desai, Pathak and Venkatramiah produced seven different opinions. One of the issues involved in the case concerned the issuance of a circular by the Union Law Minister on March 18, 1981 asking the Chief Justice of various High Courts to seek prior consent from the Additional Judges of the High Courts before their permanent appointment in any other High Court for which they were to indicate their order of preference. The response of the seven judges to this issue was recorded thus : Justice Bhagwati and Desai thought that there was nothing in the circular which would render it Constitutionally invalid;[36] for Justice Gupta the circular was of no legal consequence;[37] in the opinion of Justice Fazal Ali the circular in no way tarnished the image of judges or marred the independence of judiciary;[38] Justice Tulzapurkar held that the circular impinged upon judicial independence and therefore being violative of articles 222(1) and (4) is quashed;[39] Justice Pathak did not consider it to be binding;[40] and, Justice Venkatramiah held that circular was not invalid.[41] Similarly, each judge responded to every other issue differently thereby making it difficult to comprehend the exact ratio of the decision. It is interesting to note that despite these wide ranging differences among the judges no overt dissent was recorded in the case. Proliferation of opinions may, therefore, make the decision incomprehensible, uncertain and ambiguous.

Thus, concurrence in the Indian Supreme Court is of complex character which may move from complete unanimity over all aspects of a decision to total divergence of perception and outlook. From the behavioural point of view concurring opinions are equally the expression of individuality of judges and can, therefore, be relied upon along with the dissents for determining the vicissitudes of judges' inclinations and attitudes. But, like dissent, concurring opinions are too small in number and majority of them were written by a small fraction of the total number of judges who participated in the decision making process during the period covered here. As pointed out earlier, three judges (Beg, Krishna Iyer and Pathak) by themselves accounted for 43.71 per cent of the concurring opinions. Pathak wrote as many as 26 concurring opinions during a relatively short span between 1978 and 1981, Krishna Iyer recorded 27 of such opinions during his tenure in the Court; and Beg had written 20 separate concurring opinions in all. Four more judges, Bhagwati, Mathew, Chandrachud and Fazal Ali contributed to this kind of participation relatively more in numbers than the other judges although A.N. Sen, Kailasam and Koshal record equally high percentage of this type of response.

At least twelve judges never wrote a concurring opinion. Noteworthy among them are Ray and Tulzapurkar both of whom had two dissents each to their credit as a manifestation of their individual behaviour. These two are the only ones who have consistently adopted the extreme expression of individuality as and when they felt the need to do so without resorting to concurrence as the medium of their response. They either wrote opinions for the Court or voted for it but never sought to explain their reasons separately. Five judges (Mitter, Vaidialingam, Vardharajan, Eradi and Misra) did not record any type of individual behaviour either in the form of dissent or of concurrence. All others have resorted to both dissent as well as concurrence as medium of their individual expressions.

Judges who Dissent are likely to write Concurring Opinions

These variations in the individual judges' response pattern cannot be explained by reference to any fixed uniform pattern among any set of judges. But what appears to be a plausible correlation that may be inferred from the data on dissent and concurrence is that judges who dissent most are invariably the judges who adopt concurrence as an alternative medium of expression. This holds true in case of some judges, for instance, Beg, Bhagwati, and Mathew have made use of both the responses equally. A.P. Sen is the only judge who seems to have resorted much more often to dissent than concurrence. Krishna Iyer, on the other hand, relied exclusively upon concurring opinions and his behaviour seems to be dogmatically opposite to that of Ray and Tulzapurkar. Krishna Iyer during his seven and a half years' stay in the Court never wrote a dissenting opinion or voted for minority. This would surprise many who are familiar with his strongly held views on various issues and his dynamism, activism and liberalism which was credited to his leadership during his years (1973-80) in the Court. Pathak's propensity to write concurring opinions matches that of Krishna Iyer. In fact, in terms of percentage of his total participations, Pathak has written concurring opinions much more often than even Krishna Iyer did.

It was also noticed that Pathak wrote concurring opinions most often while he was sitting with Krishna Iyer on the bench. It is difficult to draw any positive conclusion from this kind of behaviour but it does indicate that the two judges possibly had different perception and divergence of out look which invariably impelled them to state their reasons in separate opinions. This assumption is further strengthened by the fact that two of Pathak's three dissents were registered while he was on the bench with Krishna Iyer. This serves to illustrate the point already made that in concurrence one may find a concealed dissent and that concurring opinions have often been resorted to by the judges in order to give expression to their individuality without causing a split in the decisional outcome.

The frequency with which the Supreme Court judges have been writing concurring opinions has varied from time to time. During the first few years there were few judges in the Court who often wrote separate opinions in most of the important Constitutional matters. This practice, however, became less frequent as the strength of the Court increased and so did the volume of workload in the Court. The Court became more and more fragmented and the frequency of two judge and three judge benches increased considerably. The rate of dissent and concurrence was accordingly affected and both recorded a decline in their frequency. But, whereas dissent in the Court almost disappeared, concurrence, on the other hand, was revived with renewed vigour particularly, by judges like Krishna Iyer and Bhagwati when they joined the Court in 1973. The year-wise break up of concurring opinions rendered during 1973-81 is given in the table below.

Table V : Year-wise Concurrence 1973-81

Year	Concurrent opinions	Votes + opinions	Total decisions	% of decision
1973	7	13	495	1.41
1974	15	18	462	3.24
1975	16	20	455	3.51
1976	10	14	482	2.07
1977	15	20	520	2.88
1978	18	29	290	3.44
1979	8	9	423	1.89
1980	23	26	419	5.49
1981	16	18	479	3.34
Total	128	167	4025	3.18

The table shows a steady increase in the frequency of concurring opinions during 1973-75, and except during the year 1979 the frequency of such opinions rendered in other years shows an increase over 1973 figures. In all 167 concurring opinions were written in 128 decisions of the Court. On an average every judge had 1.60 per cent participation in concurrent behaviour although, individual variations are large enough to defy any uniformity in pattern.

Nevertheless, the fact that some judges have consistently resorted to concurrence as their medium of individual expression is in itself an evidence of the difference in their approach, style and how they perceive the issues which are contested before them. While concurrence in the outcome may not normally affect the immediate decision, its potential as an instrument of change deserves further explorations. To treat concurrent opinions under the banner of unanimity is likely to create distortions in our understanding of the decision making behaviour of the Indian Supreme Court judges.

Unanimity

Unanimity from the institutional point of view would mean that the judges in the Court agree with each other over how the issues confronting the Court are to be resolved by them. It is easier to ascertain this kind of agreement among the judges where all the judges sit en-banc to hear all the cases which come before the Court for its final determination. But in a Court where majority of the cases are heard by small sub-sets comprising two or three judges each, it is presumptuous to say that unanimity exists among all the judges with regard to those issues in the determination of which majority of the members of the Court did not even participate, or if they did, not necessarily in combination with same set of judges. There is no doubt that almost 98 per cent of the decisions rendered by different division benches are unanimous in the sense that all the judges participating in a decision agree to the ultimate outcome and, the number of decisions in which one or more judges have recorded their disagreement are very small. But such disagreement which causes a split in the decision has not been necessarily a sustained dissent as is quite evident from the previous discussion and the data on dissent analysed therein. A dissent of this kind is often inadequate to project the real differences among the judges over issues that confront them in their day to day interaction in the decision making process.

The judges' individual attitudinal traits are like habits formed and concretised over long years of sustained exposure, experience and training. Their perception of problems and their outlook are fully matured by the time they are appointed to the Supreme Court. It is also expected that a small group of such versatile men who constitute a distinctive class of the governing elite are likely to differ on how certain basic issues confronting the society should be resolved. Such differences would normally be reflected in non-unanimous decisions in the form of dissenting votes as overt manifestations of their individuality. But because of several constrains discussed above such overt manifestations seem to have been very few in number. This may not mean that the judges are one in outlook and perception and hence they rarely dissent. It is more likely that the attitudinal differences of the judges in their day-to-day decision making activity get institutionally accommodated as a result of the fragmented bench structure adopted by the Indian Supreme Court. Accordingly, this kind of institutional accommodation may sometime result in bringing together judges with similar outlook on the same panel which minimises the possibility of a split in the decisions. But, in the event that this happens, the chances of different benches arriving at different conclusions in the controversies involving essentially similar issues cannot be ruled out.

For instance, in death penalty cases where the only question before the different benches has been agitated from time to time whether the accused ought to be hanged or his life should be spared the response has widely varied depending upon the composition of the bench. A conspicuous combination of three judges (Vaidialingam, Dua and Aliagiriswami) was observed to have shown remarkable consistency in their voting behaviour in the death penalty cases which they had the opportunity to decide together during 1973-74 term. In nine of the eleven cases in which they appeared together, death sentence was confirmed by them. At the same time on perusal of the voting behaviour of judges on other division benches which dealt with the issue in the same year, it appeared very plausible that any other panel of judges would have proved less unfortunate for the accuseds involved. For example, Grover, Mathew and Mukherjea bench appeared more likely to have condoned death rather than sending majority of them to the gallows. Similarly, one could not help noticing consistent effort on the part of two judges (Krishna Iyer and Sarkaria) to tilt the scale of justice in favour of the unfortunate accuseds. The two judges commuted death sentence in all the five cases in which they appeared together. An overall institutional response revealed that during this period more death sentences were confirmed than commuted.

In forty four death penalty decisions reported during 1977-79, one could immediately notice the increase in commutations over confirmations of death sentences. The voting pattern of different division benches during this period although depicted a change towards moderation at the institutional level, large variations among different panels concerning who should go to the gallows continued to persist. It was observed that while there were combinations of judges like Chandrachud, Sarkaria, Singhal, Jaswant Singh, Fazal Ali, Kailasam, Tulzapurkar and A.P. Sen who were more likely to confirm than commute a death sentence; at the other end, judges like, Krishna Iyer, Bhagwati, Desai, Gupta and O.C. Reddy appeared less inclined to impose the extreme penalty given the choice between death and life imprisonment. The instances cited here from two different time periods simply serve to illustrate that the concept of unanimity emerging out of the data could well be misleading. A discussion on the basis of these few examples atleast enables us to appreciate that the extent of unanimity in the court cannot be fully ascertained unless the focus of analysis is shifted from a mere head count of unanimous decisions to a systematic examination of the behaviour patterns of the decision making panels.

Conferences

How do the judges vote on the outcome of the cases in which they have heard oral arguments? One often finds judges in the course of hearing arguments conferring with each other on the bench. This practice as it appeared from observation of the proceedings in the court, is followed almost invariably on the smaller as well as larger benches. It is quite possible that judges make up their mind as to the outcome of the decision either after reading the briefs or immediately after hearing the oral arguments. There does not seem to be a practice of holding regular conferences among the judges after the conclusion of oral arguments.

In the daily routine matters the most likely mode of voting seems to be the brief consultations which go on among the judges while the hearing is still in progress or, immediately after the conclusion and before taking up a fresh matter for hearing. Majority of the cases fall within the category of daily routine matters and, since the opinion writing in these matters is likely to be governed by the rotation principle, the voting response of each judge is possibly asertained then and there. The heavy workload and the anxiety of judges to maintain pace with the daily cause list apparently does not leave them with much time for discussing at length the cases in which the hearing is over.

The case brief prepared by the Supreme Court Registry are supplied to the judges in advance of the hearing and, one may assume that the judges often go through the briefs before hearing oral arguments in the case. It is not however known whether all the judges follow the practice of studying the briefs before they hear the arguments or not as, at least, one High Court Chief Justice writing in his autobiography, gives an indication of a possibility that all the judges may not necessarily follow the practice of reading briefs before hand.[42]

As almost all the judges of the Supreme Court had their initial making in the High Courts, one would expect that they are likely to retain some of their habits even after they are elevated to the Supreme Court. "I think", says M.C.Chagla, "it is a mistake for a judge to go to the court after studying the case that is coming up before him. Inevitably, one makes up one's mind one way or the other after having read the papers. I agree, the decision is tentative, and one might change it after hearing counsel. But it requires a very strong mind to change an opinion once formed."[43] Referring to the practice followed by the Supreme Court judges, the author further says, "I have often discussed this question with the judges of the Supreme Court, who do an immense amount of hard work by reading Special Leave Petitions, the day before these are heard, and I have often appealed to them not to read these before hand and to decide the cases only after hearing the Bar. The answer I usually got was that it would take up a lot of time, and by reading them in advance, they were saving judicial time."[44]

No matter which view should prevail, what is important here is the fact that the pressure of workload and its speedy disposal almost invariably shows in the manner in which the judges conduct themselves on the bench. This almost inevitably reflects in the voting pattern of judges which comprises on an average 63 per cent of oral votes and, merely 37 per cent of written responses of which opinions of the court alone account for 34 per cent. Almost 97 per cent of the behavioural responses conform to a pattern of a unanimous opinion of the court in which other judges participating simply recorded their oral agreement.[45] Such a high degree of uniformity in the behavioural responses of the Indian Supreme Court judges cannot be simply attributed to the near unanimity among them as apparently projected by the number of unanimous decisions.

The post hearing conferences or discussions of the cases at a formal meeting does not seem likely even among larger benches which are normally constituted for the purpose of hearing important matters. After the conclusion of oral arguments if all the judges agree upon a unanimous outcome, the opinion writing is assigned to one of them who gets down to framing the opinion of the court. Once the draft is ready the same is circulated among all the judges. The draft is revised in view of the comments or suggestions received and, after it is finally approved by all the judges the judgment is announced.

There have been instances where the judges felt unhappy about the fact that the judge writing the opinion either could not project their views properly and adequately or, in the alternative, they did not subscribe to some of the wide propositions in the judgment which they had assented to.[46] In 1973, while writing his separate opinion in *Kesavananda Bharati*, Justice Chandrachud(as he then was) said, "there has not been enough time, after the conclusion of arguments, for an exchange of draft judgments amongst all and I have had the benefit of knowing fully the views of only four of us".[47] This suggests the possibility of different judges writing separate opinions without even having the opportunity of knowing the views of other colleagues who participated in the decision. There cannot be possibly much exchange of ideas as regards the final outcome except by way of written comments and suggestions in case it is a unanimous decision and, perhaps none where it is a split decision and the voting response has already been obtained. Justice Thakkar in his dissenting opinion in *Tulsi Ram Patel*[48] not only reinforces this impression but also demonstrates how lack of adequate communication among the judges participating in a decision may create a split where it was not warranted.

The nature of participation of judges as discussed above demonstrates how their decisional response is subjected to various factors operating at institutional as well as individual level and is not always the product of what is commonly regarded as pure legal logic. Like decision makers in other areas, judges too perform their decision making functions within a given environment which affects them and influences the decisions that they make. Judges of the Indian Supreme Court may appear to be homogeneous in their dispositions as it appears from the data on unanimous court decisions but in reality they are as different from one another as any two human beings can be. This aspect concerning judicial decision making has been further analysed in the next chapter dealing with attitudes and value orientations of judges.

Notes

1. Rajeev Dhavan, *The Supreme Court of India* 36 (Tripathi, Bombay, 1977); Hegde wrote 92 opinions of the Court in 252 decisions in which he had participated. See *id*. Table III at 36.
2. These decisions were reported in 1973-74 volumes of All India Reporter (Supreme Court), and, therefore, were included in the data.
3. *Supra*, note 1 at 36.
4. George Gadbois, "Participation in Supreme Court Decision Making" 26 *Journal of the Indian Law Institute* 15 (1982).

5. *Ibid*
6. *Id.*, at 2-4, see Table I.
7. See George Gadbois, *supra*, note 4, at 17-18; Also see Upendra Baxi, in Introduction to K.K. Mathew's *Democracy, Equality and Freedom* vi-xv (Eastern Book Company, Lucknow 1978).
8. See, e.g. Glendon Schubert, *Quantitative Analysis of Judicial Behaviour* (1959); Joel B. Grossman, "*Dissenting* Blocks on the Warran Court: A study in Judicial Role Behaviour" 30 *Journal of Politics* 1068 (1968); Herman R.C. Pritechett, *Civil Liberties and the Vinson Court* (1954); George Gadbois, "Indian Judicial Behaviour", 5 *Economic and Political Weekly*. (1970).
9. See, e.g. M. Hidayatullah, *My Own Boswell* 198 (Arnold-Heinemann, New Delhi 1984).
10. This aspect has been dealt with separately under concurrence.
11. See, Upendra Baxi, "On How Not To Judge The Judges: Notes Towards Evaluation of the Judicial Role" 25 *Journal of the Indian Law Institute* 232 (1983); see also Id., "The Travails of Stare Decision in India" in A.R. Blackshield(ed.); *Legal Change: Essays in Honour of Julius Stone* (Butterworths, Sydney, 1983).
12. George Gadbois; "The Decline of Dissent on the Supreme Court 1950-81", Ramavtar Sharma(ed.), *Justice and Social Order in India* 249 (Intellectual Publishing House, New Delhi, 1984).
13. See George Gadbois, "Supreme Court Decision Making", 10 *Banaras Law Journal* 34 (1974)
14. Upendra Baxi, *The Indian Supreme Court and Politics* 46 (Eastern Book Company, Lucknow, 1980).
15. *Id.*, at 189.
16. *Supra*, note 13 at 31-33.
17. *Supra* note 1 at 33-34; see Table I showing frequencies of dissenting and separate opinions of Judges, 1950-70.
18. 1) AIR 1973 SC 106; 2) AIR 1973 SC 1461; 3) AIR 1974 SC 543; 4) AIR 1974 SC 818; 5) AIR 1974 SC 1389; 6) AIR 1974 SC 1745; 7) AIR 1975 SC 1549; 8) AIR 1975 SC 1564; 9) AIR 1975 SC 2065; 10) AIR 1976 SC 490; 11) AIR 1976 SC 1207.
19. A.I.R. 1980 S.C. 387; A.I.R. 1981 S.C. 234; and A.I.R. 1981 S.C. 1887.
20. A.I.R. 1979 S.C. 281; A.I.R. 1979 S.C. 916, and A.I.R. 1979 S.C. 1384; In all these three decisions A.P. Sen disagreed with Krishna Iyer and Desai on a three judge bench.
21. See A.I.R. 1979 S.C. 745; A.I.R. 1980 S.C. 1896; and A.I.R. 1980 S.C. 1955.
22. *Bachan Singh* Vs. *State of Punjab*, A.I.R. 1980 SC 898, and *Minerva Mills* Vs. *Union of India*, A.I.R. 1980 SC1789.
23. *Minerva Mills., supra* note 21 at 1815-16. See also Upendra Baxi, *Courage Craft* and *Contention* foot-note 64 at 105-106 (Tripathi, Bombay, 1985).
24. *Minerva Mills, supra* note 21 at 1789.
25. A.I.R. 1981 SC 271.
26. *Supra*, note 21.
27. A.I.R. 1973 SC at 2019.
28. (1985) 3 S.C.C. 369. The draft judgment of 237 pages was circulated on the morning of July 11, 1985 less than three hours before the deadline for pronouncing the judgment. Justice Thakkar in his dissent note remarks, "it would have been appropriate if meeting of the judges constituting the Bench had been convened to seriously deliberate and evolve a consensus..." *id.*, at 526.
29. A.I.R. 1973 SC 2019.

30. A.I.R. 1965 SC 845; See, Hidayatullah J. at 862, and Mudholkar J. at 865-66.
31. A.I.R. 1967 SC 1643.
32. *Supra*, note 27.
33. A.I.R. 1978 SC 597.
34. A.I.R. 1978 SC 1675.
35. *S.P. Gupta* Vs. *Union of India*, (1984) Supp. S.C.C.87.
36. *Id.* paras 55 and 76 respectively.
37. *Id.* para 131.
38. *Id.* para 433.
39. *Id.* paras 655 and 688.
40. *Id.* para 939.
41. *Id.* para 1239.
42. See, e.g., A.R. Blackshield, "Capital Punishment in India," 21 *Journal of the Indian Law Institute* 137 (1979).
43. M.C. Chagla, *Roses in December* 125 (Bharatiya Vidya Bhawan, Bombay, 1975)
44. *Ibid.*
45. *Ibid.*
46. See Rajeev Dhavan, *The Supreme Court of India* 32 (Tripathi, Bombay, 1977)
47. AIR 1973 SC 2019.
48. (1985) Supp. S.C.C. 525-27; see *supra* note 28 per Thakkar J. at 526. See also Minerva Mills, *Supra* note 22, per Bhagwati J. at 1815

7

Attitudes and Value Orientations of Judges

Any study of groups and institutions would be incomplete without an attempt to discern the social attitudes and value orientations of the members who constitute the group. In order to find out the value orientations of our subject under discussion it is necessary to assume that judges like every one else have their value preferences which are likely to be manifested in the manner in which they decide the cases which come before them for their determinations. Their decisions can be interpreted as supporting one pattern of activity as against another "which makes them an important member of an interest group, however, temporarily and for whatever reason."[1] In other words, if such is the case then the social attitudes and value preferences of judges would be reflected in the opinions they write and in the votes they cast for or against a particular outcome. To what extent judges of the Indian Supreme Court reveal their value preferences in their decisional response examined in the previous chapter needs to be subjected to further scrutiny.

In determining the attitudinal differences among the judges almost all the behavioural studies have relied upon the individualistic behaviour of the judges.[2] Such studies have utilised for the purpose only the non-unanimous decisions in which atleast one of the judges participating in the decision has recorded his dissent as to the ultimate outcome arrived at by the majority. It is often suggested that a judge is unlikely to register his dissent unless he feels relatively strong about a particular outcome and thus, the presence of such behaviour on the Court would indicate disagreement among the judges. One of the prerequisites for studying such differences among the judges is that the individualistic behaviour of each judge must reveal certain recurrent patterns, uniformities, and consistencies over a period of time. Only if the regularities are observable that variables sufficient to explain the observed regularities can be identified.

Attempts have been made in the past to determine differences among the Indian Supreme Court judges through the non-unanimous decisions[3], but they had limited success mainly because of the 'serious handicaps' presented by the data. Three factors were clearly recognised in this regard. First, the short tenures of judges leading to their rapid turnover in the Court making it difficult to observe their responses over a reasonable time period. Second, the frequent use of small panels consisting of two and three judges to dispose of bulk of the work of the Court ruling out the possibility of all or majority of the judges to participate jointly and simultaneously on the decision making panels. Third, the quantum and character of overt dissent in the court has been such that it does not easily lend itself to behavioural analytical tools.[4] The discussion on all the three aspects presented in the earlier chapters makes it clear that during the study period the data on the Indian Supreme Court judges has become even more resistant to the quantitative methods employed in the study of attitudinal differences among the United States Supreme Court judges. Statistical methods of scaling and factor analysis were also employed to the non-unanimous decisions of the Indian Supreme Court judges by some of those studies but with limited success.

The non-unanimous decisions in the Indian Supreme Court rendered during the period under investigation, too, do not lend themselves to a systematic behavioural analysis mainly for the reason that the individualistic behavioural manifestations are too few and devoid of any recurrent pattern. They are mostly isolated expressions of disagreement among the judges and their recurrence among the same panel over similar issues is almost non-existent.

The character of unanimity in the Indian Supreme Court as discussed earlier, shows that the possibility of wider differences among the judges over various issues cannot be ruled out even though the rate of their recorded dissent has been very low. This hypothesis was tested and found plausible to a limited extent in relation to the death penalty cases. The same hypothesis is being extended here to a wider spectrum, in a modified form. The assumption here is that every single matter offers a variety of choices to a judge who is participating in the decision. Every judge, therefore, has to select among the alternatives in order to arrive at the decision. Thus, the voting response of the judge in certain identifiable subject matter areas observed over a period of time is likely to reveal some pattern in his decisional responses. According to our hypothesis therefore, it is possible to locate a judge's value preferences by utilising his total voting response manifested in both unanimous as well as non-unanimous decisions. As a corollary to this it may be suggested that since the ultimate outcome of a decision is decided by a vote and not by the manner in which the judge participates in the decision making the individualistic behaviour as manifested in the non-unanimous decisions alone can not be relied upon in determining the value preferences of the judges.[5] At the same time one may not under emphasize the importance of non-unanimous decisions in the Indian Supreme Court for the purpose of ascertaining the individual differences among the pairs of judges provided that such differences reveal recurrent patterns and are observed over a substantial period of time.

Voting Response of Judges

The data on voting behaviour presented in Table I is derived from 3445 out of 4025 decisions comprising the total universe of this study. The 3445 decisions are spread over six types of litigational activity represented by different groups classified in column 1 to 6 of the table. The two most powerful and influential groups which dominated litigation in the Supreme Court as shown in chapter 4 earlier, are the business and the state. These two groups have fought their claims among themselves, as well as against the so-called less privileged class, 'the individual' contesting his claims against the business or the state in various capacities.

It may be recalled that during the 1973 supersessions controversy, with reference to certain decisions[6] an attempt was made to project the judges as conservative elements, and the Court as an institutional supporter of the propertied class. In the post 1973 era too, similar attempts were made to classify some judges as liberal, activists, non-conformists and others, as conservatives, legalists, or conformists.[7] It is quite evident that such assertions manifestly derive their sustenance from the manner in which the

Table I : Judges' Support to Business and the State

Judge	Support to Business			Support to State		
	Busin. vs. State	Busin. vs. Worker/ Union	Busin. vs. Individ.	State vs. Individ.	State vs. Worker/ Union	State vs. Public Servant
Sikri	50.00	-	100.00	39.14	100.00	50.00
Shelat	83.33	100.00	0.00	51.07	-	66.67
V.Lingam	100.00	54.54	0.00	66.67	66.67	62.50
Mitter	0.00	100.00	-	75.00	-	0.00
Hegde	61.70	100.00	-	51.86	-	100.00
Grover	58.33	50.00	100.00	48.58	75.00	50.00
Ray	34.32	50.00	46.66	61.47	67.67	72.16
Reddy P.J	60.41	41.66	0.00	51.13	80.00	28.58
Dua	83.33	62.50	100.00	73.79	75.00	50.00
Palekar	33.33	50.00	37.50	41.80	-	54.55
Khanna	54.80	44.44	33.33	54.98	66.67	64.71
Mathew	33.96	40.00	54.54	60.76	100.00	56.42
Beg	35.41	33.33	41.66	55.83	66.67	75.44
Dwivedi	16.66	38.46	0.00	49.13	66.67	40.00
Mukherjea	33.33	50.00	100.00	52.00	100.00	42.86
Chandrachud	44.44	40.00	38.46	72.73	50.00	62.72
A.Swami	34.48	58.33	54.54	58.56	51.15	60.00
Bhagwati	69.04	61.11	55.55	43.97	0.00	52.95
Krishna Iyer	34.56	26.92	52.63	57.71	36.37	44.16
Goswami	45.09	50.00	64.28	49.72	42.86	55.00
Sarkaria	43.13	14.28	52.38	52.06	0.00	49.98
Gupta	46.66	35.71	60.00	49.73	50.00	40.55
Untwalia	50.00	57.14	64.70	50.94	25.00	57.90
Singhal	51.92	54.54	60.00	39.73	0.00	55.32
Fazal Ali	37.14	37.50	33.33	61.74	100.00	64.29
J. Singh	46.93	40.00	57.14	55.18	50.00	65.12
Kailasam	50.00	55.55	50.00	50.99	50.00	71.93
Tulzapurkar	71.42	50.00	60.00	61.12	50.00	38.47
Desai	37.50	21.42	38.46	55.79	100.00	47.83
Pathak	53.73	62.50	66.66	42.35	33.34	48.49
Koshal	52.00	58.33	0.00	42.93	50.00	42.11
Reddy, O.C	26.31	11.11	100.00	54.68	50.00	37.71
Sen, A.P	44.11	28.57	60.00	56.37	0.00	64.00
Venkatramiah	48.48	100.00	33.33	43.40	-	46.18
B. Islam	33.33	-	-	50.00	100.00	83.34
Vardharajan	0.00	0.00	100.00	36.12	-	50.00
Sen, A.N	66.66	-	100.00	36.37	-	62.50
Eradi, V.B	50.00	-	-	35.30	-	20.00
Misra, R.B.	0.00	100.00	-	50.00	-	33.34
Total Average(%)	45.53	50.80	53.39	52.35	56.97	52.85

judges cast their votes in important controversies. Invariably, such controversies occurred among groups identified in columns one to six of the table. The assumption here is that, if in accordance with the above assertions, the judges in the Supreme Court are divided on ideological grounds in their outlook towards the dominant groups and sections of society, then such inclinations should reveal in their overall voting pattern in the controversies involving those identifiable groups.

The six litigational categories shown in columns one to six account for 85.59 per cent of the decisions and include in the first three columns all matters contested between the business and the state, matters relating to employer and employee relationship contested between business employer and the employee and, matters in which business is pitted against the individual in any other capacity. In columns 4, 5, and 6, the litigational areas include all offences and any other conflict between state and the individual, the industrial dispute cases where state was one of the parties to the dispute, and the service matters where the public servant was enforcing his claim against the state.

In the foregoing discussion the value preferences of judges will be determined, not in terms of conservativism or liberalism but by simply determining the direction of their support individually for each one of the two dominant groups, the business and the state in their conflicts with each other and, as against the individual pitted against each one of them respectively in his different capacities.

The direction of each judge's support is determined on the basis of votes in the ultimate outcome of a decision and by reference to response to specific issues which may sometimes be more than one. The two independent variables used were the litigant and the subject matter involved. An attempt was made to ascertain the response of each judge in terms of favourable and non-favourable votes cast. The percentages were computed on the basis of the number of times a judge supported claims of the business or the state, divided by the total number of decisions in each category in which he had participated while he was in the Court. Thus, all the reported data on the six categories of decisions was utilised in order to determine the composite response of each judge to different categories of litigants involved in litigation before the court.

Support to the Business

(a) *In Business vs. State Conflicts:* Column one in the table shows the frequency with which each judge supported the business in its conflicts with the state. The three major areas in which the business and the state repeatedly pressed their respective claims before the Court were, taxes, regulation of business and economy by the state, and government contracts. The figures presented in column one indicate the total support which each judge extended to the business in these three areas, among others, against the state. Eight judges (Shelat, Vaidialingam,[8] Hegde, Jagmohan Reddy, Dua,[9] Bhagwati, Tulzapurkar and A.N. Sen) supported the business in more than 60 per cent of the decisions in which they participated. Particularly striking appear to be the support pattern of Bhagwati (69.04 per cent) and Tulzapurkar (71.42 per cent). Their total support to business as against the state in different subject matter areas revealed that it was highest in tax matters (77.42 per cent and 83.33 per cent respectively), relatively less prominent in regulation matters (58.33 per cent and 50 per cent), and the least in government contracts (30 per cent and 33.33 per cent). These figures suggest that the level of support extended by a judge to a litigant category may vary depending upon the subject matter of dispute. They also seem to suggest as if the two judges largely disapproved government's tax policies concerning the business. It may, however, be noted that Bhagwati and Tulzapurkar maintain relatively high support to business even under columns 2 and 3. This aspect will be further examined in relation to some of the other judges as well, particularly in view of the common belief that 'justice is blind', and it is irrelevant, who the litigants are; what the litigants have done is paramount.

Twelve judges, (Ray, Palekar, Mathew, Beg, Dwivedi, Mukherjea, Aliagiriswami, Krishna Iyer, Fazal Ali, Desai, Chinnappa Reddy, and Baharul Islam) reveal an equally strong preference (over 60 per cent support level) for the state as against the business in all such decisions in which they were a party to the decision making. These value preferences are measured without regard to the identity of the other judges who happened to be participating on the decision making panels. Thus, each judge's vote in different combinations of the decision making panels is treated as a conscious choice exercised by him either in favour of the business or the state. The fact that some judges upheld the claim of the business as against the state in over 60 per cent of the decisions they participated and, others reveal an equally strong preference in favour of the other party i.e. the state, shows that such a wide cleavage in the voting behaviour of judges could not have been a mere coincidence. The average support (45.53 per cent) being the norm, there are only seven judges (Chandrachud, Goswami, Sarkaria, Gupta, Jaswant Singh, A.P. Sen and Venkatramiah) who have demonstrated their support for the business well within the norm. The remaining thirty two judges are distinctly marked off in the extent to which they supported the business and the state, respectively. However, the fact that business was favoured on an average in 45.53 per cent decisions by the judges of the Supreme Court goes to show that the business performed fairly well as against the state in its conflicts with the latter.

(b) *In Business Employer vs. Employee Conflicts*: In this category of conflicts, the business as an employer, was pitted against a relatively weaker section, i.e., the employee and, at times against the more organised sections like the trade unions. The business apparently seems to have succeeded even more often against their employees and the unions than it did against the state. There are eight judges (Shelat, Mitter, Hegde, Dua, Bhagwati, Pathak, Venkatramiah and R.B. Misra) who supported the business employer in more than 60 per cent decisions in which they participated. On the other hand, nine judges (Beg, Dwivedi, Krishna Iyer, Sarkaria, Gupta, Fazal Ali, Desai, Chinnappa Reddy and A.P. Sen) voted for the employee and the unions in over 60 per cent of such decisions. Fourteen judges in all i.e., about 40 per cent of them reveal a pro-business leanings in the sense that their voting support for the business exceeded the average norm of 50.80 per cent. The remaining sixty per cent judges are below or well below the average support level, which means that the number of judges who supported the claims of the employees and their unions in their confrontation with the business employer was more than those who supported the business. However, in terms of total average support the business has recorded a higher percentage as against its employees than it did against the state.

(c) *In Business vs. Individual Conflicts*: The business often came in conflict with the individual in various other areas and such matters were drawn to the Supreme Court more at the instance of the business because of its capacity to undertake long and enduring litigation. Column 3 shows the support which the business received from the judges in such decisions. In all, thirty four judges participated in the disputes involving the business and the individual and eighteen i.e. 52.94 per cent of these supported the claim of the business in all such decisions. On an average, every judge supported the business in 53.39 per cent decisions which means that the eighteen pro-business judges' support for the business was obviously much above the average support level. There were, thus, only sixteen judges who had supported the individual in his claims as against the business. Of these sixteen judges, at least nine (Ray, Palekar, Beg, Dwivedi, Chandrachud, Krishna Iyer, Sarkaria, Fazal Ali and Desai) have shown consistency in their voting behaviour in terms of low level of support for the business under all the first three columns. An almost equal number of ten judges (Sikri, Hegde, Grover, Dua, Bhagwati, Untwalia, Singhal, Tulzapurkar, Pathak, and A.N. Sen) have consistently supported the business at above the average support level irrespective of the nature of the dispute and the party against whom its interests were to be protected. The remaining twenty one judges seem to have adjusted their frequency of support to the business depending upon the nature of the dispute and the party pitted against the business. For instance, Jagmohan Reddy and Khanna, both supported the business in its confrontation with the state at above the average support level, but their support for the business markedly declined when the same business appeared before them in disputes involving the employee or the individual. On the other hand, there are judges like Mathew, Mukherjea, Aliagiriswami and Goswami, who had supported the business less often in its conflicts with the state, appeared favourably disposed towards the business interest when it was in conflict with the employee or the individual.

Support to the State

(a) ***In State vs. Individual Conflicts:*** The State in the performance of a variety of functions and at various levels of decision making often comes into conflict with the individual. The fact that the State is one of the largest litigant category in the Supreme Court goes to show that a large number of disputes, between the State and the individual, creeping through the lower rung of the judicial hierarchy, finally end up in the portals of the highest tribunal. All the state-individual conflicts excepting those classified separately under columns 5 and 6 were clubbed together to form one single category presented under column 4 of the table. The major areas of conflict represented by this category concern among others, the offences, taxes, regulation matters, fundamental rights, land reforms and acquisition of property. Column 4 thus, records the pattern of response of the judges in terms of the frequency with which they supported the State as against the individual in such conflicts.

There are eight judges (Vaidialingam, Mitter, Ray, Dua, Mathew, Chandrachud, Fazal Ali and Tulzapurkar) who supported the State in over 60 per cent of all such decisions in which they participated. Particularly, of interest is the voting response of Mitter, Dua and Chandrachud, three of the eight judges, who seem to have extended their almost unqualified support to the state by upholding its claims against the individual in over 70 per cent of the decision. At the other end, there are only five judges (Sikri, Singhal, Vardharajan, A.N. Sen and Eradi) whose level of support for the state was even less than 40 per cent. In all, twenty three judges supported the State below the average level of support i.e. 52.35 per cent whereas, only sixteen favoured the State more often than the average norm. But in terms of total support to the state as against the individual, there are at least twenty five judges who voted for the State in over 50 per cent of the decisions in which they had participated.

(b) ***In State vs. Worker/Union Conflicts (Industrial Disputes)*:** Column 5 shows the amount of support the State received from the judges in industrial disputes where the State was pitted against the worker or the union. The first eleven judges (Sikri, Vaidialingam, Grover, Ray, Jagmohan Reddy, Dua, Khanna, Mathew, Beg, Dwivedi and Mukherjea) who participated in this kind of disputes, have consistently revealed a high degree of support for the State. But the State seems to have performed very poorly with the later crop of judges who joined the Court, particularly, during the seventies and the eighties. Barring a few judges like, Fazal Ali, Desai and Baharul Islam, who seem to have extended their whole hearted support to the State as against the worker and the union and Aliagiriswami whose support for the State is above the average level of 56.97 per cent, the others have supported the State much below the average norm. At least seven of the fifteen judges whose voting support for the State is below the average level have adopted more or less neutral posture by supporting the State and the workers in almost equal number of decisions. Only eight judges (Bhagwati, Krishna Iyer, Goswami, Sarkaria, Untwalia, Singhal, Pathak and A.P. Sen) have clearly revealed their options in favour of the worker/union as against the state.

(c) ***In State vs. Public Servant Conflicts (Service matters)*:** Disputes between the State and the Public servant comprise another single largest litigation category in the Supreme Court. Matters relating to the public servant's dismissal, termination, promotion, seniority, emoluments, etc., repeatedly come up before the judges, sometimes involving high financial stakes for the state. The manner in which the judges responded to the conflicting claims of the State vis-a-vis the public servant is depicted in column 6 of the table. At least, fourteen judges (Shelat, Vaidialingam, Hegde, Ray, Khanna, Beg, Chandrachud, Aliagiriswami, Fazal Ali, Jaswant Singh, Kailasam, A.P. Sen, Baharul Islam and A.N. Sen) supported the State in over 60 per cent of such decisions in which they participated. On the other hand, there are fifteen judges (Mitter, Jagmohan Reddy, Dwivedi, Mukherjea, Krishna Iyer, Sarkaria, Gupta, Tulzapurkar, Desai, Pathak, Koshal, Chinnappa Reddy, Venkatramiah, Eradi and R.B. Misra) whose voting support to the State in such disputes was even less than 50 per cent. In other words, the judges of the Supreme Court were almost evenly divided in extending support to the conflicting claims of the two parties. The remaining ten judges supported the State in 50 per cent or above, but, below 60 per cent of the decisions. The average support level for the state being above 50 per cent i.e. 52.85 per cent, the State obviously seem to have received more favourable response from the judges than the public servant. At the same time the fact that the state lost in 47.15 per cent decisions is significant from the public servants' point of view, which goes to show that the Court as an institution has kept the state on its toes.

Consistency in the Response Patterns

Table II was drawn on the basis of figures presented in columns one, four, five and six of Table I wherein the State was contesting its claims either against the business or against the individual, the worker/union, or the public servant. The judges who voted in favour of the State in 50 per cent decisions and above, were allotted a plus (+) sign, and those whose support to the State under anyone of the four columns was less than 50 per cent were assigned a negative (–) sign, indicating that they had supported more often either the business or the individual, worker/union, or the public servant as against the State. The judges in Table II, thus, are arranged according to the level of support they extended to the State in a descending order. The Table clearly shows that the first eight judges from top (Ray, Mathew, Beg, Chandrachud, Aliagiriswami, Fazal Ali, Jaswant Singh and Baharul Islam) supported the State consistently in all kinds of disputes wherever the State happened to be one of the parties to the litigation. Closely on the heels are Mukherjea, Desai, Chinnappa Reddy, Vaidialingam, Dua, Khanna, Kailasam and A.P. Sen, who have supported the State in three out of four category of disputes. But, as one moves down the order of the level of support, one would find that from Shelat to Tulzapurkar, the judges have remained more or less neutral in their propensity to support the State as against the business and the individual (including the worker/union and the public servant). The last seven judges (A.N. Sen, Bhagwati, Singhal, Venkatramaiah, Koshal, Eradi and Pathak in particular) were more inclined to favour the business and the individual than the state and have shown considerable consistency in their depicted behaviour.

At 50 per cent level, support to either group is not likely to reveal significant propensities in the voting behaviour of judges, and for that reason Table II was simply constructed to demonstrate consistency in the nature of response of each judge in symbols. However, the difference in the voting response pattern becomes more visible and prominent where a judge has consistently supported one or the other party in over sixty per cent cases as separately shown in Table III. Ray, Fazal Ali and Mathew have supported the state in over 60 per cent decisions irrespective of whether the state was pitted against the business, the individual, worker/union, or the public servant. Similarly, Beg and Baharul Islam supported the state in over 60 per cent decisions in atleast three of the four categories. In this way, out of the eight judges who had depicted pro-state response under all the four columns in Table II, only three (Ray, Mathew and Fazal Ali) maintain the

Table II : Consistency in Voting Patterns

Judge	1	4	5	6
Ray	+	+	+	+
Mathew	+	+	+	+
Beg	+	+	+	+
Chandrachud	+	+	+	+
Alagiriswami	+	+	+	+
Fazal Ali	+	+	+	+
Jaswant Singh	+	+	+	+
Baharul Islam	+	+	+	+
Mukherjea	+	+	+	-
Desai	+	+	+	-
O.C. Reddy	+	+	+	-
Vaidialingam	-	+	+	+
Dua	-	+	+	+
Khanna	-	+	+	+
Kailasam	-	+	+	+
A.P. Sen	+	+	-	+
Shelat	-	+	NP	+
Hegde	-	+	NP	+
Mitter	+	+	NP	-
Palekar	+	-	NP	+
Vardharajan	+	-	NP	+
R.B. Misra	+	+	NP	+
Sikri	-	-	+	+
Grover	-	-	+	+
Krishna Iyer	+	+	-	-
Sarkaria	+	+	-	-
P.J. Reddy	-	+	+	-
Dwivedi	+	-	+	-
Goswami	+	-	-	+
Gupta	+	-	+	-
Untwalia	-	+	-	+
Tulzapurkar	-	+	+	-
A.N. Sen	-	-	NP	+
Bhagwati	-	-	-	+
Singhal	-	-	-	+
Venkatramiah	+	-	-	-
Koshal	-	-	+	-
Eradi	-	-	NP	-
Pathak	-	-	-	-

Key: Col. 1 = Business-State disputes
Col. 4 = State-Individual disputes
Col. 5 = State-Worker/Union disputes
Col. 6 = State- Public Servant disputes
\+ = Indicates support for the State
\- = Indicates support for any other party
NP = Not participated in that category of decisions

Table III : Consistency in Voting Response at 60 and above level

Judge	1	4	5	6
Ray	+	+	+	+
Fazal Ali	+	+	+	+
Mathew	+	+	+	+
Beg	+	.	+	+
Baharul Islam	+	.	+	+
Khanna	.	.	+	+
Mukherjea	+	.	+	.
Aliagiriswami	+	.	.	+
Chandrachud	.	+	.	+
Desai	+	.	+	.
Grover	.	.	+	.
Palekar	+	.	.	.
Jaswant Singh	.	.	.	+
Kailasam	.	.	.	+
Vaidialingam	-	+	+	+
Dua	-	+	+	.
Dwivedi	+	.	+	-
Mitter	+	.	+	-
Sikri	.	-	+	.
Shelat	-	.	.	+
Hegde	-	.	.	+
Krishna Iyer	+	.	-	.
Chinnappa Reddy	+	.	.	-
A.P. Sen	.	.	-	+
Vardharajan	+	-	.	.
R.B. Misra	+	.	.	-
P.J. Reddy	-	.	+	-
Tulzapurkar	-	+	.	-
A.N. Sen	-	-	.	+
Sarkaria	.	.	-	.
Untwalia	.	.	-	.
Pathak	.	.	-	.
Bhagwati	-	.	-	.
Singhal	.	-	-	.
Eradi	.	-	.	-

Note: (a) Key to the table is the same as in Table II.
(b) The dots indicate a voting response above 40 and below 60 per cent.

consistency at 60 per cent and above level, two (Beg and Baharul Islam) maintain under three columns, two (Aliagiriswami and Chandrachud) under two columns, and one (Jaswant Singh) under only one column. In addition to these, at least one other judge (Vaidialingam) continues to support the state in over 60 per cent decisions under three of the four columns, and six judges (Mukherjea, Desai, Dwivedi, Dua, Mitter and Khanna) retain their support at that level under at least two columns.

Of the six judges towards the bottom of Table II, who had demonstrated their support in over 50 per cent decisions to any party contesting its claims against the state, none has maintained his position at 60 per cent and above level under all the four columns in Table III. Pathak, who represents extreme position in Table II, relatively improves his position at 60 per cent and above level, and appears less likely to favour any party other than the worker/union under column 5 where his level of support is maintained at above 60 per cent. Similarly, the other five judges too, lose much of their anti-state posture at 60 per cent and above level. Six judges (Jagmohan Reddy, Bhagwati, Singhal, Tulzapurkar, A.N. Sen and Eradi) continue to support the claims against the state under two of the four columns in more than 60 per cent decisions. Venkatramiah and Koshal who figure in Table II towards the bottom do not find their place in Table III because under all the four columns their level of support to any party remained well within 40-60 range.

The voting response as depicted in Table III clusters the judges according to their support to the state as against the business, the individual, the worker/union and the public servant in over 60 per cent decisions. Judges who have supported the state under all the four columns are to be found at the top and those who have supported claims against the state under any one of the columns in above 60 per cent decisions are to be found at the bottom. The voting pattern of the clusters of judges towards the top may suggest their pro-state outlook whereas, those at the bottom may not be so well disposed towards the state's claims against any other group. It may, however, be clarified that judges' response under column 5 of tables II and III may require more data to substantiate inferences drawn here because the number of total participations of each judge in such cases were too small.

Thus, if some judges of the Supreme Court have voted in favour of the claims put forth by one or the other party in over 60 per cent decisions in which they participated, irrespective of the nature of disputes, it gives rise to a strong presumption that they were most likely well disposed towards the party as such. The voting response of Justices, Ray, Fazal Ali, Mathew and Beg clearly indicates such a possibility as all the four judges reveal a consistent support to the state in almost all kind of disputes. Beg's support to the state against the individual under column 4 falls slightly short of 60 per cent, however, he voted for the state in 75 per cent decisions where the state was pitted against the public servant in column 6. Similarly, there are judges who have either supported the claims of the business or the individual (including the worker/union and the public servant) in more than 60 per cent decisions. Prominent among them are Bhagwati, A.N. Sen, Tulzapurkar, and Jagmohan Reddy.

Particularly of significance appears to be the voting response of judges who have cast over 70 per cent of their votes in favour of one or the other party. Ray, Beg, Kailasam and Baharul Islam supported the claim of the state as against the public servant in over 70 per cent decisions in which they happened to participate Mitter, Chandrachud and Dua, similarly, voted for the state as against the individual in over 70 per cent decisions. Equally important appears to be the voting response of judges like Dua, Shelat and Tulzapurkar who favoured the business class in its disputes against the state because these judges supported the business in much above 70 per cent support level.

These instances of high incidence of support extended by judges of the Supreme Court to one or the other party do suggest something more than the mere proposition that 'justice is blind', and judges are value neutral automatons who produce decisions mechanically. The pattern of their voting response as depicted above provides some evidence to suggest that they are likely to reveal their value choices in the manner in which they vote for or against the claims of litigants who come before them for the resolution of their disputes. While drawing this inference from their voting response one is not suggesting that they tilt the scale of justice consciously or deliberately for or against the claims of a particular party. It simply represents a patterned tendency to respond to stimuli which can be explained in behavioural terms as manifestation of attitudes.

Institutional Support to Business and the State Under Four Chief Justices

Table IV which corresponds Table I was prepared to show the Court's response to the two dominant groups, the business and the

State under the leadership of the four Chief Justices. This was done in order to ascertain how closely the Court responded under the leadership of the four Chief Justices to their respective response patterns as recorded in Table I, and shown in parenthesis for comparison in Table IV. The Table also seeks to project the changing response patterns of the Court as an institution under the four successive Chief Justices.

Table IV : The Court's Support to Business and the State Under the Four Chief Justices

Chief Justice	Support to Business			Support to State		
	Busin. vs. State	Busin. vs. Worker /Union	Busin. vs. Individ.	State vs. Individ.	State vs. Worker/ Union	State vs. Public Servant
Sikri	64.47 (50.00)	61.90 (N.P)	71.42 (100.00)	55.61 (39.14)	57.15 (100.00)	64.00 (50.00)
Ray	37.68 (34.32)	49.35 (50.00)	51.16 (46.66)	53.09 (61.47)	41.18 (67.67)	60.38 (72.16)
Beg	46.15 (35.41)	40.00 (33.33)	46.66 (41.66)	43.03 (55.83)	80.00 (66.67)	54.55 (75.44)
Chandrachud	52.74 (44.44)	36.11 (40.00)	54.54 (38.46)	46.70 (72.73)	28.58 (50.00)	44.37 (62.72)
Total Average (%)	47.98	46.54	53.06	50.28	44.19	53.74

Note: 1. All figures are in per cents
2. Bracketed figures indicate the respective Chief Justices own support level

It would appear from the Table that the Court under Sikri's leadership extended relatively highest level of support to the business under all the first three columns. Business was supported as against the state in 64.67 per cent of all such decisions, as against its employee in 61.90 per cent decisions, and as against the individual in 71.42 per cent decisions. On the other hand, the state seems to have done better in disputes falling under columns 4, 5 and 6 during Sikri's tenure as Chief Justice. But a sharp decline in the Court's overall support to the business is registered under Ray in all the three categories represented by first three columns. Most Significant appears to be the contrast in figures showing the Court's support to the business against the state under Chief

Justices Sikri and Ray. The two dominant groups, the business/landlord and the state had fought their battles before the Supreme Court repeatedly and the former did score a number of victories over the latter in important controversies particularly since *Golak Nath* decision in 1967. The government's increasing concern over the Supreme Court's pro-business attitude had also been expressed in no uncertain terms, and the supersessions of the three seniormost judges at the retirement of Sikri and appointment of Ray as the Chief Justice was largely viewed as an attempt to bring about the desired change in the Court. The change in the attitude of the Court under Ray did seem to have taken place, as is evident from the sharp decline in its support to the business (37.68 per cent), but can this perceptible change be credited to the leadership of Chief Justice Ray?

Three propositions can be briefly examined here in this regard. First that supersessions may have put the judges on their guard which may in turn have produced the shift. Second, Chief Justice Ray's own support to business being low (34.32 per cent), he may have succeeded to some extent in carrying his colleagues along with him. And third, the new crop of judges who joined the Court in post-Ray period may have been responsible for bringing about an ideological shift in the Court's response.

Although the argument of fear among the judges following the supersessions cannot be stretched too far at this juncture, yet there is some evidence to suggest that this may have contributed to the change to some extent. For instance, Justice Khanna in his autobiography referring to the events of 1973 admits that he "felt extremely perturbed", because in his opinion the supersessions, "were bound to generate fear complex or hopes of reward and thus undermine the independence of judiciary."[10] The Judge goes on to recall that, "the Court acquired a new complexion" and he "found perceptible change in the atmosphere."[11] Referring to the new trends in the approach of the Court, the author clearly remarks that there was a "tilt in favour of upholding the orders of the Government."[12] There is no doubt that these are only the personal views expressed by one of the judges who happened to be on the Bench at the relevant period and it would not be fair to stretch them to the point of generalisation but, at the same time, they cannot be completely considered as irrelevant till they are refuted and found baseless.

The second argument relates to the extent to which Chief Justice Ray could have carried his brother colleagues in obtaining a more favourable response for the state. This possibility cannot be ruled out altogether in view of the following factors. At least four senior most judges in the Court after Ray became the Chief Justice, namely, Palekar, Mathew, Beg and Dwivedi were favourably disposed towards the state in its disputes with the business as is borne out by their voting response in Table I. Jagmohan Reddy and Khanna were the only ones from among the seniormost judges about whom the Chief Justice could not have been so sure. With Chandrachud and Aliagiriswami then being relatively junior along with four more new judges who joined the Court in 1973, Ray perhaps, did not find much difficulty in steering the Court towards the change. This can be better described as an effortless achievement on the part of Chief Justice Ray because there was possibly very little resistance from within the Court, and moreover the conditions for change had already set in. The third argument, therefore, is an extension of the second in the sense that with the arrival of new judges possibly there was a change in the atmosphere of the Court. Alluding to this aspect, Justice Khanna writes, "the new atmosphere brought some leftist leaning on the bench and the same proved a boon for employees including some of those who were guilty of glaring acts of insubordination and indiscipline. The new trend also posed difficulty in taking disciplinary action against delinquent employees for some of the new colleagues, otherwise well-meaning and with penetrating intellect but possessed of a missionary zeal, *were ever ready to gloss over the misconduct of the employees and give relief to them just because they belonged to the category of employees*"[13] (emphasis supplied). The comparison of figures of the Court's response under all the six columns in Table IV indicated against the two Chief Justices Sikri and Ray substantially prove this proposition. The level of support in the later years under Chief Justices Beg and Chandrachud does not appear to have undergone substantial change except in the industrial dispute area where the government was pitted against the worker/union and the business employer against its employees. In the latter category of labour disputes under column 2, the Court has consistently moved from pro-business employer to pro-worker/union. Whereas, under column 5, the Court recorded the highest support to the state under Beg, and the lowest under Chandrachud. The other variations are all within the permissible range of 60-40 as applied to individual judges' voting response in Table III.

The three propositions examined above show that a perceptible change did occur in the Court's attitude under Ray for which among other factors, the most likely appears to be the change in the composition of the Court. This conclusion further serves to illustrate that the value preferences of judges play an important role in shaping their responses which affect the decisional output of the Court.

The respective Chief Justices' own voting response as it appears from Table IV has been quite at variance with that of the Court under their leadership. As against four favourable votes of Ray and three of Beg, their respective Courts reveal two and one at sixty per cent response level. Sikri's Court, similarly, approximately went along with him in one of the four areas shown in the table. Chandrachud's own predisposition was completely at variance with that of his Court under his leadership. Chandrachud supported the state in two of the four categories in which state was one of the parties in over 60 per cent decisions, whereas his Court supported the business, the individual, the worker/union and the public servant more often than it supported the state under his leadership. This finding is in conformity with what has been pointed out earlier that the Court under Chandrachud's leadership appears to have been more fragmented than it was either during Beg or Ray's tenure as Chief Justice. On the basis of these findings it is possible to say that the successive Chief Justices although not necessarily, were at logger heads with the institutional response towards many issues under their stewardship, but did have very different orientation from the majority of the court. The Chief Justices may have been able to influence the judges' response on the decision making panels in which they participated in a limited number of important controversies which for obvious reasons may not get adequately reflected in the total decisional response of the court.

Thus the analysis of the judges' voting response in the decision making process spread over a period of time transcends the conscious and penetrates deep into the sub conscious to bring out those factors influencing their decisions which would otherwise remain concealed under the myth of judicial neutrality. To say that judges of the Indian Supreme Court are homogeneous because of their relatively uniform backgrounds, training and experiences as almost all of them were elevated from the various High Courts, and therefore they are likely to respond more often in similar ways is a proposition which can not be sustained atleast in view of the empirical evidence adduced here.

Notes

1. Jack W. Peltason, "A Political Science of Public Law", 34 *South Western Social Science Quarterly* 51-54(1953).
2. See, e.g. David W. Rohde and Harold J. Spaeth, *Supreme Court Decision Making*, Passim (W.H. Freeman, San Francisco 1976). H.J. Spaeth, *Supreme Court Policy Making: Explanation and Prediction* Passim (W.H. Freeman, San Francisco, 1979).
3. George Gadbois, "Indian Judicial Behaviour", 5 *Economic and Political Weekly* 153 (1970); see also *Id.* "Selection, Background Characteristics, and Voting Behaviour of Indian Supreme Court Judges, 1950-59" in Schubert and Danielski, *Comparative Judicial Behaviour* 221, (Oxford University Press, 1969); Id. "Supreme Court Decision Making", 10 *Banaras Law Journal* 1 (1974). See also, V.S.K. Haranath, "Supreme Court of India: 1950-70 — An empirical enquiry into Judicial Behaviour", 7 *Journal of Constitutional and Parliamentary Studies* 116 (1973).
4. George Gadbois, *supra*, note 3, at 38 (1974).
5. Sydney Ulmer, "The analysis of behaviour patterns on the U.S. Supreme Court," 22 *Journal of Politics* 629 (1960).
6. *Golaknath*, A.I.R. 1967 S.C. 1643; *Bank Nationalisation* A.I.R. 1970 S.C. 564; *Privy Purses*, A.I.R. 1971 S.C. 530, and *Kesavananda Bharati*, A.I.R. 1973 S.C. 1461.
7. Upendra Baxi, *The Indian Supreme Court and Politics* 125 (Eastern Book Company, Lucknow, 1980)
8. Vaidialingam had participated in only one decision involving business and the state in which he supported the business which accounts for his 100 per cent support.
9. Dua participated in twelve such decisions and he supported business in ten of them accounting for his 83.33 per cent support to business. He also maintained his relatively high support to business under columns 2 and 3 indicating his overall response pattern more favourable to the business group irrespective of the subject matter of the dispute.
10. H.R. Khanna, *Neither Roses Nor Thorns* 63 (Eastern Book Company, Lucknow).
11. *Ibid.*
12. *Ibid.*
13. *Id.* at 63-64.

Part IV
Conclusion

8

Conclusion

The general picture that emerges from the study reveals that the Supreme Court as an institution is more than a mere decision-making machine. It is a functional organisation which performs its activities with a view to achieve certain objectives, goals and desired ends. Its decision-making activity is no doubt subject to certain established norms of interpretation but, at the same time, involves a complex interaction of human and organisational or institutional factors. Since the Court is an intrinsic part of the political system, its interaction with the other organs of governmental system like the legislature and the executive are also likely to influence its activities. In an overall appraisal of the Court as an institution, therefore, one must emphasize the need to view the Court not as a simplistic legal entity but a dynamic component of the political process as such.

The study, while focussed primarily on the institutional factors, has also taken into considration the influence of some of the external factors which the Court encounters and comes into contact at various levels. Although, the Supreme Court owes its existence wholly to the Constitution of India, its institutional resources to a large extent are controlled by the legislature and the executive. Parliament has the power to sanction number of judges that would be required by the Court from time to time. Similarly, the President (the executive) carries the final say in matters of selection and appointment of its judges.

Despite the wide jurisdiction conferred on the court its institutional resources did not receive much attention either from the Constitution makers or later on from the successive governments. The Supreme Court, with limited resources and heavy responsibilities, found it extremely difficult to cope with the increasing work load almost from its very inception. Ad hoc measures like periodic increases in the Court's strength, appointment of ad hoc judges now and then, increase in the working days by cutting down on its vacations and increase of manpower by slicing the court into smaller division benches could not contain the swelling docket of the court.

These measures essentially related to the administrative and management spheres which lie within the exclusive domain of the Chief Justice of India who is the leader of the Court. In this respect, the appointment of the Chief Justice assumes special significance.

An examination of the appointments of the successive Chief Justices of India reveals that the leadership of the Court has been changing hands rather too frequently because of the seniority convention which enabled the seniormost judge next in line to almost automatically step into the highest judicial office. While this convention ensured impartiality in the appointments, it left little scope for a clear articulation of the distinctive role of the Chief Justice and accordingly evolve criteria for his selection.

The Chief Justice's role in the appointment of his colleagues in the Court is particularly significant in the Indian context. An analysis of the appointment process shows that the Chief Justice has had an important say in the choice of nominees for the Supreme Court. However, since appointment of judges is not the exclusive prerogative of the Chief Justice, the acceptance of his recommendations in this behalf by the executive would largely depend, among other factors, upon his intrinsic qualities of leadership by which he can persuade and influence the latter's discretion in matter of appointments.

The power to appoint judges virtually amounts to determining the composition and character of the decision makers which is likely to influence and shape the decision making activity of the Court as an institution. The question whether the executive at any time consciously made use of its prerogative with a view to influence the institutional output of the Court by appointing certain kinds of judges cannot be answered conclusively. However, the events leading to the supersessions in 1973 and 1977 do provide credible basis for such an assumption. It is generally believed that the superseded judges were victimised because of their purported stand against government in certain important decisions. One may as well argue that the government actions were primarily motivated by a desire to influence and change the institutional response by having a Chief Justice of its own choice. Considering the role of the Chief Justice in the selection and appointment of judges and in the constitution of benches in the Court the government's anticipation was perhaps not far wrong as is partly borne out in the changes depicted under Ray and Sikri. It may be recalled that about the same time arguments about the social philosophy of judges were advanced and the need to induct 'committed judges' to the Court was emphasised. Whether or not any attempt was made to ascertain the social philosophy of the judges who were appointed thereafter, such arguments clearly reveal the thinking of those who were entrusted with the task of appointing judges to the Supreme Court.

The fact that almost all the appointments to the Court were made from among the senior judges or Chief Justices of the High Courts gives an inevitable impression that the Supreme Court judgeships have been reserved for them so that the 'deserving ones' can be rewarded with a judgeship in the apex court as they approach their retirement. This impression is not without substance as almost 50 per cent judges were appointed with a term of less than six years in the Court. As against this, only nine judges had a minimum of ten years in the Court. The practice of appointing judges in their fairly advanced years coupled with delays in filling the vacancies has caused rapid fluctuations in the composition and character of the Court adding to its crisis due to the docket explosion.

At the same time, an examination of the work of the Court and the structural arrangements of its decision making process reveal that a variety of factors influence and condition the judges' response. Although, the Court enjoys variety of jurisdictions, almost 75 per cent of its work comes through two channels of access i.e. the Original Writ petitions under article 32 and the special leave jurisdiction under article 136 of the Constitution. Both these channels of access being discretionary, the Court could effectively arrest the mounting arrears by evolving rigid standards and carefully devised screening process for cases coming under these jurisdictions. Particularly in the area of special leave jurisdiction the Court has added no less than 65 per cent of its total docket. Obviously, therefore, special leave jurisdiction is the main feeder to its swelling docket and despite the institutional constraints the Court has failed to evolve a screening or in the alternative adopt a more principled approach to admissions in this area. Moreover, such a liberal use of the special leave jurisdiction by the court is likely to create a crisis of confidence among the High Courts whose place in the hierarchy of judicial system particularly in a federal set up needs to be reinforced rather than compromised in any way.

The geographical spread out of the work of the Court clearly establishes its national character. The data on regional distribution of appeals suggests a possible correlation between the size of the state by population and the number of appeals from its High Court travelling to the Supreme Court. The figures also indicate that the Court has not been simply putting its stamp of approval on the High Court decisions. It has overruled almost 49 per cent of the High Court decisions on an average which were subjected to its scrutiny.

The composition of litigants in the Court suggests that a fairly wide section of the Indian society has had access to the apex court. All the same for most of the time the Court has been kept busy by the government and the business class. Although, the Court's business in terms of subject matter is almost illimitable, there appears to be a large concentration of tax matters, rights of public servants and labour disputes.

The Constitution of division benches which perform the decision making function of the Court is within the exclusive prerogative of the Chief Justice who may determine the number of such benches to be constituted, their size, composition and the nature of work to be assigned to them. Except of course, the minimum number of judges on a division bench should not be less than two, and in case the matter involves the interpretation of the Constitution, the number of judges must not be less than five. A comparison of the data on constitution of benches by four Chief Justices Sikri, Ray, Beg and Chandrachud reveals that bench assignments, the type of bench formations and the character of their compositions may vary under different leaderships. Similarly, the rate of participation of judges in the decision making process is also likely to vary under different Chief Justices. At the same time some of the factors like the size and nature of the docket, number of judges available for assignment, utilization of the available strength with a view to maximise the decisional output and accommodation of judges according to their inclinations in particular subject matter areas, or otherwise, may influence the Chief Justice in the exercise of his discretion.

The role of the Chief Justice assumes special significance in relation to the bench structures as he has the exclusive prerogative to constitute division benches, determine their number, size, composition and work that they will perform. For the purpose of decision making, every single assignment technically amounts to a fresh warrant of appointment issued by the Chief Justice this time enabling a judge of the Supreme Court to participate and decide a case. In this sense it is an extremely powerful tool in the hands of the Chief Justice who may use it consciously to exclude a judge from participating in a particular decision. In controversial issues having far reaching social, political or economic consequences, this power can be effectively used by the Chief Justice with a view to influence the decisional outcome.

The volume of work had apparently necessitated the constitution of division benches in the Court from the very beginning. As the pressure of work further increased the size of benches too was reduced to provide more manpower. This process continued till one finds that over 95 per cent of cases were being disposed of by panels of two and three judges. This process of fragmentation of the Court into small panels, realistically speaking, has destroyed the Court concept and brought into existence a division bench which only represents a fraction of the Court. The implications of this arrangement for the High Courts and subordinate courts throughout the country which are bound not only by the ratio of the decisions of the Supreme Court but also by its obiter dicta, can be of far reaching consequences.

Different interpretations of the same provision by different panels are likely to create uncertainty as well as multiplicity of interpretations—a situation which would be comparable to different High Courts interpreting the same provision in different ways. In addition to this, the immediate parties before the different division benches may get differential treatment under more or less similar situation. This aspect has been demonstrated in relation to death penalty cases in order to show that the fate of the accused under such circumstances would depend upon whether his case is to be decided by a bench which is more likely to confirm, or commute the death sentence. Differential treatment is likely to create serious problems of credibility for the Court in the long run.

The discussion on the nature of participation makes it clear that 63 per cent of the total decisional response comprises oral votes cast by the judges and the remaining 37 per cent consisted of written opinions. Of the total written opinions 98 per cent were opinions of the Court, and barely about 2 per cent were written as concurring or dissenting opinions. It was found that judges considerably vary in the extent to which they write opinions of the Court. Apart from the personal attributes of judges, institutional factors like the role of the Chief Justice in determining the participation rate of judges and that of the presiding judge's option to assign opinion writing partly accounted for such variations.

Dissent in the Court during this period has been relatively low, invariably a solitary venture and non-recurring. On the other hand, judges have shown a tendency to write concurring opinions more often. Concurring opinions often express differences in outlook and perception, and to that extent they may be termed as dissent in disguise. From the behavioural point of view such opinions are important as they provide an alternative medium to the understanding of individualistic behaviour. In addition, it has been demonstrated with the help of death penalty cases how the statistical impression of the Court's unanimous behaviour may be misleading as chances of different benches arriving at different conclusions in controversies involving essentially similar fact situations may not be ruled out.

The nature of participation of judges in terms of oral votes, written opinions, separate concurring opinions and dissenting opinions, is to a large extent determined by their own personal attributes as also by the institutional factors like the work load, participation in bench formations and the extent to which they are involved in the decision making process. For instance, heavy workload and time factor may discourage many judges from writing their own opinions in concurrence or dissent even if they wish to write one.

Junior judges while participating with senior colleagues may out of hesitation or respect decide to suffer silence for some time, as many fresh appointees felt that the senior judges in the Court were very sensitive in the matter of seniority. A host of other similar factors not necessarily dealt with in this study may determine the nature of response of a judge, and the choices he makes in selecting among the alternatives presented before him in the issues which he decides. To say that judges of the Supreme Court make their decisions exclusively within the legally permitted logical framework would amount to mystifying the judicial role of the judges.

Finally, in order to test the hypothesis that 'judges are value neutral automatons who produce decisions mechanically', the aggregate voting response of each of the 39 judges in relation to six specified categories of subject matter and parties to the dispute was utilized and their individual propensities to respond was recorded. The fact that judges have supported one or the other party to the dispute in 60 to 70 per cent of the decisions in which they participate involving same kind of issues do suggest their preference for a particular value. Further, an analysis of the Court's aggregate voting response under four Chief Justices revealed that the institutional support to the business as against the state sharply declined from 64.47 per cent under Sikri to 37.68 per cent under Ray. This would not happen if the judges were merely interchangeable parts of the decision making process.

During the last three and a half decades since its inception the Supreme Court of India has shown its inner strength and vitality. It has guided the Constitutional developments in the country and given it a new philosophical dimension. It has nourished its fundamental right jurisdiction almost with parental care. A new jurisdiction was evolved by the Court, namely, epistolary jurisdiction which enabled it to take into its protective arms the weaker and the exploited sections of Indian Society. In addition to all these, the Court through its wide appellate jurisdiction assumed leadership in almost every sphere of the law. This is by no means a small achievement on the part of the Court.

On the other hand, its mounting arrears assumed threatening proportions so much so that today they are posing a challenge to its credibility as an apex court. This study, apart from seeking to explain the inner dynamics of its decision making process, highlights some of its major constraints.

The problem of arrears cannot be isolated from its institutional strategies. In fact, it is believed that a careful monitoring of cases by the Court coming through its special leave jurisdiction can go a long way in solving the bulk of the problem. In addition to this the adoption of better techniques of docket management also appear to be equally essential to prevent accumulation and help speedy disposal of cases. Besides these measures, it is of utmost importance that the Chief Justice and the judges of the Supreme

Court be appointed with longer tenures and with better regard for the institutional requirements of the Court, and here the executive will have to do some real hard thinking.

The expanding docket of the Court over the years, and its inability to find ways and means to quicken the pace of disposals, or in the alternative exercise more restraint on its discretionary access channels, have no doubt caused stagnation and delays in the highest Court of the land - causing serious problems of accountability. But this is essentially a problem which given the right kind of leadership and a few extra resources can be solved to a large extent. The problem of arrears is not exclusively the Court's problem. It has to be seen in the wider context of litigious culture which rapidly overtook the Indians with the introduction of formal laws and legal institutions by the British. It is also a problem which cannot be dissociated from the legal profession as such and the kind of professional ethics it has pursued. Nor, the government can absolve itself of its role in contributing to the arrears by pursuing a policy of unprincipled litigation and dragging every possible dispute to the apex Court.

Postscript

There is always an unavoidable gap between the completion of a study and its publication. In the mean while some changes are bound to occur in the court both at the institutional level as also in the environment within which it operates and performs its decision making function. The changes that have taken place in the course of time are sometimes to the advantage of the study in so far as they can be used to test the inferences drawn from the data which inevitably has to be limited to a particular time span.

In the case of Indian Supreme Court, however, there is not much that seems to have changed at the institutional level over the years except in the exceptionally rapid turnover of its leadership as well as in the composition of its decision makers. The subsequent governments, irrespective of their party affiliations, have almost religiously followed the seniority convention in the appointment of Chief Justice of India. Consequently, the court has had ten Chief Justices (including Chief Justice Ahmadi who took over from M.N.Venkatchaliah at his retirement on 25-10-1994) appointed within a short span of nine years since Chief Justice Chandrachud retired in July, 1985, giving on an average even less than a year to a Chief Justice to lead the court. This is a very significant change in the pattern of continuity in its leadership if one compares with the average of about two years term enjoyed by the Chief Justices during the first three decades of course with a few notable exceptions. The change is no doubt indicative of further instability in the leadership of the court which has remained a predominant feature of the appointments to this highest judicial office. It is also a matter of concern that the successive governments have failed to articulate clearly the distinctive role that the Chief Justice of India is called upon to perform within and outside the institution and accordingly evolve a distinct criterion for his selection.

In terms of the composition of its decision makers, once again, the only significant change discernible is in the frequency of turnover of judges in the court. There have been forty four appointments made to the court since January, 1981(R.B.Mishra, the last judge covered by the study joined the court on 30-1-1981) in about 13 years time including those of Justices S.B.Majumdar and Sujata Manohar announced in September and October, 1994 as against a total of seventy one appointments made during the first three decades. Thus the average frequency of appointments in the court went up from approximately 2.2 in the first three decades to over 4 appointments every year in the eighties and the first half of the nintees. Although this change may be partly due to the increase in the number of judges in 1985 when the strength of judges in the court was enhanced from 18 to 26, yet it fails to account for such a phenomenal turnover in the composition of the court within such a short period.

The only possible explanation for exceptionally high mobility in the membership during the subsequent period perhaps lies in the short tenures for which most of the judges were appointed to the court. An examination of the 44 appointments made since 1981 in fact reveals that the majority of the judges had a tenure of not more than 3 to 5 years, with a few having a term of 6 to 8 years, and the remaining eight or nine judges were appointed for a term ranging between 8 and 10 years. None was however given a term of ten years or more. Among the relatively younger judges appointed during this period were Ranganath Mishra (1983-91) and R.C. Patnaik (1991, but for his untimely death in May 92, would have served till the year 2000) both from Orissa High Court, A.M.Ahmadi (1988-97) from Gujarat High Court, Kuldip Singh (1988-97) from the Punjab Bar, J.S.Verma (1989-98) from Rajasthan High Court, M.M.Punchi (1989-98) from Punjab & Haryana High Court, S.C. Agarwal (1990-98) from Rajasthan High Court, A.S. Anand (1991-2001) from Madras High Court, and S.P.Barucha (1992-2002) from Karnataka High Court.

Even in terms of High Court seniority of the judges other than those who were already Chief Justices, majority of them were elevated to the Supreme Court when they were about to retire or had one or two years' service left before their retirement from the High Court. Quite obviously, therefore, most of the judges selected for elevation to the Supreme Court were well advanced in their age and occupied seniormost positions in their High Courts. This not only supports the earlier finding but also shows that age and experience continue to play an important role in the selection of judges from the High Courts.

The regional and communal considerations too have been equally prominent in the 44 appointments made in the post 1981 period as was observed in the context of the first seventy one judges appointed in the court since its inception. Almost Sixteen out of the eighteen High Courts are represented in these appointments with 4 each going to Karnataka, Calcutta, Madras and Allahabad, 3 each to Gujarat, Andhra Pradesh, Rajasthan and Bombay, 2 each to Kerala and Orissa and 1 each to the remaining five High Courts. The regional character of these appointments, however, has changed with more judges being appointed or transferred from outside the region to the High Courts now than it was the case with earlier judges. For instance, the appointments of Yogeshwar Dayal (1991), B.P. Jeevan Reddy (1991), G.N. Ray (1991), A.S. Anand (1991), N.P. Singh (1992), S.P. Barucha (1992) and V.Sujata Manohar (1994) may be representative in character only to the extent of representing the High Court from which their elevation took place. The 44 appointments also appear to be fairly representative in terms of giving representation to major religious communities which goes to show that the regional and communal considerations continue to play a significant role in the appointment of judges to the apex court.

The only distinctive feature of the appointments in this period appears to be that for the first time two women judges i.e., M.S.Fathima Beevi(1989-92) and V.Sujata Manohar(1994-98) both from Kerala High Court were elevated to the apex court. In a way Justice Kuldip Singh's elevation from the Bar after a long gap of 23 years can also be of some reassurance to the lawyers community that after all the government has not forgotten them altogether, while the Academics are left to wonder even after four and a half decades as to what has happened to the 'distinguished jurist'. Thus, the basic character of the court's composition has by and large remained unchanged except that there is now a quicker turnover in both its membership as well as its leadership which has been changing hands rather too frequently.

The rapid turnover of judges in the court in the post 1981 period, however, need not give the impression that the government has discharged its obligation in filling up vacancies in the court with utmost punctuality as against its earlier shoddy performance. The role of the government in judicial appointments in general and appointments to the Supreme Court in particular has been far from satisfactory and continues to be so. The vacancies are never filled up in time and in fact even the present court has only 20 as against the sanctioned strength of 26 judges.

With the pressure of work in the court being heavier than what it was in the seventies and its decision making process as fragmented as ever, the judges are most likely to continue to function under the same institutional and environmental constraints as discussed in the context of 39 judges who served the court during the third decade. The demands on the court's justice system have always far exceeded its institutional resources. Over the past four and a half decades, neither the successive governments nor the leadership of the court have been able to evolve an equilibrium which is so essential for the development and healthy growth of any institution.

Appendix

PROFILE OF 29 JUDGES WHO SERVED THE SUPREME COURT, 1973-81

Name	Date of Birth	Religion	Education		Pre High Court Experience	High Court Experience	Appointed to Supreme Court	Miscellaneous
			General	Legal				
1	2	3	4	5	6	7	8	9
1. Sikri, S.M.	26.4.1908	Hindu	Cambridge	Lincoln's Inn.	Adv. Lahore H.C. 1930-49; Income Tax; Asst. Adv. Gen. Punjab 1949-57 Adv. Gen.Punjab 1951-64	None	Apptd. on 3.2.64 Age: 55.10; Retd. 26.4.73	Member, Law Comm. 1955-58 Delegate to Int. Conferences 1947-63.
2. Shelat, J.M.	16.7.1908	Hindu	Elphinston College, Bombay and University of London	Inner Temple	Adv. Bombay H.C. 1933-48; General Practice, Member of Higher Judicial Service 1948-57	Judge, Bombay H.C. 1957-60, Judge & Chief Justice, Gujarat H.C. 1960-66	Apptd. on 24.2.66; Age: 57:7; Resigned 30.4.73	Author of Akbar and Contributor to Munshi: His Life and Work
3. Mitter, G.K.	24.9.1906	Hindu	Patna College and University of London	Lincoln's Inn	Adv. Calcutta H.C.; General Practice 1934-52	Judge, Calcutta H.C. 1952-66	Apptd. on 29.8.66; Age: 60; Retd. 24.9.71	Appointed Adhoc Judge, S.C. 1971-72
4. Vaidialingam, C.A.	30.6.1907	Hindu	Presidency College, Madras	Madras Law College	Adv. H.C. 1931-53; Civil & Criminal Practice, Govt. Pleader 1953-57	Judge, Kerala High Court 1957-66	Apptd. on 10.10.66; Age: 59:4; Retd. 30.6.72	Father was former Judge of Madras H.C. Appointed Adhoc Judge 1972-73
5. Hegde, K.S.	11.6.1909	Hindu	St. Aloysius College, Manglore	Madras Law College	Adv. Mysore H.C. 1936-47; Civil & Criminal Public Prosecutor & Govt. Pleader Mysore 1947-51	Judge Mysore H.C. 1957-66; Chief Justice High Court 1966-67	Apptd. on 17.7.67; Age: 58:1; Resigned: 30.4.73	Member Parliament 1952-57; and 1977-79 also Speaker Lok Sabha

contd. . . .

Name	Date of Birth	Religion	Education		Pre High Court Experience	High Court Experience	Appointed to Supreme Court	Miscellaneous
			General	Legal				
1	2	3	4	5	6	7	8	9
6. Grover, A.N.	15.2.1912	Hindu	Amritsar and Govt. College, Calcutta	Cambridge Christ College	Adv. Lahore & Punjab H.Cs. , Company & Income Tax, 1936-50 & 1950-57 respectively.	Judge Punjab H.C. 1957-68	Apptd. 12.2.68; Age: 56; Resigned 27.4.73	Became Chairman Press Commission
7. Ray, A.N.	29.1.1912	Hindu	Ripon School & Presidency College, Calcutta	Oriel College Oxford & Gray's Inn	Adv. Calcutta H.C. 1940-57; Practised on Civil Side	Judge Calcutta H.C. 1957-69	Apptd. on 1.8.69; Age: 57:7; Retd. 29.1.77	Vice President Asiatic Society 1965-67; President Society for' Welfare of Blinds (W.B.)
8. Reddy, P.J.	23.1.1910	Hindu	St. George Gr. School, Hyderabad, Deccan City of Leads School, University of Leeds, England	Trinity Hall, University Cambridge and Gray's Inn.	Adv. Bombay, Hyd. and Madras H.Cs. 1937-46 Judicial Service 1946-52 Commercial, Company Tax & Revenue Practice.	Judge, Hyderabad H.C. 1952-56; Judge and Chief Justice A.P. High Court 1956-69	Apptd. on 1.8.69; Age: 59:7; Retd. 23.1.75	Delivered Ashutosh Lectures, 1978, published by Calcutta University in 1982
9. Dua, I.D.	4.10.1907	Hindu	Frontier H.S. Peshawar; Daba H.S. Jallundhar; and F.C. College, Lahore	Law College, Lahore	Adv. Lahore H.C. 1933-50; Punjab H.C. 1950-58; Practised on Civil side	Judge Punjab H.C. 1958-66; Judge &Chief Justice Delhi H.C.1966-69	Apptd. 1.8.69; Age: 61:10; Retd. 4.10.72	Chairman, State Bar Council 1958; Adhoc Judge, S.C. 1972-73
10. Palekar, D.G.	4.9.1909	Hindu	Govt. H.S., Kamar; Elphinsten College, Amritsar	Govt. Law College, Bombay	Adv. Bombay H.C. 1934-39; Civil & Criminal Judicial Service 1939-61	Judge, Bombay H.C.1961-71	Apptd. 19:7:71; Age: 61:10; Resigned 4.9.74	Father, a leading Lawyer

contd. . . .

Name	Date of Birth	Religion	Education		Pre High Court Experience	High Court Experience	Appointed to Supreme Court	Miscellaneous
			General	Legal				
1	2	3	4	5	6	7	8	9
11. Khanna, H.R.	3.7.1912	Hindu	DAV High School; Hindu College & Khalsa College, Amritsar	Law College, Lahore	Adv. Lahore H.C. 1940-50; Punjab H.C. 1950-52; Judicial Service 1952-62; Practised Civil Cases	Judge Punjab H.C. 1962-66; Judge & Chief Justice Delhi H.C 1966-71	Apptd. 22.9.71; Age: 59:2; Resiged 12.3.77	Law Minister in Janata Govt. for 100 hrs. Chairman, Law Commission
12. Mathew, K.K.	3.1.1911	Hindu	St. Ephrein's English H.C. Mandanam; Arts College, Trivandrum	Law College, Trivandrum	Adv. Travancor & Kerala H.Cs. 1939-60. General Practice, Adv. Central Kerala 1960-62	Judge, Kerala H.C. 1962-71	Apptd.4.10.71 Age: 60:9; Retd. 3.1.76	Became Chairman, Law Commission; Press Commission; Wrote Democracy, Equality & Freedom.
13. Beg, M.H.	22.2.1913	Hindu	St. George School, Hyderabad; DCSW Sussex; Trinity College, Cambridge	Lincoln's Inn	Adv. Allahabad H.C. 1942-63; General Practices; Also taught Law in Meerut	Judge Allahabad H.C. 1963-66; Chief Justice Himachal H.C. 1966-71	Apptd. 10.12.71; Age: 58:10; Retd. 22.2.78	Became Chairman, Minority Commission
14. Dwivedi, S.N.	1.10.1913	Hindu	Govt. H. School, Hamirpur; Ewing Xian College, Allahabad	Law College, Lucknow	Adv. Allahabad H.C. 1943-59; Civil Practice Govt. Standing Council 1954-55S	Judge Allahabad H.C. 1959-72	Apptd. 14.8.72; Age: 57:7; Died in Office: 8.12.74	Arrested for participating in freedom movement.

contd. . . .

Name	Date of Birth	Religion	Education		Pre High Court Experience	High Court Experience	Appointed to Supreme Court	Miscellaneous
			General	Legal				
1	2	3	4	5	6	7	8	9
15. Mukherjea, A.K.	20.1.1915	Hindu	Presidency College & Sanskrit College, Calcutta; School of Oriental Studies, London.	Gray's Inn	ICS, 1937-50; Adv. Calcutta H.C. 1951-62; Practised Original Side.	Judge, Calcutta H.C. 1962-72	Apptd. 14.8.72; Age: 57:7; Died in Office: 23.10.73	None
16. Chandrachud, Y.V.	12.7.1920	Hindu	Nutan Marathi Vidyalaya, S.P. College & Fergasa College Pune; Elphinstone College, Bombay	Law College, Pune	Adv. Bombay H.C. 1943-58; Practised Civil & Criminal Cases, Govt. Pleader 1952-61 Law Teacher 1949-52	Judge Bombay H.C. 1961-72	Apptd. 28.8.72; Age: 52:1; Retd. 12.7.85	Held longest tenure as Chief Justice of India
17. Allagiriswamy, A.N.	17.10.1910	Hindu	Roman Catholic School, Board H. School; and Presidency College, Madras.	Law College, Madras	Adv. Madras H.C. 1936-41 Civil & Criminal Work. Judl. Service 1941-60; Govt. Pleader 1960-66	Judge Madras H.C.1966-72	Apptd. 17.10.72; Age: 62; Retd. 17.10.75	Died on 15.2.83
18. Bhagwati, P.N.	21.12.1921	Hindu	Eliphinston High School & Govt. Victoria College, Palghat.	Govt. Law College, Bombay	Adv. Bombay H.C. 1946-60	Judge Gujarat H.C. 1960-67; Chief Justice 1967-73	Apptd. 17.7.73; Age: 51:7; Presently CJI due to retire 21.12.86	Father N.H. Bhagwati former SC Judge; Partici-pated in freedom movement.

contd. . . .

Name	Date of Birth	Religion	Education		Pre High Court Experience	High Court Experience	Appointed to Supreme Court	Miscellaneous
			General	Legal				
1	2	3	4	5	6	7	8	9
19. Krishna Iyer, V.R.	15.11.1915	Hindu	Distt. Board H.S. Quallands & Govt. Victoria College, Palghat.	Govt. Law College, Madras	Adv. Madras & Kerala H.Cs. 1938-68; Worked in Civil & Criminal cases.	Judge, Kerala H.C.1968-70; Member, Law Commission 1970-73	Apptd. 17.7.73; 57:8; Retd. 15.11.80	Minister in Kerala Govt. 1957-59; Eloquent Speaker & Versatile Writer
20. Goswami, P.K.	1.1.1913	Hindu	Sibsagar Govt. H. School and Cotton College, Gauhati	Earl Law College, Gauhati	Adv. SC, Calcutta & Gauhati HCs. Practised Civil, Criminal, Court & Labour matters.	Judge & Chief Justice of Gauhati H.C. 1967-73	Apptd. 10.9.73; Age: 60:8; Retd. 1.1.78	First Judge to be appointed to the SC from North Eastern Region
21. Sarkaria, R.S.	16.1.1916	Sikh	B.N. Khalsa Poly. & Govt. Mehindra College, Patiala; Govt. College, Lahore	Govt. Law College, Lahore.	Adv. 1937-43; Practised Civil & Criminal Cases; Joined Judl .Service 1943-67.	Judge Punjab & Haryana H.Cs. 1967-73	Apptd. 17.9.73; Age: 57:8; Retd. 16.1.81	Headed Sarkaria Commission
22. Gupta, A.C.	1.1.1917	Hindu	Mitra Institution, Bhowanipur & Presidency College, Calcutta	University Law College, Calcutta.	Adv. Calcutta H.C. 1945-64; Practised Civil, Criminal & Court Cases.	Judge Calcutta H.C. 1964-74	Apptd. 2.9.74; Age: 57:8; Retd. 1.1.82	Father was a lawyer; First Non barristor Judge from Calcutta H.C. appointed to SC.
23. Untwalia, N.L.	1.8.1915	Hindu	Sitamarhi H. E. School & G.B.B. College Muzaffarpur.	University Law College, Calcutta.	Adv. Patna H.C. 1944-58; Practised Civil, Company, Tax & Court Cases.	Judge and Chief Justice, Patna H.C. 1958-74	Apptd. 3.10.74; Age: 59:2; Retd. 1.8.80	None

contd. . . .

Name	Date of Birth	Religion	Education		Pre High Court Experience	High Court Experience	Appointed to Supreme Court	Miscellaneous
			General	Legal				
1	2	3	4	5	6	7	8	9
24. Fazal Ali, S.M.	20.12.1920	Muslim	Patna Collegiate School and Patna College	Patna Law College	Adv. Patna H.C. 1944-58; Practised Civil, Criminal, Revenue & Court Cases	Judge & Chief Justice J&K H.C. 1958-75	Apptd. 2.4.75; Age: 54:4; Died in Office	Father, Sir S. Fazal Ali, Former Judge of S.C.
25. Singhal, P.N.	15.10.1915	Hindu	Allahabad & Lucknow University	Law College, Allahabad	Worked as Munsif Magistrate, Legal Rememberance & Law Secretary in formerAlwar State; Distt. & Sessions Judge.	Judge & Chief Justice Rajasthan H.C. 1961-75	Apptd. 6.11.75; Age: 60:11; Retd. 15.10.80	Worked in various capacities in the State & Central Govts.
26. Jaswant Singh	25.1.1914	Hindu	Mirpur(now in Pakistan) and Lahore	Law College, Lahore	Public Prosecutor in Mirpur, Jammu & Srinagar; Asstt. Adv. Gen. & Adv. Gen. J&K 1948-67	Judge and Chief Justice J&K H.C. 1967-77.	Apptd. 23.1.76; Age: 62; Retd. 12.9.80	Heading One-man Commission on Allahabad H.C.
27. Kailasam, P.S.	12.9.1915	Hindu	R.K. Mission's Home, P.S.H. School, Malayapur & Presidency College, Madras	Law College, Madras	Adv. Madras H.C. 1938-60; Did Civil & Criminal Work. Public Prosecutor & AG Madras H.C.	Judge & Chief Justice Madras H.C. 1960-77	Apptd. 3.1.77; Age: 61:4; Retd. 12.9.80	None
28. Tulzapurkar, V.D.	9.3.1921	Hindu	Wilson H. School & Wilson College, Bombay	Govt. Law College, Bombay.	Adv. Bombay H.C. 1942-56. Practised Civil & Criminal Cases; Judicial Service 1956-63	Judge Bombay H.C. 1963-77	Apptd. 30.9.77; Age: 56:6; Retd. 12.9.80	None

contd. . . .

Name	Date of Birth	Religion	Education		Pre High Court Experience	High Court Experience	Appointed to Supreme Court	Miscellaneous
			General	Legal				
1	2	3	4	5	6	7	8	9
29. Desai, D.A.	9.5.1920	Hindu	Jamanabai Sink School; Dehen H.School & M.T.B. College, Surat.	Sarjanik, Law College, Surat	Adv. Bombay H.C. 1945-60; Practised Tenancy, Land Revenue & Labour Cases, Judicial Service, Gujarat 1960-68	Judge Gujarat H.C.1968-77	Apptd. 30.9.77; Age: 57:4; Retd. 9.5.85	Was Chairman, Law Commission of India
30. Pathak, R.S.	25.11.1924	Hindu	St. Joseph H. School, Ewing Xian College, Allahabad.	Allahabad University	Adv. Allahabad H.C. 1948-62; Practised in Tax Company, labour & Court matters.	Judge Allahabad H.C. 1962-72; C.J. Himachal H.C. 1972-78	Apptd. 20.2.78; Age: 53:3; Due to retire: 25.11.89	Father G.S. Pathak, Renouned Lawyer and Former Vice President of India
31. Koshal, A.D.	7.3.1917	Hindu	Public H.S. Ahmedgarh; Farman Xian College Lahore & Govt. College, Ludhiana	Law College, Lahore	Pleader 1936-48; Adv. Punjab H.C. 1948-60; Civil & Criminal Practice; Judicial Service 1960-68	Punjab & Haryana H.C. Judge 1962-72; C.J. Punjab & Haryana H.C. 1977-78	Apptd.17.7.78; Age: 61:4; Retd. 7.3.82	Legal Remembrancer & Law Secy. to Govt. of Punjab 1966-67
32. Chinappa-reddy O.C.	25.9.1922	Hindu	London Mission H.S. and Goty Loyda College, Madras.	Law College, Madras	Adv. Madras & Hyderabad H.Cs. 1947-67; Civil and Criminal Practice.	Judge Andhra Pradesh H.C. 1967-76; Judge P&H H.C. 1976-77; Returned to A.P. H.C. 1977-78	Apptd. 17.7.78; Age: 55:10; Due to Retire: 25.9.87	None

contd. . . .

Name	Date of Birth	Religion	Education		Pre High Court Experience	High Court Experience	Appointed to Supreme Court	Miscellaneous
			General	Legal				
1	2	3	4	5	6	7	8	9
33. Sen, A.P.	20.9.1923	Hindu	Dinanath School; Hislip Collegiate H.S. and SC College Nagpur.	Law College, Nagpur	Adv. Nagpur H.C. 1947-56; M.P. H.C. 1956-67; Adv. Gen. M.P. Practised Revenue & Tax Cases.	Judge Madhya Pradesh H.C. 1967-76; Raj. H.C. 1976-78; & C.J. M.P. H.C. 1978.	Apptd. 17.7.78; Age: 54:10; Due to retire: 20.9.88	None
34. Venkatramiah, E.S.	18.12.1924	Hindu	D.B.H. School & Inter College, Mysore; Maharaja's Cotton College, Gauhati.	Law College, Pune	Pleader Bangalore 1946-48; Adv. Mysore H.C. 1948-70; Adv. Gen. H.J.S., Practised Civil & Criminal	Judge Mysore 1970-79	Apptd. 8.3.79; Age: 54:3; Due to Retire: 18.12.89	Appointed Oneman Commissioner on Chandigarh Transfer. 1986.
35. Baharul Islam	1.3.1918	Muslim	Gurdon H. School, Nalbari, Cotton College, Gauhati.	Aligarh Muslim University, Faculty of Law.	Adv. Gauhati H.C. since 1951; Practised in S.C. also between 1951-72.	Judge and Chief Justice, Gauhati H.C. 1972-80	Apptd. 4.12.80; Age: 62:9; Resigned in Feb'83	Member, Rajya Sabha 1962-72; contested Lok Sabha Elect. & Won
36. Vardharajan, A.	17.8.1920	Hindu	Municipal H.S. Tirupattur Voorches College & Loyota College, Madras.	Law College, Madras.	Adv. Madras H.C. 1944-49; Judicial Service 1949-73	Judge Madras H.C. 1973-80	Apptd. 10.12.80; Age: 60:4; Retd. 17.8.85	He was the first among the Hindu Scheduled Castes to be elevated to S.C.

contd. . . .

Name	Date of Birth	Religion	Education		Pre High Court Experience	High Court Experience	Appointed to Supreme Court	Miscellaneous
			General	Legal				
1	2	3	4	5	6	7	8	9
37. Sen, A.N.	1.10.1920	Hindu	Harisinge H.S. School, K.N. College & Scotterch Ch. College.	University Law College, Cal. Inner Temple.	Adv. Calcutta H.C. 1947-65; Practised Civil Cases.	Judge and Chief Justice, Calcutta H.C. 1965-81	Apptd. 28.9.81; Age: 60:4; Retd. 1.10.85	None
38. Eradi, V.B.	19.6.1922	Hindu	Zamarin School & College, Calicutt; Xian College, Madras.	Law College, Madras.	Adv. Madras & Kerala H.Cs. 1945-67; Practised Tax, Civil & Criminal Matters.	Judge & Chief Justice Kerala H.C. 1967-81	Apptd. 30.1.81; Age: 58:7; Due to retire: 19.6.87	Appointed Chairman of National Commission on consumer Protection
39. Misra, R.B.	15.6.1921	Hindu	K.G.H.S.	Allahabad	Adv. Allahabad H.C.	Judge, Allahabad	Apptd. 30.1.81;	None

Bibliography

Books

Abraham, Henry J.; *The Judicial Process* (Oxford University Press, New York 1980).

Antulay, A.R.; *Appointment of a Chief Justice* (Popular Prakashan, Bombay, 1973).

Austin, Granville; *The Indian Constitution: Cornerstone of a Nation* (Clarendon Press, Oxford, 1966).

Baxi, Upendra; *The Crisis of Indian Legal System* (Vikas, New Delhi, 1982).

Baxi, Upendra; *The Indian Supreme Court and Politics* (Eastern Book Co., Lucknow, 1980).

Baxi, Upendra; *Courage Craft and Contention: The Indian Supreme Court in the Eighties* (Tripathi, Bombay, 1985).

Chagla, M.C.; *Roses in December* (Bharatiya Vidya Bhavan, Bombay, 1974).

Dhavan, Rajeev; *The Supreme Court of India: A Socio-Legal Critique of its Juristic Techniques* (Tripathi, Bombay, 1977).

Dhavan, Rajeev; *The Supreme Court Under Strain: The Challenge of Arrears* (Tripathi, Bombay, 1978).

Dhavan, Rajeev and Jacob, Alice; *Selection and Appointment of Supreme Court Judges: A Case Study* (Tripathi, Bombay, 1978).

Easton, David; A Systems Analysis of Political Life (John Wiley and Sons, Inc. New York, 1965).

Freund, Paul A.; *The Supreme Court of the United States: Its Business, Purpose and Performance* (Meridian Books, The World Publishing Co. Cleaveland, 1977).

Gajendragadkar, P.B.; *To The Best of My Memory* (Bharatiya Vidya Bhavan, Bombay, 1983).

Griffith, J.A.G.; *The Politics of the Judiciary* (Fontana/Collins U.K., 1977).

Hidayatullah, M.; *My Own Boswel* (Arnol-Heinemann, New Delhi, 1984).

Jain, M.P.; *Indian Legal History* (Tripathi, Bombay, 1966).

Khan, Sir Shafa'at Ahmed; *The Indian Federation, Macmillan* and Co. Ltd., London, 1937.

Khanna, H.R.; *Neither Roses Nor Thorns* (Eastern Book Co., Lucknow, Year not stated).

Lewis, Anthony; *Gideon's Trumpet* (Random House, New York, 1964).

Mahajan, M.C.; *Looking Back* (Asia Publishing House, New Delhi, 1963).

Murphy, Walter F.; *Elements of Judicial Strategy* (University of Chicago Press, Chicago, 1964).

Murphy, Walter F. and Pritchett, C.H. *Courts, Judges and Politics* (Random House, New York, 1974).

Nayar, Kuldip(ed); *Supersession of Judges* (Indian Book Company, New Delhi, 1973).

Pylee, M.V.; *Constitutional Government in India* (Asia Publishing House, New Delhi, 1965).

Pylee, M.V.; *The Federal Court of India* (Manak Talas, Bombay, 1966).

Rao, B. Shiva; *The Framing of the Indian Constitution Select Documents* Vols. III & IV (1966).

Reddy, P.J.; *Liberty, Equality, Property and the Constitution, Ashutosh Lectures for 1978*, (University of Calcutta, Calcutta, 1982)

Rohde, David W. and Spaeth, Harold J.; *Supreme Court Decision Making* (W.H. Freeman, San Francisco 1976).

Schmidhauser, John R.; *The Supreme Court: Its Policies, Personalities and Procedures* (Holt, Rinehart and Winston, New York 1963).

Schubert, Glendon; *Quantitative Analysis of Judicial Behaviour* (Free Press, 1959).

Setalvad, M.C.; *My Life: Law and Other Things* (Tripathi, Bombay, 1971).

Sharma, Sri Ram; *The Supreme Court in the Indian Constitution* (Rajpal and Sons, Delhi, 1959).

Speath, Harold Jr.; *The Supreme Court Policy Making* (W.H. Freeman, San Francisco, 1979).

Articles

Baxi Upendra; "The Constitutional Quicksands of Kesavananda Bharati and the Twenty-fifth Amendment" S.C.C. *Journal*, 45-67, (1974).

Baxi Upendra; "Introduction" to K.K. Mathew's *Democracy, Equality and Freedom*, I- LXXXV (Eastern Book Company, Lucknow, 1978).

Baxi Upendra; "Appointments of the Chief Justice and Justices of the Supreme Court" A Key note paper read at the Bar Council Seminar on Judicial Appointments held on October 17-19 (1980)- A monograph.

Baxi Upendra; "Who Bothers About the Supreme Court: The Problem of Impact of Judicial Decisions" 24 *Journal of the Indian Law Institute*. 848-862 (1982).

Baxi Upendra; "The Travails of Stare Decisis in India" in A.R. Blackshield(ed) *Legal Change: Essays in Honour of Julius Stone*, 34-51 (butterworths, Sydney, 1983).

Baxi Upendra; "Taking Suffering Seriously: Social Action Litigation in the Supreme Court of India" in Rajeev Dhavan et al (ed) *Judges and the Judicial Power*, 289-315 (Tripathi, Bombay 1985).

Bhoj Raj; "Decision Making" AIR *Journal*, 110-113 (1968)

Blackshielf, A.R.; "Capital Punishment in India" 21 *Journal of the Indian Law Institute* 137-226 (1979).

Chakraborty, Manas; "Chief Justices of the Supreme Court of India: 1950-1978", 17 *Political Science Review* 78-91 (1978).

Chakraborty, Manas; "Indian and American Supreme Court Judges - A Comparative Study of Background Characteristics, 1950 - 74" 21 Political Science Review 57-72 (1982)

Dixit, Y.P.; "The Judiciary and Political Appointments", AIR *Journal* 2-3 (1959).

Flango, Victor E. et al; "The Concept of Judicial Role" 19 *American Journal of Political Science* 277-290 (1975).

Gadbois, George H.; "Evolution of the Federal Court in India", 5 *Journal of the Indian Law Institute*, 19-45 (1963).

Gadbois, George H.; "Indian Supreme Court Judges - A Portrait" 3 *Law and Society Review*, 317-336 (1968).

Gadbois, George H.; "Selection Background Characteristics and Voting Behaviour of Indian Supreme Court Judges, 1950-1959", in Glendon Schubert and David J. Danelski (ed)

Comparative Judicial Behaviour, 221-256 (Oxford University Press, New York, 1969).

Gadbois, George H.; "Indian Judicial Behaviour" 5 *Economic and Political Weekly*, 149- 166 (1977).

Gadbois, George H.; "The Supreme Court of India: A Preliminary Report of an Empirical Study", 4 *Journal of Parliamentary Studies* 33-54 (1970).

Gadbois, George H.; "Supreme Court Decision Making" 10 *Banaras Law Journal*, 1-49 (1974).

Gadbois, George H.; "Participation in Supreme Court Decision Making" 24 *Journal of the Indian Law Institute*, 1-23 (1982).

Gadbois, George H.; "The Decline of Dissent in the Supreme Court,1950-81" in Ram Avtar Sharma(ed) *Justice and Social Order in India*, 261-79 (Intellectual, New Delhi 1984).

Gadbois, George H.; "The Supreme Court of India as a Political Institution" in Dhavan et al (ed) *Judges and the Judicial Power* 250-67, (Sweet and Maxwell, Bombay 1985).

Gibson James L.; "Judges' Role Orientations, Attitudes and ; Decisions", 72 *American Political Science Review* 911-24 (1978).

Goldman, Sheldon "Backgrounds, Attitudes and the Voting Behaviour of Judges, 31 *Journal of Politics* 214-22 (1969).

Grossman, Joel B.; "Social Backgrounds and Judicial Decision Making" 79 *Harvard Law Review*, 1551-64 (1966).

Grossman, Joel B.; "Social Backgrounds and Judicial Decisions: Notes for a theory", 29 *Journal of Politics*, 334-57 (1967).

Jacob, Herbert; "The effect of the Institutional differences in the Recruitment Process: The Case of State Judges" 18 *Journal of Public Law*, 104-19 (1964).

Schubert, Glendon; "The Study of Judicial Decision Making as aspect of Political Behaviour" 52 *American Political Science Review*, 1017-22 (1958).

Tulzapurkar, V.D.; "Judiciary: Attacks and Survival" A.I.R. *Journal* 9-18 (1983).

Index